A View from Life's Edge

Global Perspectives on Aging

Series editor, Sarah Lamb

This series publishes books that will deepen and expand our understanding of age, aging, ageism, and late life in the United States and beyond. The series focuses on anthropology while being open to ethnographically vivid and theoretically rich scholarship in related fields, including sociology, religion, cultural studies, social medicine, medical humanities, gender and sexuality studies, human development, critical and cultural gerontology, and age studies. Books will be aimed at students, scholars, and occasionally the general public.

Jason Danely, *Aging and Loss: Mourning and Maturity in Contemporary Japan*
Parin Dossa and Cati Coe, eds., *Transnational Aging and Reconfigurations of Kin Work*
Sarah Lamb, ed., *Successful Aging as a Contemporary Obsession: Global Perspectives*
Margaret Morganroth Gullette, *Ending Ageism, or How Not to Shoot Old People*
Ellyn Lem, *Gray Matters: Finding Meaning in the Stories of Later Life*
Michele Ruth Gamburd, *Linked Lives: Elder Care, Migration, and Kinship in Sri Lanka*
Yohko Tsuji, *Through Japanese Eyes: Thirty Years of Studying Aging in America*
Jessica C. Robbins, *Aging Nationally in Contemporary Poland: Memory, Kinship, and Personhood*
Rose K. Keimig, *Growing Old in a New China: Transitions in Elder Care*
Anna I. Corwin, *Embracing Age: How Catholic Nuns Became Models of Aging Well*
Molly George, *Aging in a Changing World: Older New Zealanders and Contemporary Multiculturalism*
Cati Coe, *Changes in Care: Aging, Migration, and Social Class in West Africa*
Megha Amrith, Victoria K. Sakti, and Dora Sampaio, eds., *Aspiring in Later Life: Movements Across Time, Space, and Generations*
Cristina Douglas and Andrew Whitehouse, eds., *More-than-Human Aging: Animals, Robots, and Care in Later Life*
Casey Golomski, *God's Waiting Room: Racial Reckoning at Life's End*
Claudia Huang, *Dancing for Their Lives: The Pursuit of Meaningful Aging in Urban China*
Corinne G. Dempsey, *A View from Life's Edge: Discovering What Really Matters with Older Women Across the Globe*

A View from Life's Edge

• • • • • • • • • • • • • • • • • •

Discovering What Really Matters with Older Women Across the Globe

CORINNE G. DEMPSEY

Rutgers University Press
New Brunswick, Camden, and Newark, New Jersey
London and Oxford

Rutgers University Press is a department of Rutgers, The State University of New Jersey, one of the leading public research universities in the nation. By publishing worldwide, it furthers the University's mission of dedication to excellence in teaching, scholarship, research, and clinical care.

Library of Congress Cataloging-in-Publication Data

Names: Dempsey, Corinne G., author.
Title: A view from life's edge : discovering what really matters with older women across the globe / Corinne G. Dempsey.
Description: New Brunswick, New Jersey : Rutgers University Press, [2025] | Series: Global perspectives on aging | Includes bibliographical references and index.
Identifiers: LCCN 2025005267 (print) | LCCN 2025005268 (ebook) | ISBN 9781978844643 (paperback) | ISBN 9781978844650 (hardcover) | ISBN 9781978844667 (epub)
Subjects: LCSH: Older women—Psychology. | Aging—Psychological aspects.
Classification: LCC HQ1061 .D435 2025 (print) | LCC HQ1061 (ebook) | DDC 305.26/2—dc23/eng/20250220
LC record available at https://lccn.loc.gov/2025005267
LC ebook record available at https://lccn.loc.gov/2025005268

A British Cataloging-in-Publication record for this book is available from the British Library.

Copyright © 2026 by Corinne G. Dempsey
All rights reserved

No part of this book may be reproduced or utilized in any form or by any means, electronic or mechanical, or by any information storage and retrieval system, without written permission from the publisher. Please contact Rutgers University Press, 106 Somerset Street, New Brunswick, NJ 08901. The only exception to this prohibition is "fair use" as defined by U.S. copyright law.

"Here I Am, Lord" by Dan Schutte text © 1981, OCP. All rights reserved. Used with permission.

"I Carry a Torch in One Hand" by Rabi'a al 'Adawiyya from *Doorkeeper of the Heart: Versions of Rabi'a*, translated by Charles Upton. Used with permission.

"Door Never Closed" by Rabi'a al 'Adawiyya from *Radical Love: Teachings from the Islamic Mystical Tradition*, translated by Omid Safi. Copyright © 2018 by Omid Safi. Used with permission of Yale University Press.

"Vulnerability" by David Whyte from *Consolations: The Solace, Nourishment, and Underlying Meaning of Everyday Words*. Copyright © 2014 by David Whyte. Reprinted with permission from David Whyte and Many Rivers Company, Langley, WA.

References to internet websites (URLs) were accurate at the time of writing. Neither the author nor Rutgers University Press is responsible for URLs that may have expired or changed since the manuscript was prepared.

∞ The paper used in this publication meets the requirements of the American National Standard for Information Sciences—Permanence of Paper for Printed Library Materials, ANSI Z39.48-1992.

rutgersuniversitypress.org

Dedicated to the memory of my mother,
Frances Dempsey (1929-2024)

Contents

	Icelandic Language Notes	ix
	Introduction: A View from the Edge	1

Part I Landscapes

1	Crossing Frontiers in the San Francisco Bay Area	15
2	The Forces of Nature in Northern Iceland	29
3	Sacred Relations in South India	43
4	On Their Own Terms: The Sisters of St. Joseph	59

Part II The Real

5	Where Does It Hurt? Rejecting and Revising God and Religion	75
6	Critical Junctures: Love and Loss	95
7	Lost and Found: The Fruits of Letting Go	115

Part III The More

8   Death and Nature: Portals into the Wondrous More   137

9   Unearthly Entities: Angels, Deities, Spirits, and Saints   157

10 Frameless Presence: Encounters with the Unshakable
    Unknown   179

    Conclusion: Finding Our Place at the Edge   199

    Acknowledgments   209
    Notes   213
    Bibliography   223
    Index   231

Icelandic Language Notes

I keep to original spellings of Icelandic names and specialty terms because letter variations are few and simple to learn. Here are a few pronunciation tips:

á	*ow*, as in *cow*
æ	*i*, as in *like*
ei	*ay*, as in *way*
ö	*e*, as in *bed*, but with rounded lips
ð	soft *th*, as in *father*
j	*y*, as in *yes*
þ	hard *th*, as in *thick*

A View from Life's Edge

Introduction

• • • • • • • • • • • •

A View from the Edge

> The most important experiential source of knowledge about what it is to live a finite life is neglected by the same culture that needs its wisdom.
>
> **JAN BAARS,** "Aging: Learning to Live a Finite Life"

This book was my mother's very good idea. A few months after she and my father had moved into a retirement community in the San Francisco Bay Area, while filling me in about some of the fascinating women she'd been meeting, she was struck by a thought: "You should stay here and write a book about *us*!" For decades, Mom had watched me fly to the ends of the earth—literally, between South India and northern Iceland—to learn about people's practices and beliefs. She may have been kidding (and later denied saying this), but I liked the idea of meeting her new friends. It also occurred to me that such a project could morph into a cross-cultural study, a good excuse to meet with older women in South India and northern Iceland as well.

Over a span of five years, from 2016 to 2020, I ended up interviewing ninety-one women over the age of eighty, some twice, with 124 recorded conversations in all. The fieldwork was an honor and a joy unlike any of my other ethnographic adventures, having much to do with the gusto with which so many entered into conversation, almost as though they were waiting for me to show up.[1] At first, this willingness to share caught me by pleasant surprise. I now see it as an unsurprising symptom of later life, where a view of what really matters can sharpen. As gerontologist Jan Baars puts it, "If everything could always be postponed, nothing would really matter. Only in a finite life can something be really at stake and can life gain its full depth in this very moment."[2] In other words, we owe much of our late-life clarity to impending death.

What this confident clarity boils down to and what this book is ultimately about is a reckoning with a reality that older age forces upon us: that life lies outside our control. This we learn through death's imminence but also upon losing things—faculties, abilities, friends—as the years advance. Our orientations must adjust for sanity's sake, even if in fits and starts. Key to the process and also what this book is about is a loosening of structures and certitudes normally meant to keep life's unwieldiness at bay, held more tightly in some cultures and by some people than others. The stories and opinions that women shared with me repeatedly reflected this loosening, a chipping away at the illusion that any of us, at any stage, are captains of our own perfectly sailing ships. It is a countercultural realism that often leans into wonder, a curiosity at life's precarious edge that is not the same as hopelessness. What has been important for me to glean and now to pass on faces a double challenge, however. Inasmuch as we strive to deny, out of fright, life's finitude, we deny older adults their voices. A central conundrum of ageism is that we silence out of fear that which could quell our fears.

But this is not how this book project began. Because my area of study is religion, I prepared for my first round of California interviews by reading up on literature that explored religion and spirituality among older adults, written mostly by sociologists of religion and chaplaincy professionals. Armed with findings from this research, I arrived at my mother's retirement community where women eagerly shared their memories and life philosophies. Yet when we turned to questions informed by this research, much of which assumed that religiosity or spirituality, narrowly construed, deepens for people in later life, we lost steam. The topic of religion itself wasn't the problem. Women enjoyed reflecting on their upbringings—mostly Christian, one Jewish, one Buddhist, and a few fairly secular. It was the assumptions behind my questions that grated.[3] Momentum returned as women recalled for me what were often gripping accounts of religious uprooting, as many had moved out West as young adults and, along the way, had traded the old for the new. Even cradle Californians had stories of shifting religiosities to tell.

Encouraged by this emotionally charged theme of uprooting, I was relieved to have found a framework to replace my initial less-than-helpful sense of direction. I created a computer folder that I called "Spiritual Evolutions," ready to be filled with transcripts from northern Iceland and South India, where I planned to hear how, when, and why women's beliefs and practices changed over time. Instead, upon venturing beyond California, I quickly learned that Spiritual Evolutions was also a fairly useless theme.

My destination in Iceland has long been the town of Akureyri, Iceland's "northern capital." Here, friends and contacts helped me locate nineteen women willing to meet with me in the summer of 2017 and again in the following spring. All were nominally Lutheran, and more than half had grown up on remote farms where, during the long dark winters, the nearest church was often impossible to reach. In the summer, farmwork left little time for anything else. Surrounded by unwieldy forces of nature, nearly all the women, even those from town, spoke of finding sanctity and power in the landscape itself. Formal religiosity, if it existed at all, was usually homespun. Women reflected on how their lives had changed over the decades: once steeped in hardship, they now felt comfortable and safe. Yet my questions about how their religiosity had shifted over time stopped them in their tracks. Shaking their heads, several offered an old Icelandic adage: *Lengi býr að fyrstu gerð.* First things last the longest.

The tropical, densely populated South Indian state of Kerala is in many ways Iceland's opposite. Here, formal religion is richly diverse, where Christians and Muslims live alongside the Hindu majority, representing about a quarter each of the population. Far from languishing, religiosity is impossible to ignore, as saints, deities, and sacred symbols crowd both public and domestic spaces. Similar to Iceland, friends and contacts helped me find participants, thirty-two in all to accommodate Kerala's economic diversity and a fairly equal mix of Hindus and Christians typical of the region most familiar to me. Accompanied by two of my students during the 2017–2018 and 2019–2020 winters, we heard life stories saturated in religiosity that sounded nothing like those in Iceland. Yet when we asked how their commitments and practices evolved over time, conversations again came to a halt. What was given in childhood, nearly everyone insisted, remained.

In summer and fall of 2019, when I met with twenty Sisters of St. Joseph (SSJs), founders of the university where I teach, I had long given up on

Spiritual Evolutions. Yet to my surprise, nearly every sister I met told dramatic, unsolicited departure stories. The most wrenching had to do with entering the convent in the first place, usually straight out of high school, leaving one or both parents heartbroken. Another involved living through Vatican II reforms in the 1960s and 1970s that propelled a convent exodus across the country. The sisters I met, who had stayed, recalled radical changes in their religious lives as well as in their own conceptions of God. Many looked back at the severity of their early convent years, at how far they'd traveled since then, with a sense of disbelief.

Tossing Spiritual Evolutions to the wind, my wildly successful plan became to simply enjoy the process. Finding it impossible to generalize about what religion or spirituality looks like in older age, I had to trust that another framework would make itself known. Clear from the start was that my broadly pitched questions invited women to reflect on what mattered most to them. Dredging up memories, a sense of gravity settled in naturally. For some, the ease with which they stepped into this space took them by surprise. On a number of occasions, someone who had filled our time with captivating stories and forthright opinions would confess that, leading up to our meeting, she'd worried she would have nothing to say. Together we'd laugh at how wrong she'd been. Emotions charged most of our conversations, moving me as well.

On several occasions, I invited the women I interviewed in California to gather at one of their community parlors to update them on my travels. At one gathering, after sharing photos and stories from Kerala, noting cultural patterns along the way, I asked the group what they felt might set them apart, as Californians. Ann, a transplant from New Jersey, suggested that "superficiality wins the day" in California. "People will say the easy thing, not the thing that really requires a whole lot of thought or depth. Whenever I get to that place," Ann said, "I get very emotional. And it's hard for me to hold back the tears—not because I'm sad, particularly, but because of the deep meaning for me." Finding this last point familiar, I mentioned how women often teared up during our exchanges, not necessarily due to sorrow, but because they were connecting to something deep and true. Women around the room, many of whom had misted over during our meetings, nodded in recognition.

While some Californians may shy away from deep exchanges, this wasn't the case for the women I met, as our parlor group attested. Nor was it true anywhere else. While this willingness, if not entitlement, to dive deep could be chalked up to their many years on earth, a greater factor seems to be their position near life's end. As occurs with those living with terminal illness, such states of precarity, as worded by anthropologist Michael Jackson, have the capacity to "wrench a person out of his or her habitual routines of thought and behavior," altering perspectives in ways that "philosophical choice or idle curiosity" simply cannot.[4] Pushed to the surface at life's edge, such perspectives are what give structure to this book. Loosened from habitual routines of a youth-oriented, death-denying culture particularly insistent in mainstream U.S. culture, they furthermore call for our attention.[5]

Ageism and Fear of the Edge

While older-age perspectives are inarguably worth passing on, in our ageist determination to deny our eventual demise we too often sideline such views along with the elderly and infirm themselves—pesky reminders. Out of fear, we portray older adults "almost as another human species," as Baars puts it, "demented or wise but not in a perspective of one's own possible future with all its uncertainties and promises."[6] In a blog kept during her final years, Ursula Le Guin derides what she sees as a particularly American form of denial, encouraging "geezers" to think they're not really old. "Encouragement by denial, however well-meaning, backfires," Le Guin writes. "Fear is seldom wise and never kind. Who is it you're cheering up, anyhow? Is it really the geezer?" Being told that "old age doesn't exist is to tell me I don't exist. Erase my age, you erase my life—me."[7]

Another particularly American response to aging is our booming antiaging industry, one with growing global appeal. Promoting vigorous, active lives for the elderly, "successful aging" campaigns fueled by consumer capitalism prey on our fears of inadequacy as we advance in years, further stoking our denial. Those who cannot manage to "age successfully" despite a plethora of antiaging products, procedures, and activities for sale are made to feel like failures.[8] This deficit for which the individual is made to feel responsible is magnified by a moralism that views good things as happening to good people and bad things, like aging, as happening to bad people.[9]

Ageism is furthermore unique among bigotries in that it thrives relatively unquestioned. As proclaimed by Margaret Morganroth Gullette, it's time we recognize ageism for what it is: "We have already learned that the 'woman problem' turned out to be sexism, not the supposed nature of women. The 'Jewish problem' was and is anti-Semitism, not Jews. The 'Negro problem' is still squarely racism. Now the whole world is said to be facing the 'graying

Nations problem': too many old people, sickly, unproductive, costly, selfish.... We shouldn't be shocked to find that the problem isn't old people, it's ageism."[10] Ironically, distinguishing ageism from other bigotries is that it's the only "ism" related to a universal condition, "a prejudice against our future selves."[11]

The work to be done is thus to dismantle the binary that we either succeed or fail at aging, accepting instead inevitable late-life complexities.[12] As psychoanalyst Stanley Leavy points out, if we view older age in solely positive or negative terms, "we miss the possibility of this as being a novel and productive time that offers something new and specific due precisely to its limitation." This offering exists "not in spite of physical and mental limitations, but joined with them."[13] In her critique of the "ageless self" promoted by the antiaging industry, Sarah Lamb similarly proposes "meaningful decline." Noting the paradox, she insists, "But isn't the fact that no person can live forever, or stay the same, what gives human life much of its meaning and urgency?"[14]

This antiageist logic in which meaning is found in decline parallels the paradoxical themes that steer this book, where life's riches have a way of asserting themselves when we are perched at its edge. Attending to a realism that often comes to the fore near life's end, making way for wonder, we might catch better sight of what it means to live fully.

The (Ir)relevance of Religion and Spirituality

As I aim to throw my own small wrench into ageism's vicious cycle of fear and denial, I make use of the tools at my disposal. While this sometimes involves addressing religiosity directly, formal religion was usually beside the point when women reflected on matters and memories most important to them. In such cases, concepts borrowed from religious traditions were often useful for fleshing out countercultural perspectives and linking conversations across contexts.

As will become clear, the concepts I've found especially helpful for unpacking paradoxical late-life logics draw from Buddhist traditions. The Tibetan practice called "Four Thoughts That Turn the Mind to the Dharma" offers a quintessential example. Duplicating edge-of-life scenarios, it encourages a firmer grasp of life's impermanence, requiring sustained meditation on the fact that everything we have we could lose tomorrow or in an hour.[15] A foundational discipline that brings the truth of impermanence to the forefront of daily life, it forces people against the grain. Helping practitioners see how everyday assumptions can mislead us, that permanence and personal agency are in fact impossible illusions, its insights are similar to those reported near life's end. While it would be unfair to expect advancing age to confer the wisdom needed to live at peace in an ever-changing, imperfect reality outside our control, we do find clear traces in women's reflections.[16]

While tools from my discipline have at times come in handy for thinking through older women's perspectives, this is not the same, to be clear, as labeling them "religious" in the narrow sense—as scholarship on ageing often does.[17] This not only risks running us off course but would be an imposition to many, especially women from Iceland and California for whom formal religion was irrelevant or, in some cases, hurtful. Also, to be clear, I am not equating advanced age with a type of religious discipline, as its attendant sorrows and losses are not something people tend to chase after, no matter how much enlightenment might ensue.

Jennifer Ortegren helpfully suggests a dislodging of "religion" from its narrow confines by applying instead the Sanskrit term *dharma*. Often translated as "religion," dharma more amply refers to "that which holds the world together." Highlighting matters of critical importance that include forces both internal and external, within and beyond our grasp, dharma sets cosmic and mundane experiences on equal footing. Viewed as such, it is a framework that encompasses more holistically the tangle of significances that holds life together at its edge.[18]

Some might want to suggest "spirituality" as a helpful term, as less loaded than "religion" and more recognizable than "dharma." Recall how I did apply this word at the start, when Spiritual Evolutions was my go-to framework. Yet I discovered that the term was not only too narrow to encompass what mattered to women across locales but that it also wasn't necessarily less loaded than "religion." In fact, "spirituality" ended up being fairly useless in most settings.

This brings me to another California story.

Preparing for my first round of interviews, aware that many of the women I planned to meet had few or no formal religious ties, I inserted the words "spiritual" and "spirituality" into my list of questions. In part, this was my way of following the lead of the literature I'd been reading that insisted that people become more spiritual as they age, even if they didn't identify as religious. It turns out that the Californians I met didn't conform well to the literature not only because they didn't meet the projected trends but because "spirituality" rankled. For those who had rejected religion, this supposedly benign term often seemed a way of sneaking it through the back door. For many, the word simply sounded trite.

Helen held both positions. On the morning of our initial meeting, we bumped into one another at the dining hall. She had just read the interview questions I'd sent and wanted to let me know upfront that she "had problems with the word 'spirituality.'" She later explained how the term implied "godly forces" that didn't resonate with her. Plus, she had been turned off by the overuse of "spiritual" and "spirituality" that seemed to "burst forth from everyone" during the 1990s.

A handful of others in California expressed their annoyance with the term "spirituality" by bringing up the Day of the Spirit as a case in point. With eyerolls, they told me how the Day, an annual event hosted at the community's headquarters, was a total waste of time. My mother recalled how new residents would get "hooked in" by workshop titles that sounded interesting. But as far as she knew, no one went more than once. Mom ended up going twice because, as campus president, she was made to go a second time. With a laugh, she told me how during the hour-long bus ride home people were "really bitching" about the Day. When she passed this feedback on to headquarters, they responded by insisting that residents needed *some* sort of spirituality program. Months later, a rabbi and a staff member came to their campus for a special session. Setting up one of the parlors with paper, crayons, markers, and colored chalk, they invited attendees to express their spirituality through freestyle art and then to share out with the group. Mom recalled feeling so irritated that she just sat at her place, not drawing. With a slow shake of her head, she said, "It was pathetic." After several more attempts at workshops, attendance dwindling, headquarters dropped the idea altogether.

While "spirituality" landed awkwardly in California, it gained zero traction outside the United States. I was already aware that it didn't translate well into Icelandic, complicated by local spirit traditions that gave the word a very different meaning. In India, the term just didn't land at all. It doesn't translate well into Malayalam, the language spoken in Kerala, but the bigger obstacle had to do with how formal religion loomed so large there. Even English speakers familiar with the concept had no need to cloak their religiosity under the benign cover of spirituality. The outliers in this case were the Sisters of St. Joseph, who readily referred to personal beliefs and practices as "spiritual" versus "religious" matters related to the Church.

I thus avoid using "spirituality" as a blanket term. I also question its seeming safety, heard in the common assurance that a person is "spiritual but not religious." This standard disclaimer, as Robert Orsi notes, can be traced to an Enlightenment-era privileging of mainline European Christianity as properly modern "good religion," its qualities aligned with spirituality today. "Bad religion," by contrast, involves practices perceived as stuck in "an earlier stage in the timeline of human development," associated with people "in other parts of the world and with skin colors other than white."[19]

Left unchecked, this same spiritual/religious or secular/religious divide carries unfair inferences about levels of freedom and social advancement for women across contexts. Some might assume, for instance, that the traditional religious commitments of the SSJ sisters and women in India translate to social conservatism and constraint. As noted by Rosi Braidotti, such assumptions typically held by Euro-American secular feminists presume that "'our women' (Western, Christian, white or 'whitened' and raised in the tradition of secular Enlightenment) are already liberated," while "'their women' (non-Western, non-Christian, mostly not white and not whitened, as well as alien to the Enlightenment tradition), however, are still backward and need to be targeted for special emancipatory social actions."[20] Inverting these caricatures, the SSJs and Indian women of means I met had achieved levels of education and professional accomplishment well beyond their largely secular Californian and Icelandic peers.

Women's View from the Edge

I decided to interview only women for a host of reasons. Most practically, to be honest, when searching for people over eighty to meet with me, women were easier to find. Also, when collecting stories from people across cultures, it made sense to limit the pool to one gender to help rein in comparative themes. Four years into the process when the SSJ sisters joined in, I was especially grateful to have limited the project to women. Another reason has to do with my interest in amplifying perspectives marginalized by ageism that are further sidelined by sexism. In her discussion of "ageist alarmism" in the United States, Margaret Cruikshank notes how our so-called ticking time bomb set to decimate our economy essentially refers to older women who live longer than men and will more likely be poor as they enter old age.[21]

During my second visit to Kerala, I decided to ask some of the women what they thought. Why might it be a good idea, I asked, to interview them rather than men? Since many of our exchanges in India revolved around formal religion, they often responded that women were more likely to be religiously inclined and thus would have more to say. Teresa was adamant: "Because women are closer to prayers and to God!" Startled by her proclamation, she backed up and quietly added, "I don't know why. I'm mostly at home saying prayers." As those of us listening broke into laughter at her sudden shift in gears, Teresa turned to her grandson beside her, the only man in the room, to ask his opinion. He agreed. "I would say that women understand God better. For men, it will only be lip service. They will say the prayers, or whatever, and then go on to the next thing." Annamma C. offered something similar, that women tended to be more sincere in their religiosity while men often skipped their prayers. Her granddaughter sitting next her added, about the men, "They just want to have a good time and enjoy." A male friend who had joined us laughed, "Right. The women are praying for their men."

Women in Kerala also felt it was easier for them to enter into deep conversation. Ammini suggested, her daughter nodding beside her, that it was more natural for women to "talk about matters of the heart, while men would be embarrassed and tongue-tied." Grace, the most effusive of Kerala's storytellers, reasoned, "You feel a little freer to talk with women. That is the way." Seeing me nod in agreement, she became more insistent. "Men, they're inclined to hide their feelings. They won't tell you the truth. But women, they will say what has come to their heart. They will say it out!" Annamma also asserted that women are better listeners. "Whatever is good, they will take it seriously. They will take it into their hearts."

I agree with my Kerala friends. Initially surprised by older women's readiness to share matters of the heart, I have found this to be a specialty near life's end. It also seems that a lifelong place at society's edge, with less to lose, encourages veracity when conditions are right. Le Guin notes, "It's often easier for women to trust one another, to try to speak our experience in our own language." She moreover insists that "when women speak truly, they speak subversively—they can't help it: if you're underneath, if you're kept down, you break out, you subvert. We are volcanoes. When we women offer our experience as our truth, as human truth, all the maps change. There are new mountains."[22]

This speaking from the heart can be its own kind of disruption. It's part of what makes women's late-life clarity so compelling. Having lived through subtle and straightforward diminishments for close to a century, nearing life's edge can be emboldening. Insights, as such, become double-edged.

Contents

Divided into three parts, the book is organized according to themes heard across contexts with part I, "Landscapes," setting the stage. Drawing on women's early-life recollections, its four chapters highlight qualities unique to each place. Here we find that, just as aging bodies shape late-life orientations, earthly terrain shapes formal belief systems.

Part II, "The Real," explores women's commonsense challenges to religious, social, and cultural conventions and expectations. In chapter 5, we learn how institutional religions were lifelines for some women and devastations for others. Across scenarios, systems worthy of rejection were those where divinity reigned in judgment from on high while those that endured were entrenched in the messiness of life itself. In chapter 6, women reflect on life's greatest joys, loves, and victories that, it turns out, were consistently embedded in contexts of pain, loss, and abandonment. Illustrating late-life inclinations to poignancy, their stories confirm how precarity not only is intrinsic to life's fullness but magnifies its preciousness. Chapter 7 features women's two most commonly recited life lessons: to let go of expectations and to trust in an abiding goodness. Seemingly at odds, they offer a clear-eyed hope that, unearthed at life's edge, is applicable at any stage.

Part III, "The More," relates encounters with forces beyond our recognizable world that, like life itself on the brink, represent a teetering between what can and cannot be understood or controlled. Again, we see how the view from life's edge is productively unhinged from normative expectations, where wonder proves more fruitful than intractable certitude. In chapter 8, women reflect on death and nature, favorite topics that served as wondrous portals to the more, whose appeal was often tied to their capacity to overwhelm, confound, and humble. Chapter 9 describes encounters with ethereal entities who, staying predictably in their religious and cultural lanes, call into question colonizing assumptions about women's religious agency and authority. In chapter 10, "frameless presence" accounts sidestep cultural, religious, and earthly logics altogether. Recalled by women across three of the four settings, these long-ago events were as indescribable as they were unforgettable, suggesting an unshakable unknown that underlies everyday existence.

"Finding Our Place at the Edge" concludes the book by considering why what matters near life's end matters. I rally perspectives from critical gerontology, disability studies, and mystical theologies whose social critiques dovetail with older women's stories and perspectives. Echoing the counterintuitive, countercultural themes resounding throughout the work, these approaches likewise recognize uncertainty, imperfection, and dependency not as problems to be solved but as realities essential to human flourishing. Together they offer a counterforce to the impossible demands imposed by religious, economic, and political systems holding sway in much of our world today.

It is my hope that stories and reflections born of late-life precarity so generously shared can magnify our appreciation for what really matters. Discovering what it means to be more fully human in the company of older women, we might uncover new maps that, as Le Guin puts it, are truer to form than the standard-issue ones that too often lead us astray.

Part 1

Landscapes

● ● ● ● ● ● ● ● ● ● ● ● ●

1

Crossing Frontiers in the San Francisco Bay Area

● ● ● ● ● ● ● ● ● ● ● ● ●

Although all of the four interview settings were familiar to me, my strongest ties are to the redwood-tree-lined retirement community in California. As Fran's daughter, I had semi-insider status and my regular visits to see her helped me stay in good touch with the women I interviewed. I've watched how the years have treated them, each in their own way, and mourned the passing of a good few, including my mother in late summer 2024.

Staying in touch usually meant sharing a meal at the dining hall or lingering for a chat when bumping into someone on the grounds. On several occasions I organized gatherings at one of the campus parlors where I would share photos and stories from interview trips elsewhere. Near the end of one such session, I wanted to hear more from the women around the room about their religious migrations, a repeating theme during our conversations. About three-quarters of the Californians I met had moved westward as young adults, their physical uprooting usually followed by religious departures. Even the California-born had stories of religious shifts to tell. I explained that while spiritual fluidity was clearly a national trend today, they seemed a generation ahead of the curve. The group, about half of whom identified as religious "nones," agreed that they were unlike their non-Californian peers in this way. Women who were transplants confirmed that the friends and relatives they'd left behind tended to stay put religiously, as well.

I asked what they thought it was about California that encouraged this fluidity. Some offered logistic explanations; when moving across the country and away from home, traditional bonds naturally loosened or broke. Others chalked it up to the state's frontier culture that was hospitable to fresh ideas, or to a soft climate that encouraged optimism and openness. Kay, who often thought about this difference in the context of the Bay Area, told us that she envisioned the Golden Gate Bridge as a gateway, as offering a kind of refuge. "You know, we weren't enclosed. We somehow had these windows open that drew people here, people who were wanting or searching or trying to create a better living."

This chapter takes up Kay's point. Tales of religious migrations that older Californian women shared, unlike what one often hears from generations in their wake, had little to do with the enticements of spiritual experimentation and innovation. Rather, most women described being propelled by frustrations and self-doubt, by a "wanting or searching or trying" to feel less at odds with external expectations. It is a sense of being out of sync that parallels what older adulthood can feel like in an ageist society, a topic we will circle back to at the chapter's end.

The Stories

Lolly

Lolly was one of the two Californian women I interviewed who lived outside the retirement community. When she greeted me at her duplex apartment wearing a slim-fitting black sweater and black and gray yoga pants, I was taken aback. Although aware that she had recently retired as a yoga instructor, I wasn't prepared to meet an eighty-five-year-old inhabiting the body of someone half her age. In constant motion during our interview, Lolly would stand jauntily or wave her arms overhead while making a point, sometimes dashing to the next room to fetch photos to flesh out a story.

Raised in an Italian Catholic enclave in Utica, New York, Lolly moved to California when her husband took a job at Stanford University. She had been giving birth to children in rapid succession during this time, five in seven years. Told that birth control was a sin, she felt helpless to do anything about it. Yet when her fifth child was born prematurely, weighing in at two and a half pounds, matters changed. Lolly explained, "The pediatrician came to see me and said, 'We're going to do everything we can do,'" and then sped off to save her baby. Pounding the table with tears in her eyes, she recalled how, left alone in her anger and grief, she had pounded her white hospital sheets, proclaiming, "*No*body's going to *tell* me what to *do* with my *body* again." Quieting her voice, she said, "This was the moment when I said, 'I am leaving. I am no longer a Catholic.'"

By the time Lolly reached her early forties, she was suffering from arthritis "from head to toe." Prescribed Valium and a neck brace, she became fairly useless at home. She eventually tossed out both the collar and the Valium around the time someone suggested she try yoga. This, as Lolly put it, hooked her for life. At the front line of a burgeoning movement, in the first graduating class at San Francisco's Iyengar Yoga Institute, she traveled to India to study with Iyengar himself. In 1980, Lolly and a partner opened a yoga studio that they geared toward healing. She explained how a workshop she regularly taught, "Hands and Feet and Everything in Between," was modeled after her mother's work as the neighborhood healer. A devout Catholic, her mother had integrated prayer into her practice, and in a similar way yoga had become, as Lolly put it, "my new religion."

Near the end of our first conversation, Lolly described a more recent turn to Buddhism. "It's kind of like when you make snowmen. You roll the snowball down the hill and you get another layer, and another layer." Lolly demonstrated, her arms rounding and rolling the expanding layers. "That's how it was for me. The yoga was one layer. And Buddhism was sort of like the envelope." Buddhism's greatest appeal for Lolly was how it had reversed the damaging effects of her Catholic upbringing. "You know what Buddhism says. It's, 'Be yourself. Be present. Listen. . . .' I never felt, with the Catholic Church, that I counted. Now I feel like I count, just the fact that I'm in this body and I'm alive. I've lived my life and I'm getting ready to go on to the next step." Shaking her head, she said, "So, I don't see me hanging on a cross with nails in my feet and in my hands and with a gash in my chest, and with a crown of thorns on my head. I don't see myself as a bad person. I feel so fortunate to have found a *sangha*, a community."

Paddy

Paddy and I met in her retirement community apartment, brightly lit to accommodate her failing eyesight. Physically sturdy at ninety-two, she spoke with a soft Canadian accent, her blue eyes twinkling mischievously when recalling stories from her childhood. Raised just outside Winnipeg, "in the dead center of the Prairie," Paddy grew up in a Pentecostal family with "a *lot* of church*,*" as she put it. "I listened to an awful lot of hell and damnation when I was growing up." She told me how entire Sundays were dedicated to church. Her parents also went on Wednesday evenings, and her mother was fully dedicated to missionary circle activities. "There was just an awful lot of church," she repeated. "And I started thinking, 'What is there besides this?'"

Resistance began early for Paddy. "I started questioning the Sunday school teacher, who was a very small, sweet little lady." With a sigh she added, "And now I'm kind of sorry that I did it." Paddy also targeted her pious grandmother whose morning prayers would fill the house. "Mamma would say, 'Now be quiet, girls, Grandma's having her prayer time.'" Paddy chuckled. "One day, I said to Grandma, 'Grandma, I learned something in Sunday school. The Bible says you should go into your closet and close the door and pray quietly. But you don't do that, do you?'" Paddy smiled wryly. "And that drew a line between Grandma and me a little bit."

The ultimate disconnect for Paddy was when, at age twelve, her beloved mother was sent to spend three years at a tuberculosis sanitarium. "My life just fell apart," she recalled. When her mother returned, Paddy announced that she wasn't going to go to church anymore. She had begun to question God's existence but didn't admit this, even to herself, until later. At the time, she explained that the services were simply too noisy. "I just didn't feel there was any dignity to it. I remember that the minister played a trombone up on the altar." With admiration, Paddy recalled how her mother never pressured her to stay. Free to find a church that suited her, she eventually joined her future husband's Congregationalist Church. Admitting with a chuckle that their services "were very bland," she added, "but at least there wasn't a lot of screaming and yelling."

When Paddy, her husband, and their six small children moved to California, they continued their Sunday routine for a while. This, she emphasized, was no small feat. But "on this one particular Sunday, we had just got all into the car. And I went right back to my childhood questioning. And I thought, 'Oh, this is church, is it? Is this what's important?' And I looked at Duncan and I said, 'I'm going to say something.' And he said, 'Okay, what do you want to say, honey?' I turned around and said, 'Is there anyone here who would like to stay home today?'" Paddy reenacted her children's big eyes, hands thrust in the air, "'Yeah!' And I said, 'Okay. Your father and I are very tired. We've worked hard all week. And so, I want everybody to behave themselves the whole day. Go on and get your good clothes off.'" Paddy sat back with a smile. "We never went back to church."

Although her clean break from "a lot of church" was without regret, Paddy spoke of pieces worth keeping, like the Bible's teachings about kindness and compassion. Watching all six of her children leave religion behind completely, she followed her mother's example. "I talk to the girls about religion every once in a while. They both say, 'Well, I don't believe in any of that, Mom.' So, I think back to Mamma and say, 'Well that's all right dear. You just do what you have to do. And you just think about the Ten Commandments. They're good to remember.'"

Nora

Once a resident at the retirement community, Nora moved into her husband's home after they married while both were in their nineties. My mother, a friend of Nora's, joined me for our visit. Slight of build and prone to cold, Nora met us at the door in a flannel shirt buttoned to the top. Using a walker, she led us to chairs set up around a card table in their living room, to a spot where sun beams streamed in from the garden window.

Nora's upbringing also brimmed with "a lot of religion" that, unlike Paddy, she relished. She spent her first fourteen years in northern China, raised by American parents. Her mother, a Congregationalist missionary, gave up her work after marrying Nora's father, a lawyer who was Catholic. On Sundays the family went to services at both churches, which Nora loved. Ensuring equal opportunity, Nora's parents asked their five children to wait until they were twenty-one to choose their religious path. Dividing up evenly, Nora and her oldest sister followed in their mother's footsteps, the two middle sisters joined a convent, while their brother remained "an agnostic searcher."

Nora attended college in New England where she met her husband while he was in med school. In 1956, they moved to the Bay Area for his residency. It was at this point, deeply involved in her Presbyterian church, that Nora began to cast about. "I was really searching for a place to fit in," she explained. "Y'know, I was a round peg—and there were a lot of square holes running around." For a while she felt that if she could just become more active, she would somehow fit in. "So, I joined the choir and I taught Bethel and I got involved in Bible Study Fellowship. And I thought all of that would make it possible for me to fit." Nora shrugged. "And nothing really fit." When I asked why she thought this was, she sighed. "I wanted to say that I was a Christian who believed that Jesus died for our sins—you know, all of that. That unless you believed that Jesus died for your sins, you were not saved. And I *wanted* to believe that and I would *say* that I believed that. But there was a part of me that just didn't believe." With incredulity sounding in her voice, she added, "All those years. And I was really active."

"How many years?"

Nora looked over at my mom and we waited. She eventually said to her, "You don't know. But you're nice to look at." As we burst out laughing, Nora said, "Goodness. Probably twenty, twenty-five years." As we marveled at her persistence, Nora intoned, "All. Those. Years."

"And you were deeply involved."

"Deeply involved."

"And *trying*."

"And trying." Nora told us how she even went on two mission trips to Eastern Europe. "And the second time I thought, 'What am I doing here? I have to get out of here!' I just didn't fit. I didn't fit what they were talking about. I didn't fit what they were doing. I didn't fit with the people we were visiting, what they were creating. I thought it was wonderful that they were doing that. But I just didn't fit. I just plain didn't fit."

Nora eventually met with a pastor from a Presbyterian church who she knew to be open-minded. Admitting to him that she simply couldn't believe what the church taught, she recalled his response, while looking her straight in the eye: "We are mutual heretics!" Agreeing to be Nora's spiritual director—to walk with her, as she put it—he freed her to believe as she did.

During our second meeting, when I asked Nora if she had a life lesson to share, she said, without skipping a beat, "Our job—and I think this is really what Jesus and all the other sages have said—is to bring light *in*. Bring in the light. As my mother would say, 'I look for the light in people.'" Choking back tears, she concluded, "So that's our job. So that's it."

Nestled within each of Lolly, Paddy, and Nora's tales of religious departures is an indebtedness to their beloved, pious mothers. Each described, with tears, how profoundly she still missed her. While unapologetically veering from childhood religiosities, each held onto a maternal lifeline. Lolly's career as a yoga instructor, a healing practice that became her "new religion," was her way of walking in her mother's footsteps, who also was a healer. Paddy's unquestioning support for her children's views was her way of honoring her own mother's support during her wayward teenage years. Nora's determination to look for the light in others stayed true to her mother's life motto. Leaving mothers behind logistically and religiously, the heart centers of their childhoods lived on through them.

The two remaining migration accounts are from women born and raised in California. True to trends, their religious upbringings were less traditional than their transplanted peers. Yet both described a similar discomfort, if not despair, with ill-fitting ideologies. Eventually arriving at frameworks that made sense to them and, more importantly, where they made sense, their experiences were, like those just described, a kind of homecoming.

Eleanor

Eleanor's corner apartment was filled with finely crafted wooden furniture—elegant and stately, like Eleanor herself. Her remarkable recounting of her religious migrations thus took me by surprise. After we'd finished our interview, as I was nearly out the door, she admitted that she rarely spoke of such things. With a laugh, she said, "And I didn't even have to pay you!" Momentarily confused, I caught on and laughed along before heading back into the sunshine.

Born in 1928, Eleanor was raised by a banker father and a staunch Presbyterian mother. The family hit a turning point when, as the United States was entering World War II, her mother attended a conference in San Francisco organized by the Oxford Group that promoted peace through what they referred to as "moral rearmament." Eleanor recalled how her mother became "very captured" by the movement while she, a teenager at the time, was also swept up, "dazzled by these fabulous ideas, ideas of absolute honesty, absolute purity, absolute unselfishness, and absolute love." Soon to be renamed Moral Re-Armament (MRA), the movement wasn't exactly a religion, as Eleanor described it, but was based on a three-step formula in which "God has a plan for the world. And if you listen, God will speak to you. And if you obey, God acts."

Backing up slightly, Eleanor recalled how she had become an atheist a few years earlier, while preparing for her confirmation in the Presbyterian church. "I don't think I discussed it with anyone. I just thought, 'I don't think I believe in any of this anymore.'" But when the MRA came along, "I was still utterly susceptible to ideas that say, 'We know how the world works. And we know how you can help make it work.' Somehow when you're so unsure about life, you're just beginning to learn, and somebody comes along and says, 'Here's the answer: If you do this, you'll get that'—which is a totally reductive view—but it's a totally compelling idea for people at that age. If someone comes and says, 'Okay, this is how life is.' Phew!"

The summer between her junior and senior years of high school, Eleanor and her older sister volunteered at the MRA training center on Mackinac

Island in Michigan, where she was further swept up by its ideals. Returning the summer after her senior year, she decided to stay on rather than go to college in the fall. Eleanor's older sister had made the same decision, as did her younger sister a year later. She recalled how her father was broken by the news. "It was really hard. But later on, at some point, he said, 'Remember girl, no matter what you decide or what happens, I'm for you. No matter what.' This was his way."

In Mackinac, Eleanor was tasked with renovating a hotel, preparing guest homes, and serving in the dining room. She also began performing in choirs and plays that toured the country and, eventually, traveled through Europe, India, and Pakistan. These productions featured messages about healing factions, Eleanor explained, "between husband and wife, in families, in farms. Eventually, you see, it was between nations. It's a worldwide effort that, as it's metamorphosed, has moved in different directions."

This was Eleanor's life for seventeen years. Then, as put it, she was "gently pushed out." This she only realized when rehearsals began for a new play, *The Vanishing Island*, and she wasn't invited to take part. "And I thought, 'Oh?'" Eleanor looked shocked. "I always just kind of went places." The reason, she surmised, was that after the curtain came down, cast members were expected to go out into the audience, to "meet people and get into this deep conversation where you would help them change." Eleanor was happy if she had "a real job to do," as she put it. "But none of the conversion stuff. I hated doing that. I would always try to find a way out." In Germany on her final assignment, Eleanor recalled how, when it came time for her to leave, "I just didn't know who I was, where I was, or what I was doing, or why."

Trying to imagine how this must have felt, I said, "You were kind of rudderless."

"Absolutely," Eleanor nodded. Returning home at age thirty-five, she recalled, "My mother didn't know what to do with me. She used to say, 'If you could decide whether to get things done in the morning or in the afternoon'—because I'd have breakfast and then go back to bed, and then I'd have a long nap. Of course, I was in a deep depression, which I didn't know." Her greatest fear, that she would be "cast out into the darkness," had come true.

Eventually Eleanor applied and was accepted at UC Berkeley. To work through some of her general degree requirements before the start of fall semester, she took a summer biology class at a local community college. This is where her worldview shifted, in an instant. Unable to remember the exact lesson, Eleanor recounted the moment when she was prompted to think "about the universe, the vastness of it, what an incredible amount there was. And then about the seashore and the grains of sand and how much there was of everything beyond any understanding or human comprehension." Realizing that "there was more than any one single brain could put together," she gleefully concluded, "God is a myth!" The epiphany was liberating for Eleanor, who had "tried and tried and tried and tried to somehow build a relationship with God, determined that 'I will learn and I will change and I will evolve.'" It was in this moment that she realized, "But no, you're you. You're just going to be you. And that was okay, that I could just be me."

Not wanting to leave me with the wrong impression, Eleanor added, "I get unhappy with people who try to badmouth Moral Re-Armament. Because it did do a lot of very fine things. And there are a lot of people who found real healing through applying its principles. The fact that it's also done damage to a lot of people . . ." She shrugged, "Well, what doesn't?"

Jan

Jan, who had the bluest of blue eyes, possessed what seemed to be an unflappable equanimity. When facing a dire cancer diagnosis, she was certain that all was well with the world, that she was held in the arms of God. Her religious migration story, like Eleanor's, took me by surprise.

Born in Southern California in 1926, Jan was an only child to a waitress mother and a truck-driver father whose rocky marriage ended when she was fourteen. Her mother died soon after, at age thirty-six, of alcoholism. Jan's childhood "anchors," her grandparents originally from Iowa, would bring her along to their Methodist church, where Jan latched onto the idea "that there was a Father in heaven looking out for me—because I didn't know for sure if my dad was going to be around or not." Her baptism at age seven reinforced this: "I was just so into what it meant, that I was now a real child of God. I was a *real* child of Jesus. I was *really* . . . Now I was really adopted."

Married to her high school sweetheart, Jan described the two of them as half-heartedly religious. When they moved to the Bay Area, they attended a Methodist church and enrolled their two daughters in Sunday school. Eventually, they lost interest. "So, we all dropped out and started going camping." Jan chuckled. "And then when I started back to church, Gayle was in . . ." Jan sighed. "I've had a complicated life. Gayle, my eldest daughter, she finally committed suicide."

My heart dropped. "Oh. I'm so sorry."

Jan explained how, while suffering from bipolar disorder, her daughter had started rebelling during her senior year of high school. So, Jan started going back to church. "I don't know what I was thinking. Maybe I was hoping she'd come to church with me." Although she was unable to convince her daughter to join her, Jan found that prayer helped keep her "from falling apart." Becoming more involved, even serving as a deacon, she again stopped going over time.

It was during this lull that Jan took a parapsychology course at a local junior college. Learning of her psychic abilities, she began doing readings for classmates. As news of her talents spread, with requests from strangers flooding in, matters got out of hand. Struggling to reconcile her Christian faith with her readings, Jan began to feel, as she put it, "I was going goofy with the whole thing." Eventually deciding to settle matters once and for all, as she recalled, "I fervently prayed to God to take this gift, or curse—whatever it was—away from me. And I saw Jesus. I saw Jesus and he said," Jan lifted her outstretched her arms, "'Come to me.'" In the wake of this event, Jan joined a local Evangelical church and never looked back. With a shrug she concluded, "So anyway, that was part of my spiritual journey. I always say that God put me on a long leash and just let me explore. And when it was time to pull me in, Jesus just said," Jan outstretched her hands and brought them together with a clap, "'Come to me!' I mean, it was that fast."

Similar to how Lolly, Paddy, and Nora held tight to maternal lifelines, Eleanor and Jan's migrations brought them full circle. Feeling like a failure amid the MRA's certainty about God's role in the world, Eleanor found relief and self-acceptance in her return to her teenage atheism. Jan's childhood thrill at being "a *real* child of Jesus," adopted by a Father who would never leave, returned in a flash after decades of long-leash exploration.

Out of Sync in an Ageist Society

I conclude with another parlor exchange that took place after sharing photos and stories from Kerala. With twenty minutes remaining in our allotted time, I asked the group if they might tackle a million-dollar question: What did they want to be called? I suggested that the label "elderly" often carried negative connotations, to which they agreed. A search for a baggage-free term seemingly a worthy pursuit, we were off and running.

Helen began by questioning the question. She wondered whether "elderly" was necessarily disparaging, as it implies different things to different people. In agreement, Judy considered the relativity of the term, "since a fifteen-year-old looks elderly to a ten-year-old."

Word options came next. Kip offered "experienced," followed by a thoughtful silence.

Susie suggested "post-maturity," prompting light laughter.

My mom offered "wisdom," to which Helen responded, "not always." This brought on another wave of laughter. More words were tried out, with "elders" seemingly gaining traction.

Eleanor suggested, "How about survivors?" to which Jan interjected, "I like 'not dead yet,'" provoking more light laughter. As more words were tried out, with "elders" still sticking, I suggested that the term might not box people in as much as "elderly." Helen flatly disagreed. "Elder *is* a box, though," she insisted, "in that all the wannabes in this culture, when looking to Native American people, fall in love with the sense of *elders*." To the sound of light laughter, Helen concluded, "It's a huge box."

"You're right," I conceded. "Can we appropriate it?" Helen shook her head.

Back to the drawing board, Judy suggested, "I like the neutrality of 'people over eighty.'" Mary Jo quipped, "I want a T-shirt that says, 'I'm eighty-five and still alive!'" Waiting for the laughter to die down, Pat told us about an article she'd read recently about fashion marketers who were trying to promote a clothing line for older women without making them sound old. "They were trying to decide between 'mature' and 'experienced.' They finally decided on the 'experienced' woman." To sounds of general approval, my husband Nick, sitting in a back corner, couldn't resist. "Oh, but that doesn't sound good, though!" Seeing his point, the room erupted in laughter, peppered with comments like, "Yeah, watch out!" "I know!" and "That's advertising for you!"

Aware that a consensus wasn't building, I pointed this out, adding that the indecision was instructive. The difficulty of recognizing age without disparaging or romanticizing, I suggested, is real and rooted in ageism. People agreed. This raised for me a related question. "Is there value in being older? In other words, why am I bothering to talk to you and your counterparts in other parts of the world? Is there a benefit to talking to people over eighty? If so, what is it?"

Thoughtful silence.

Still searching for a label, Kay said, "One thing could be 'Voices of Experience,' because that's something we have for sure in our lives: experience." Thrusting her hand up, Jan said. "You can call us WEMs: Wise, Experienced, Mature." Joining the acronym quest, Judy suggested, "Wise Older Women, that's WOW." This prompted a new crest of laughter as the conversation continued, flipping from acronyms to cultural approaches to aging, the relative nature of wisdom, and the unique contributions of every generation.

FIGURE 1.1 Parlor gathering in California. Corinne's mother is the tall one in the middle of the back row. Photo by author.

Switching gears and slowing the pace, Eleanor reflected on the potential usefulness of this project to older women themselves. "I think it's interesting to discover the universality, to recognize that you're not alone. You're not isolated. Others are going through the same thing. It would be good to somehow express that. Because your experiences are in some ways very different but you're all on the one path, approaching the end."

This struck a chord. To the sound of supportive murmurings, I suggested, "I think when ageism boxes people in and devalues them it also isolates them. So, what I hear you saying, Eleanor, is that we are complicated people with memories and challenges all our own, but a life position near its end is something you share and is valuable."

"You have a broader perspective," Eleanor concurred.

My mother, always the timekeeper, noted that lunchtime was closing in. "We're going to have to wrap it up here if you want to get a group photo!" Taking the cue, I thanked everyone, and we launched into haphazard maneuvering, everyone with opinions about who should stand or sit where, according to height and mobility.

Above the din, Jan insisted, "I don't want to be sitting. I'm not a sitting person."

Eleanor-of-stately-stature replied, "Well then, don't be short!"

Jan laughed, "That's why I'm short, because I've walked myself down into a stub!"

Eventually lined up in rows against the window, Pat noticed we were backlit. With further furniture scooching and bodies rearranged against a nearby wall, Nick snapped our photo.

It's not surprising that we made little progress finding an acceptable word for long-lived people. Common terms like "elderly," which no one liked, can't help but soak up the ageism in the water. New labels that stick are bound to do the same.[1] We are moreover bound to fail when we try to categorically describe the final decades of a long life since older age, perhaps more than any, contains infinite variety. Although I didn't mean to, I gave these women an impossible task.

But we did start closing in on something, thanks to Eleanor, whose indisputable point was that the women in the room were together "approaching the end." This, I've learned, is something that over-eighty women across cultures have little trouble facing. Also self-evident is that while nearing life's edge can clarify the view, late-life challenges can feel isolating, made worse when ageism makes one feel at odds with the surrounding world.[2]

This state in which internal truths clash with external impositions, where attempts at self-acceptance strain against demeaning cultural messaging, is what so many of my Californian friends described when sharing their religious migration stories for which the above accounts are just a small sampling. Their stories brimmed with effort, with "wanting or searching or trying" to make sense of their worlds, to fit in and to count as worthy humans. Yet these stories also resolve. Moving beyond estrangement and self-doubt, they are ultimately accounts of arriving "home." Ageism's storylines, on the other hand, leave people stranded.

Arriving at life's final frontier, it seems especially shameful that the women who have struggled against and overcome ill-fitting expectations in life are now faced with more of the same. Along with Eleanor, my hope is that by bringing their accounts to light, they might feel less alone, less out of sync. To begin, there is perhaps some consolation in recognizing that, although each compilation of life experiences is distinct, "we're all on the one path approaching the end."

2

The Forces of Nature in Northern Iceland

● ● ● ● ● ● ● ● ● ● ● ● ●

Moving on from the Bay Area, land of sunshine and religious fluidity, we arrive in Iceland, where nature's demanding forces appear to relegate religion to the sidelines. More specifically, we arrive in Akureyri, Iceland's "northern capital," population twenty thousand as of this writing. Nestled between mountains to the east and Iceland's longest fjord, Eyjafjörður, to the west, the town hosts a maze of walking paths with stunning views at every turn. This was how I usually wound my way to women's homes, most of whom lived on their own. Their solo situations set them apart from the others, from the communal residences in California and at the SSJ Motherhouse and from the extended family homes in Kerala. Yet Icelandic homes felt anything but lonely, as photos of smiling children, grandchildren, great-grandchildren, and the occasional great-great-grandchild crowded women's walls and display cabinets, testament to the extra-large family that was once the rule.

My regular companion during these visits was Olla, a graduate student in philosophy at the University of Akureyri. Her reassuring presence, her help with translation, and our post-interview discussions of Icelandic cultural trends were indispensable to the process. Reveling in every conversation, we joked that our greatest challenge was making a respectable dent in the snack-feasts that women would set out for us: cheeses, breads, fruits, jams, homemade pastries, and always a pot of strong coffee.

FIGURE 2.1 A winter's evening in Akureyri. Photo by Svavar Alfreð Jónssón.

Also distinguishing Icelandic women from the others was that their first decades were lived during an era of countrywide hardship, when the buffer between humans and nature's unwieldy forces was much thinner than it is today, when poverty was pervasive and serious diseases raged. While those raised on farms grew up particularly vulnerable to the elements, Akureyri-born women shared stories of family struggle, as well.

Another Icelandic difference was in older women's reluctance to be interviewed, to the surprise of my friends and contacts. Before I arrived, I was assured that the women they assigned to me—mothers, grandmothers, aunts—would be happy to share their stories. Yet after I arrived, ready to schedule our meetings, we repeatedly learned that they had misjudged. While about half of these women were willing to meet, the rest vaguely insisted that they had nothing to say. With further help from friends of these friends, I eventually gathered nineteen women to meet with us.

On occasion, Olla and I would mention this confusion during our interviews. Most women were not surprised. Some felt that people shied away because the topic of religion made them uneasy (which couldn't have been the reason, since our invitation was simply to share stories). Over snacks at her kitchen table, Inga went on to explain that people worried they'd be judged if they talked about their faith. "I feel I can talk about these things to my good friend and I can talk to you because you ask the right questions and you're so willing to listen."

Olla agreed. "My feeling is that if we talk about our faith openly in a circle of people, people will think we're crazy."

"It's *definitely* like that," Inga nodded. "You just don't talk about this."

Not sure what they meant, I asked, "People will think you're crazy?"

"People think you're crazy if you mention God or anything related to that," Olla said. "Even if you're celebrating Christmas or you're somewhere for a christening, you don't talk about *God*." Turning to Inga, Olla said she was surprised to hear this from her, assuming this pattern to be more common among younger people. Inga disagreed. She illustrated her point by describing a childhood bedtime scene that Olla and I had already heard from several women, where parents would tell their children to "say something beautiful" (*farðu með eitthvað fallegt*) before bed. This, Inga explained, was code for "say your prayers," helping people to avoid mention of prayer or God. "Our grandparents or parents were there to teach us bedtime prayers or to do the sign of the cross when we got dressed after bathing. Otherwise, we just didn't talk about it."

In the following accounts, we hear how, especially for older women raised on farms, formal religiosity had difficulty competing with Iceland's tenacious forces of nature. Women's reticence to speak with me—whether about religion or about life in general—can also be traced, it turns out, to early-life precarities not shared by younger generations. But first, childhood stories.

The Stories

Svala

Svala's childhood accounts were set in the remote western fjords where Iceland's larger-than-life terrain is especially hard to ignore. Recalling her outback childhood with affection, she would often gesture to her favorite painting of her farm in Lambadalur Valley, hung above the couch where Olla and I sat. Despite her joyful reliving of these early memories, we agreed that members of today's younger, "softer" generations could never manage, let alone imagine, such a childhood.

As was customary for farm children in her day, Svala was homeschooled until, at age ten, she joined a *farskóli* taught by a traveling teacher. Farskóli classes were usually held at farm homes big enough to fit children from surrounding farms. The traveling teacher would usually stay for two weeks at a time, move on to two other farms for two weeks each, then return for another two-week stint. Svala's class with around fourteen students was especially large, so classes were held in a community building rather than a farm. Since this was too far for her to walk to and from every day, she stayed with relatives Monday through Saturday. Once classes finished at around three o'clock on Saturday afternoons, she would walk home to Lambadalur. The trip, she told us, took an hour and a half, if she hurried. The oldest of five siblings, she spent two years traveling it alone.

Olla looked over at me and repeated, "And she was ten years old."

Aware that winter months would have two hours of dim daylight at best, I was incredulous. "In the dark?"

Svala smiled. "I was so glad after two winters had passed because then two more children—my sister and the neighbor boy—were old enough to come to school. Then there were three and that was much better."

Still stunned, I asked, "Were you ever afraid when you walked home alone?"

Svala insisted that she was never afraid out in nature. On second thought, she said, "But at the farm where I stayed, there was a guy working there who loved to tell me stories about sea monsters. So, at the last part of the way home I would walk on the beach, because above the beach was really swampy and wet. So, I walked on the beach and sometimes there were birds that got startled and flew—and of course I couldn't really see them. Sometimes I thought, 'Could this be a sea monster?'" Olla and I laughed uneasily. Svala continued, "But I was never really afraid because I was born in nature. My father would take me fishing in the sea and I was there when we herded the sheep. I was used to walking across streams and rivers. So, I was never afraid of nature."

From age fourteen through seventeen, Svala went to a boarding school in Reykjaness on the other side of the mountain and across the fjord from her farm. Students from her area would go to school in the fall and return only in the spring, since travel over Christmas break wasn't possible. Their fall trip began with a ferry ride to Ísafjorður, the closest town, where the children would then board a postal boat that made stops to deliver mail and collect milk from the farms. Although two other boarding schools were slightly closer to her farm, Svala chose Reykjaness because of its slightly shorter academic year. Another perk was the hot springs that emptied into the school's swimming pool and onto a nearby beach, popular spots for students to meet and swim.

Once a year the Reykjaness students would go to church, a trip that required a fjord crossing and a hike over a mountain, which took them all day. For this reason, they couldn't plan in advance but had to wait for a period of stable weather. At Svala's farm, the closest church was also hard to reach much of the year due to the rough and roadless terrain. As was typical in farm country, services were mostly held in the winter, when travel was difficult. In the summer, church was out of the question because everyone including the pastor had farm work to do. "Since summer was when we used to stock up for the winter, people didn't have time to go to church," Svala explained. "But we didn't really go in the winter either because it was just too far." Olla interjected for my benefit that Svala used the traditional word *lífsbjargartíminn* for summer rather than the standard *sumar*. Its literal meaning, "life's salvation time," was appropriate given the life-and-death importance of the short harvest season.

Typical of rural Icelanders of her generation, Svala's family would hold a weekly *húslestur*, literally, "house reading," instead of going to church. Her great-grandfather would select chapters from the Bible for her father to read, followed by hymns. "Sometimes I got really sleepy when they were reading from the book," Svala recalled. "But I quickly learned, at a young age, to sing along."

For college Svala moved to Akureyri, where she met her future husband. Since then, her religious practices continued to be homegrown, like most of the women we met. Near the end of our second interview, as Olla and I sidled up to her kitchen table filled with snacks, we watched Svala walk to the far side of her sitting room. With the sun setting behind her, she wordlessly lit a white candle alongside a photo of her deceased husband. After standing in silence for a moment, she returned to our table. This tradition of sunset candle-lighting for loved ones is common in Iceland among young and old alike. The Icelandic saying *Ég kveiki á kerti fyrir þig*, "I'll light a candle for you," is a way of assuring someone—while avoiding religious language—that they will be held close.

Ingibjörg

Born in 1926, Ingibjörg was ninety-three when we met at the home of a mutual friend, Sirra. Raised in the western fjords across the river from Svala, Ingibjörg was the youngest of fifteen children whose oldest sister was Svala's mother. When Olla and I arrived at Sirra's house, Ingibjörg was already there. Dressed in sensible farmer's attire, she quietly sized us up during introductions, her no-nonsense demeanor clear from the start.

Ingibjörg began by laying out for us what it was like to grow up in Lambadalur Valley a generation before Svala, when grinding poverty was a matter of course. Ingibjörg's father had started out as a *vistarband* farmer, a common form of indentured servitude when Iceland was under Danish rule. As she described it, her mother made do by knitting, sewing, and patching every stitch of material in the house to clothe their fifteen children. Her father, who spent part of the year at sea, sold the fish he caught to buy oil and other necessities. "But sometimes there was no fish," Ingibjörg said. "Sometimes there was nothing to eat."

Ingibjörg recalled fervent nighttime prayers during winter storms when her brothers would be out at sea and her father no longer fished. "Everyone slept together in the same room in the old days," she explained. "So, I would hear my mom saying to my dad, 'Where are my boys now? What are they doing?' He would say, 'Well, the wind is blowing from the north now, so they are probably stationed in that area where they wait for the wind to die down.' He would comfort her by telling her, 'I know the ocean. I know exactly where they'll be when the wind blows from the north or the south.'" After this, her parents would pray for their sons, "that everything would be okay and that they would come home."

Poverty compounded the usual challenges of getting to church for Ingibjörg's family. "There were three rivers to cross, that you just had to walk through," she explained. "And you wouldn't go into the church with wet shoes, so you needed to bring another pair of shoes with you. But we didn't have a second pair, so we just didn't go."

Like Svala's family, Ingibjörg's held a húslestur on Sundays where her mother read from the Bible and her father led the singing. Brightening at the memory, she told us how her parents, both with strong voices, had met in a small church choir on a farm. "So, they knew every hymn and every folk song that was popular at that time. And then they had all these children and all of us could sing really well. So, it was like a little service with its own choir—a beautiful ceremony right there in our home." Reveling in the scene, she described how she and her siblings would be on their best behavior, how they kept the fire going with fuel that was otherwise used sparingly. "Although there was no running water in the house, everything was done so we would all be clean and our hair combed." Ingibjörg sighed. "These were truly festive occasions."

Ingibjörg told us how the two boys that she planned to marry, both fishermen, were "taken by the ocean," one at a time. After the second one died, she said with a smirk, she decided she was "all through with boys." Relocating to the south end of Akureyri's fjord to help her ailing sister, Ingibjörg met her future husband and eventually settled down to raise a family and run a farm.

Ásdís

Although childhoods in Akureyri town were in many ways different than Svala's and Ingibjörg's, religiosity remained a private matter . While church was easily accessed and ran year-round, most families didn't go. At the same time, Sunday school was a popular option for town children, something that would have been impossible on the farms.

Ásdís's home was filled with family artwork rather than photos. On display were paintings by her recently deceased art teacher husband, her daughter's work that I recognized from shops downtown, wood carvings by her father, and other enticing pieces by her children and grandchildren. Healthy and agile at eighty, Ásdís was stylishly put together. Born and raised in town, she described her religiosity as eclectic. Drawn to spirit work (*andleg mál*) and a member of Akureyri's Theosophical Society, she had been practicing meditation and yoga for decades. "I am, at heart, a mix of all kinds of things," she told us.

Ásdís and her five brothers grew up in the basement of an old schoolhouse where their parents eked out a living as housekeepers for Davíð Stefansson, a famous Icelandic poet who lived above them in the same building. Her religious upbringing was fairly typical, with nighttime prayers passed on by her mother while her father, who played the violin, taught the children hymns. She and her brothers attended Sunday school, after which the family would gather around the radio to listen to services. Ásdís told us how she once asked her mother why they didn't attend services in person. Her answer was that church was for the upper classes, referring to the Icelandic business class as well as the wealthy Danes who settled in town. "The middle and lower classes didn't go to church," Ásdís explained, "because they felt their coats or their shoes weren't good enough." Yet her mother insisted that they were not poor. "We didn't have much, but we weren't poor."

Ásdís's most cherished practice was lighting a candle at sunset. She used this time to pray for those in need, who "have a wound to bandage," as she

FIGURE 2.2 Ásdís with a childhood toy carved by her father and family artwork. Photo by author.

put it. Near the end of our second interview, she led Olla and me to a small hallway table to show us her "family circle," an African candleholder with five dark brown clay figures surrounding a thick white candle. Two people she was currently praying for, she told us, a grandson and another young man, were both sick. "It's not often that I pray out loud. But this is my way, to light a candle."

Naninga

Naninga welcomed Olla and me into her home just three weeks after her husband, Jón, had passed away. Her son, a Lutheran priest and a friend of mine, rightly guessed that a visit might lift her spirits. With a sweet, high voice and beautiful dark-brown almond-shaped eyes, Naninga spoke of being anchored, from the start, in a strong Lutheran faith. It was a lifelong commitment that set her apart from all the other Icelandic women we met.

Our conversation began with condolences. I told Naninga how I had admired the photos and heartfelt tributes her son had posted of his father on Facebook. Taking this in, she reflected on the deep faith she and her husband had shared. Thinking back further, she recalled how her fondest childhood memories were of the times she spent with her grandparents who lived above them in their Akureyri flat. Her grandmother, who was on the YMCA missionary board, would host gatherings every other week where women would come to knit and do needlework to sell and raise funds for missionary work. "They also sang together and had these good prayer meetings," Naninga recalled with a smile. "I loved being there with them."

Aware that her church-bound faith was unusual for Icelanders, Naninga was grateful for what had been passed down to her as well as for how it had continued. She told us how her grandchildren, especially the girls, looked forward to sleeping over at her house when they were young, to sharing her nightly routine of reading from the Bible and saying prayers. "I think they felt this was important and good. They enjoyed it. It was relaxing for them. And obviously their parents have taught them well to pray."

Aðalheiður

Aðalheiður was one of the two women Olla and I met in an assisted living facility. We were joined by her son, Hlynur, who added layers of warmth and memory to the conversation. We arranged ourselves in Aðalheiður's small room so that she had a good view of us. Olla and I sat side by side on a small couch with Hlynur in a chair beside us. Aðalheiður, perched on the side of her bed, sat facing the three of us.

Raised on a farm in eastern Iceland, Aðalheiður was one of nine siblings preceded by nine half-siblings from her father's first wife. Unlike Svala and Ingibjörg's farm families who stayed put, Aðalheiður's spent winters in the village where her father repaired fishing boats and summers at a small farm ten kilometers away. Although the village church was within walking distance during the winter, services were sporadic since the priest had to serve several churches at once.

Like Naninga, Aðalheiður revered her "very religious" grandmothers who taught her to pray and to sing hymns. Smiling at the memory, she recalled sharing a room with one of them. "I remember when I woke up in the morning, sometimes I'd see my grandmother all dressed, sitting on her bed, and saying prayers for the day." When I asked how her approach to religion had changed over the years (a question I learned to stop asking), this at first confused Aðalheiður. Once she understood, she shook her head adamantly, "Lengi býr að fyrstu gerð." First things last the longest. Recalling again her beloved grandmothers, she said, "If the foundation is strong, it holds."

At this, Aðalheiður switched gears. Noting how her own children hadn't kept their foundation, she eyed Hlynur. "I remember when Gunnar left the church. I can't remember who told me because he didn't tell me himself. It stung me a little bit."

Hlynur looked startled. "It stung you a little?"

"Yes, it stung. I was so surprised. The worst thing about it was that I had to tell my mother." Filling the silence that followed, Olla asked why Gunnar left. Aðalheiður mused, "I don't know. Nobody knew."

Hlynur interjected that of course people knew. It had to do with the politics of the 1960s. In Icelandic, he said, "He was very left. And I am too." In English he added, "I'm no longer part of the Church either."

Knowing this to be typical, I quipped, "So Gunnar broke the ice."

Hlynur nodded, "He broke the ice."

"So, we can blame *him*," Olla said, making us laugh.

Aðalheiður stayed serious. Quick to redeem her son, she said, "I still find Gunnar a good person even though. He's always cheerful and upbeat."

Hlynur added encouragingly, "Yes, he probably has some kind of religion even though he's not in the Church."

"*Já já.*" Aðalheiður nodded. "But I found this a challenge."

Realizing his mother's disappointment for the first time, Hlynur said, "Of course. At the time, it must've been." Assuring her that she did her job well, he reminded her of how she would read Bible stories to her children and bring them to church on special days. Leaving the Church, he insisted, had nothing to do with her. "I think it was just a matter of circumstance and timing that people turned out not to be very religious. Maybe it had nothing to do with the Church, even. They just didn't want to be part of the system."

Sigríður H.

Sigríður H., also from the east of Iceland, was ninety-three when we met. Unlike the others, her childhood farm family was well-to-do. Surrounded by turf houses, hers was the first in the area to be made of stone. Hardship arrived nonetheless when, at age five, Sigríður's mother died, leaving her eleven children to be raised by extended family members. Earning a degree at a women's college in Uppsala, Sweden, Sigríður returned to Iceland to marry a farmer whose grandfather, a pastor-farmer, had built a church next to his farmhouse.

When we met Sigríður, she had just returned from a choir tour in Scotland the day before. Still living at her home along with one of her sons and

FIGURE 2.3 Sigríður outside her family's farm church. Photo by author.

his family, she greeted us at the entryway elegantly dressed in a knee-length black wool skirt and black-patterned stockings. Leading us to her living quarters at the top floor, she bounded up two flights of stairs to a large room with wide windows that opened onto views of the mountains encircling the farm. A table in the center was heaped with homemade pastries, cheeses, breads, and jam.

Like most of the women we met in Iceland, Sigríður told us that she'd learned to say prayers at bedtime and to make the sign of the cross after washing and putting on a clean shirt. Not wanting to make too much of this, she said, "These were just things that grown-ups were expected to teach children at that time. It was just something we did. Before we went to bed, my father would always tell us, 'Say something beautiful,' which meant that we were supposed to say our prayers." Sigríður's religiosity continued to be lukewarm despite the countless hours she'd spent singing in church choirs, from her teens up into her nineties,. "But that was more for the music than for the religion," she insisted. "After I was confirmed around the age of fourteen, I soon grew out of my religion. After that point, I didn't say prayers. But I've been a part of the mass for such a long time. I know how to answer the priest and, in a choir, you are supposed to participate.... But the thought behind it, I don't think much of that."

Svana

Svana was the most insistently nonreligious woman that Olla and I encountered in Iceland. When we arrived at her house, she admitted to nearly ducking out of our interview, feeling unsure about where our conversation might go. Her uncertainty, a mismatch for her confident demeanor, dissolved as soon as her stories started rolling.

Born in 1932, Svana was raised on a small farm in the Borgadalur Valley just east of Akureyri during an era when poverty was the rule, as she described it. "At that time, it was a crisis for everyone. A bad time, really. People were poor. I remember my first years: there was no electricity and no telephone. In 1937 we got the first telephone line. The heat went from coal to propane gas only in 1970." Like other farm children, Svana entered the farskóli system at age ten. She recalled with amusement how their traveling teacher would "carry the school in a suitcase, just some maps, some books, and a blackboard." Three years in, her father and teacher, who pegged Svana as "a hard worker and a good learner," scraped up funds from extended family and sent her to a boarding school in Akureyri. During her second year, she contracted polio, confining her to bed in Akureyri for months. "It wasn't easy at that time—no roads, no cars, really. I remember when I did go home, it was with the snowplow over the mountains."

Before her final year at boarding school, Svana's family ran out of money. Taking leave to earn school fees herself, she ended up, at age seventeen, as a farskóli teacher. Svana laughed, "So, I traveled with my suitcase to the farms!" Fetching a photo album from across the room, she showed us a black-and-white picture of herself and five of her students. Peering over it together, we agreed that it was nearly impossible to tell the teacher from the students. After teaching for a year, Svana held down two jobs in Akureyri while she finished boarding school. Moving on to earn her teaching degree in Reykjavík, she returned home to Borgadalur to found its first stationary school to replace the farskóli system. For forty years she served as teacher and head mistress. During the first ten years she performed all duties on her own, eventually hiring teachers, staff members, and a bus driver.

When our conversation eventually steered its way toward the topic of religion, it lost momentum. Svana explained that, in Borgadalur Valley where she grew up, no one she knew held a Sunday húslestur, nor did parents teach their children to pray or to cross themselves after taking baths. Yet Svana wanted to be clear that she didn't have anything against the Church, per se. "Of course, priests came to our school to talk to the children and we maybe played some music or sang some hymns. But we were not hypocrites of faith. We knew all the hymns, the Christmas hymns and everything, which is important to participate in. But we weren't hypocrites."

Stuck on the word "hypocrite," I asked what she meant. This was hard for Svana to explain so I later asked Olla. As she understood it, when people used the word in this context it implied a skepticism of "churchy" Icelanders, of those who spoke openly about God and their faith. People were suspicious of such talk since no one, they felt, could be *that* holy.

Landscape Lessons

This suspicion returns us to the challenge of finding women willing to share their life stories with us that, as I see it, is related to the problem of speaking openly about religion in Iceland. Margrét had some thoughts on the former. An international correspondent who began her career as the second woman ever to work for Iceland's major newspaper, *Morgunblaðið*, she was used to sharing her opinions. Margrét felt that women of her generation held back since so many had spent most of their lives as housewives. "They aren't expected to express themselves and, even if they do, their ideas are more or less suppressed by men." Grateful for the changes wrought by the women's movement in the 1970s, Margrét shrugged. "But men will still somehow steal their ideas. They will steal their ideas and then pretend that it came from some men." Thinking for a moment, she added, "It's amazing what I have seen and heard and experienced through my life."

After our four-hour-long, wonderfully stimulating conversation with Margrét, as Olla and I were nearly out the door, she admitted that she had actually been dreading our meeting. Shocked, I suggested that perhaps she wondered who these strange people were, barging into her home. Margrét shook her head. She'd worried, she told us, that "as an old lady, I would have nothing to say." Beaming a beatific smile, she said, "But you've made my day."

Margrét's confession suggests that, along with sexism, internalized ageism may also have led women to resist meeting with us. This makes sense. Yet since older women in the other three locations were overall eager to share their stories and opinions, who lived in places where sexism and ageism are thriving to different degrees, this can't be the whole story. As suggested in the introduction, older women's willingness to engage seems to come from a clarity about what really matters that can surface at life's edge. It's a late-life confidence that seems to override socially prescribed self-doubts in many instances.

We're left, then, to wonder about the particular strength of Icelandic women's reticence. In the wake of her mother-in-law's surprising refusal to be interviewed, my friend Hulda offered another possibility. When she wrote to tell me that this otherwise enthusiastic storyteller insisted that she didn't have anything to say, I told Hulda that others were backing out for similar reasons. Recognizing this uncertainty as a pattern among older women, Hulda joked, "If you were to ask them what their favorite color is, they would still have a problem answering it. What if the answer is not correct?!" Speculating further, she recalled her mother-in-law telling her that, as a girl, people would coach her to say "I don't know" when asked her opinion. Hulda suspected this had to do with life's hardships, a way of protecting family secrets. She also felt it was meant to protect the girls themselves since Icelanders tended to dislike "know-it-alls," especially girls.

Iceland's countrywide hardship that lasted well into the twentieth century is a variable that sets it apart from other three locations. It also starkly separates the older generations from the rest who don't always understand their ways. The connection Hulda made between early-life precarity and the training of girls to guard their opinions I'd heard from some of the older women as well, when we asked them why they thought their peers shied away from us.

A disdain for know-it-alls returns us to Inga and Olla's exchange at the start of this chapter, to a fear of judgment when speaking of one's faith or, to use Svana's word, of being cast as a hypocrite. A general disdain for self-promotion is a recognized feature among Nordic people, known in English as the "Law of Jante."[1] It seems that life-threatening natural events commonplace in Iceland such as avalanches, volcanic eruptions, and storms at sea have further enforced this law. Those who wield too much confidence might come across not only as socially inappropriate but as disrespectful to the wilds that put you in your place. Know-it-alls will have their comeuppance.

Standing back, it thus seems that larger-than-life terrain contributes to Icelandic women's disengagement from formal religion on several accounts. As we've seen, the country's harsh and bountiful seasons literally blocked people's way to church back in the day. During this time, when buffers between humans and an untamable landscape were thinner, people were trained in humility that, in turn, created a disdain for overconfidence, including presumptions tied to faith.[2] Finally, listening to Icelandic women's reflections on what matters in life, so often shot through with the majesty, power, and sanctity of nature itself (stay tuned), one might wonder how any religious system unhinged from the natural world could possibly compete.

3

Sacred Relations in South India

●●●●●●●●●●●●●

The physical and religious terrain of Kerala could not be more different than Iceland's. Here, where temples, churches, and mosques enliven a densely populated tropical landscape, saints and deities shower prosperity onto businesses, receive prayers at roadside shrines, and ensure safety for travelers. In contrast to sitting rooms populated by family photos in Iceland, sacred images in Kerala hovered over women's doorways, lined kitchen ledges, and held forth in *puja* or prayer rooms. Human portraits sometimes mingled among them, yet these tended to be of straight-faced matriarchs and patriarchs who, having passed on, conferred blessings as well.

Interviews in Kerala also tended to be like small parties. Family members would often help with translation or supply details when memories dimmed. Friends and neighbors would sometimes arrive to listen in. On both trips to Kerala, I was accompanied by my two students, Haley and Paige, who added youthful charm to each setting, offering their own questions and insights along the way.

Adding to the festive feel of these meetings was the gusto with which the older women partook. During our first winter trip, on the heels of my summer stint in Akureyri, this rather astounded me. Where I'd struggled to find nineteen women to meet with me in Iceland, thirty-two interviews fell into place in about half the time in Kerala. Reasons for this aren't immediately clear. Many of the women we met in Kerala had endured hardships, as in Iceland, yet this didn't seem to dim their willingness to share their stories. While Kerala's front-and-center religiosity may have fueled their enthusiasm, we didn't lose momentum when moving on to other topics. It's possible that the status typically given to older adults in India, where older women are often the designated storytellers, gave them added confidence.[1] Yet the same could be said of Icelanders, who often treasure their older relatives for the same reasons.

Another way to think about Iceland-Kerala differences is to consider how each place draws the line between public and private domains differently. In Iceland, where older women were taught to guard themselves from strangers, such lines were drawn boldly. In Kerala, hazier lines were evident not just in women's willingness to open up about themselves but in their physical expressions, warmly holding one or both of my hands during our exchanges, clasping a knee or arm for emphasis. These differences also support anthropological theories in which socially porous societies, like in Kerala, host "enchanted" worldviews in which gods and spirits mingle among humans. Socially buffered societies, by contrast, are deemed to uphold so-called modern, disenchanted worldviews. Beneath these theories is often the assumption that the standard to which we're all headed, as a culture grows out of enchantment and into modernity, is the buffered, guarded state.[2]

Such theories and assumptions dissolve, however, when considering how Iceland's buffered society includes a lively spirit-filled worldview. The country also seems headed in the "wrong" direction, as the need to guard one's privacy appears to be waning over time, especially among younger generations who are growing up less vulnerable to the elements. From this angle, Kerala's social porosity seems less tied to an "enchanted" nonmodern worldview than to an openness made possible by its more hospitable, tropical terrain.

Speaking of hospitable terrain, we can also chalk up Kerala's remarkable religious diversity to its tropics. Annually buffeted by monsoon winds and rain, its climate is ideal for growing spices and its location perfectly aligned for trade ships to blow in from the Middle East. With thousands of years' traffic across the Arabian Sea, Kerala's majority Hindu community has been joined by Christians and Muslims who make up roughly a quarter each of the total population. Most of Kerala's Christians belong to one of several denominations within the Syrian Christian community that traces its roots to St. Thomas the Apostle, believed to have arrived on a trade ship.[3] Because my earlier work in Kerala was in areas with high concentrations of Christians, two-thirds of the women we interviewed were Christian. These include socially elite Syrian Christians and, at the other end of the economic spectrum, Dalit converts who were mostly members of the British-based Church of South India.[4] The rest of the women we met were Hindus from a range of backgrounds.

While conversations in Kerala were a study in contrasts unlike anywhere else, women uniformly described being steeped, from the start, in devotional practices. Religious routines in Kerala, unmatched even by the Sisters of St. Joseph, were also less indebted to doctrines and distinctions than to the sacred entities that blessed and sustained them.[5] Eager to share their stories of sacred intimacy, worries about being pegged as hypocrites, as in Iceland, couldn't have been further from their minds.

The Stories

Sarojini

Sarojini had just turned ninety when Haley, Paige, and I visited her home. My friends Sujatha and Shobha, friends of Sarojini's daughter-in-law, Shayla, took the day off to drive us from Ernakulam to their remote village. Sarojini lived in the ancestral home where she was raised, handed down through generations of women as was custom among Kerala's matrilineal Nair community. Walking had become difficult for Sarojini, so we met in her bedroom, led there by Shayla. On the way, we passed the family puja room where portraits of Sarojini's mother, grandmother, and great-grandmother looked down on us from above the entrance. As is typical of Hindu devotion in Kerala, the deities who received prayers and offerings inside mingled across sectarian lines.[6]

Dressed in a white sari with red trim, Sarojini greeted us from a chair in her room. Shayla had arranged seating in a semicircle around her so the six of us could sit close. Shayla claimed the chair to Sarojini's left, her right arm draped over her mother-in-law's shoulder for most of our conversation. I was given a seat on a cot to her right, helping me to catch her softly spoken words.

Sarojini began by telling us that her mother died when she was two and a half. Her grandmother, her great-grandmother, and her mother's "very strict" oldest brother looked after her and her younger brother until they were sent to school in Ernakulam, where their father had moved and remarried. Their preschool years and holiday breaks at home were bookended by prayer. At five o'clock every morning, their uncle would wake the children to bathe in the

FIGURE 3.1 Sarojini with Corinne and Haley to the left, Shayla and Paige to the right. Photo by Shobha Menon.

pond. He would then pass them off to their grandmother, who would walk with them to the nearby goddess temple for prayers. At sunset, the family would wash up and gather in front of the house to light an oil lamp. Seated next to the lamp, Sarojini and her brother would "pray the names of God." This, she told us, could be anyone: Rama or Krishna, Shiva or the Goddess.

Sarojini's bedroom was like a second puja room. Across from where we sat, deity images covered the two walls surrounding her sleeping cot, poised to bless and protect her. During a lull in our conversation, Haley noted the gold chains peeking out from around Sarojini's neck, prompting her to show us the four medallions she had tucked into her sari, imprinted with some of these same deities: a baby Krishna lying across a gold leaf, a baby Krishna chakra-mandala, and the goddesses Bhagavati and Lakshmi. Asked if she had a favorite, Sarojini said without missing a beat, "Guruvayur Appan. The baby Krishna."

Shobha then drew our attention across the room to the same Krishna, whose image was strategically placed just above the head of Sarojini's cot. She also mentioned that the image of Lord Shiva on the adjacent wall she had painted herself. As the rest of us enthused over Shobha's handsome Shiva, Sarojini smiled, waiting to get us back on track. Once we'd quieted down, she told us how she sometimes complained to baby Krishna at night. "I ask him, 'Why are you doing this to me?' 'Why are you giving me pain?'" But by morning, she assured us, the pain would be gone. When I reflected back to Sarojini how special Guruvayur Krishna must be for her, beyond all the others, she nodded. "My children are almost all gone, living all over the world." Sneaking a glance at her daughter-in-law, who smiled back, she said, "But he's always been with me and always will be."

Pennamma

Pennamma was ninety-six when we met. Like Sarojini, she was lovingly cared for by her daughter-in-law. When Haley, Paige, and I arrived at their family home located in a small backwater village, her daughter-in-law, Reeni, greeted us at the front steps along with four dogs of different shapes and sizes, three of them rescued strays. Heading inside, we passed through a high-ceilinged entry room with saint statues stationed above the doorways. On the main wall, a gold-framed image of Mother Mary with child Jesus, both wearing crowns, was flanked by four family portraits: Pennamma's deceased husband, his brother, his parents, and his grandmother.

Pennamma waited for us in the sitting room, her favorite dachshund-pug mix nestled at her feet. She was wearing white cotton attire that, once standard issue for Syrian Christians, is still worn by some women of her generation: a V-neck top (*chatta*) with sleeves reaching just above the elbows and a cloth (*thuni*) wrapped around the waist to make a skirt.[7] Pennamma took us in with a quiet seriousness as we settled in and introduced ourselves. When we began our conversation by asking Pennamma about her childhood, her face brightened. She had grown up in a family of eleven children, she told us, when life was "without a care." Especially precious were summer holidays in the hills, where she and her siblings and cousins would climb trees and play games. She told us how the family would attend daily mass during the holidays and gather for morning and evening prayers at home. "I grew up in an atmosphere of prayer," she said, something she'd maintained throughout her life.

Underlining this last point, Reeni told us, "Her entire day is spent in prayer."

"The entire day?"

"She leaves for church around six fifteen every morning and attends mass. Then, the first thing she does when she comes home is that she goes and stands there, below the statues," Reeni pointed to the entry room. "For about five minutes she's standing there, and praying. Then she has a routine. She has her breakfast, she sleeps, and again she's in her room saying her rosary and prayer.

Then she comes up front where she has her collection of books and her Bible. So, I join her there every day at five o'clock." Reeni smiled at Pennamma. "From five to six, it's mom-in-law time. Until then, she waits for me to come. And while she waits for me, she reads the Bible and says her prayers and her novenas."

Paige asked Pennamma whether she prayed for anyone in particular. Shaking her head, she said, "I take the names of everyone in our family and pray. I pray for my eight children, taking everyone by name, and I pray for the grandchildren." Doing the math, Haley counted up to twenty-one grandchildren.

"No wonder all day is in prayer," I said.

Reeni nodded, "Sometimes I ask her if she might do some other thing and she will say, 'I don't have time, after all my prayers.'"

Ananda Lakshmi

Ananda Lakshmi, from northern Kerala, was in Ernakulam for a monthlong visit with her daughter when we met with her. We were introduced by her granddaughter, Priya, who responded to a request for interviews that my friend Sujatha had posted on an All Ladies League app. Arriving at their family home, Priya lead Haley, Paige, and me to their sitting room where her parents were seated on a cot set against a wall. Once we'd settled in, we watched as Ananda Lakshmi emerged from the puja room, oil lamps burning in the background. Wearing a gold-trimmed off-white sari, she chuckled to herself as she took her place in a large cushioned chair.

Priya and her mother began by filling us in on their goddess-worshipping Thiyya community from northern Kerala. Proud of their heritage, they were eager to put Ananda Lakshmi in the spotlight. Haley, Paige, and I then introduced and explained ourselves, telling the group how much we were enjoying our time in Kerala. As I turned to Ananda Lakshmi, inhaling to ask our first question, she smiled widely and blurted, "I really don't know anything." Taken aback, we all laughed. I insisted, "No, no, don't say that!" Laughing along, Ananda Lakshmi said, "Now that I am old, I just pray, morning and evening. That is my favorite thing to do." I reassured her that this is something we wanted to hear more about. But first, I wondered if she had any childhood memories to share. Closing her eyes, working to recall, Ananda Lakshmi said that she was number six in a family of fifteen children. Beyond that, she remembered very little.

So, we moved on to her religious practices. Ananda Lakshmi told us how her day began at four thirty each morning when she bathed, lit oil lamps

Sacred Relations in South India • 49

FIGURE 3.2 Ananda Lakshmi. Photo by Haley Saba.

before the deities in the puja room, then spent an hour and a half in meditation and prayer. This included yoga postures: "Surya namaskaram. Chandra namaskaram also. I used to do Chandra namaskaram five times, then Surya namaskaram ten times." I asked whether this was hard to keep up at ninety. As Ananda Lakshmi shook her head, her daughter inserted that their doctor actually wanted her to cut back on the yoga postures, as they were straining her back.

Priya wanted to impress upon us that the most important part of her grandmother's routine was that she loudly chanted mantras and Sanskrit passages from the *Devi Mahatmyam*, Hymn to the Great Goddess. Impressed, I asked if she had memorized these passages. With Priya nodding in my peripheral vision, Ananda Lakshmi leaned in with a laugh and said, "I have *not* memorized them!" As our conversation continued, we heard stories of how the goddess to whom she chanted loudly, from memory or not, was central to her existence, heaping miracles upon her life.

Grace

Born into a well-to-do Syrian Catholic family like Pennamma's, Grace had no trouble dredging up childhood memories. Tech-savvy, she had responded to Sujatha's All Ladies League app request herself and invited us to her thirteenth-floor apartment. Married to an army lieutenant, Grace had spent most of her adult life in Delhi and Bangalore. Earning a bachelor's in economics, she ran her own successful sock business in Delhi for many years. Similar to other older women in Kerala who had achieved professional success, this did not diminish her deep religiosity, handed to her in childhood. Unarguably the most enthusiastic storyteller of anyone we met, Grace held out a bangled arm to warn me as I got ready to switch on the voice recorder: "I just want you to know, I'm not one to give short answers!"

As was often the case for women born into families of means, Grace grew up with daily mass and family prayer time. Their evening sessions were some of the most intense I'd heard in Kerala. At seven every night, Grace told us, her family of thirteen children would meet in their prayer room, the Christian equivalent of a puja room populated by saints rather than deities. "Candles would be burning, and my father would stand at the front with all the children around. And he would dedicate each of us into the Sacred Heart of Jesus." Throughout these hour-long sessions the children were made to kneel. "We were to stay on our knees. And if we sat down, my mother had a stick and she would," Grace swiped with her arm, "'Tuck!' 'Get up!' But if you were sick or something like that, you were allowed to sit down. Sometimes we would say," Grace made a troubled face, "'Oh I am paining!'" As the three of us laughed, Grace nodded, "I was good at it! Then we'd say the angelus. After that, we'd say the rosary. After that, there would be a reading about a saint's life followed by a short prayer, offered to a different saint each month. For St. Joseph it would be March. For Mary it would be in May."

Marveling at the intensity, I said, "And you would all be on your knees."

"Yes." Grace chuckled. "We had a servant called Jose, Malayalam for Joseph. So, when we were saying the litany, the prayer for St. Joseph, he would be there, on the side and sometimes he'd be sleeping. So instead of saying, 'Praise you,' or whatever it was that we were saying, he'd say, 'Endo? Endo? Endo?'"

I translated, "What? What? What?"

"So, he would say that and we'd all start laughing. And my father would say, 'No laughter! No laughter!'" Grace laughed.

Grace recalled warmer religious moments with her mother. "My mother used to sit us in her lap and tell us about Jesus, about his beauty and how he is God and how he comes into your heart when you receive communion. And she used to teach us prayers and told us that when you pray a hundred times you are making a satin cloth for Jesus to come inside you, to lie in there."

Grace told us how she continued her Catholic devotions throughout her adulthood, rising early to pray the rosary before daily mass. Then at age sixty-five, while battling a chronic illness, she underwent a healing experience that led her to Pentecostalism, transferring her religious zeal to a new framework. Although we didn't learn this until midway through our first meeting, we could have guessed by looking around the room, where walls and end tables featured framed passages from scripture with no saints in sight.

Grace was also one of the handful of women in Kerala, both Hindu and Christian, who offered to bless us before we left. Always agreeable, Haley, Paige, and I huddled tightly together, Grace's hands touching each of our heads as she prayed for our safety, that Jesus would surround us with his light and drive away any darkness within.

Thanks to Jestin, a doctoral student at Mahatma Gandhi University at the time, we also visited the homes of seven women living in Dalit colonies. Their stories of childhood poverty are part of the enduring effects of Kerala's slave trade history that, although abolished in 1855, continued to rupture Dalit families well into the 1930s. While land reforms in the 1960s entitled the formerly enslaved to the plots of land where they'd been living for generations, many still worked for the same landowners, making full autonomy slow in coming.[8] All but one of the Dalit women we visited were members of the Church of South India (CSI), founded in Kerala by British missionaries. Despite CSI's Anglican roots, the Holy Spirit loomed large for its Dalit members, making them seem more Pentecostal than mainline Protestant.

Rahel

Rahel's home, across the lane from a pineapple field and surrounded by papaya, jackfruit, and coconut trees, was part of a Dalit colony built on land purchased in the early 1900s by the CSI Church. Wearing a white V-neck chatta top and a blue-and-white plaid *mundu*, she bounded out to greet us, Bible in hand, shouting, "Alleluia! Praise God!" in Malayalam. After introductions and more praising, she led us to a circle of plastic chairs set up on her porch. Directing me to the seat to her left, she gripped my hand, letting go only when she needed both hands to tell a story.

Rahel painted her childhood hardships in broad strokes. Her father died when she was two, sending her mother back into the rice fields to work and leaving her older brother to look after his three sisters. Once she reached school age, Rahel was charged to care for her younger sister, and thus never received formal education. From adolescence onward, she worked in manual labor. Rahel described her husband's childhood as even more impoverished than hers, his family forced to eat rice paddy remains normally fed to the cows. When they were first married, they barely scraped by, selling foraged medicinal plants at the Kottayam market.

A major life event for Rahel was when, at age fourteen, she received the Holy Spirit during a retreat and "became a child of God." From then on, she was a regular at Wednesday evening prayer meetings where she would dance and sing in the Spirit. After marrying, she supported their Dalit colony church by working in the kitchen. Back when the building was just a mud hut with a cow dung floor, her husband helped the priest gather coconut fronds to replace the roof every year. Today, however, the church is a proper cement structure with a tile roof, just like her own home. "Whatever we had to suffer, we held on tight to God," she told us. Slapping Jestin's arm with a laugh, she said, "So God resurrected us from the bottom of the earth!"

Rahel also admitted to a brief lapse in faith a while back, when her husband was still alive. Since their return, however, their blessings multiplied. "Our well used to go dry in the summertime, but after we came back to God, it never went dry." Tightening her grip on my hand, leaning toward Haley and Paige, she said, "We are even more blessed now that we've returned to God. We have so much water in the well, we've made a tank and built pipes so we can share our water with others."

Propelled by a sudden thought, Rahel jumped up to fetch her Bible. Thumbing through to Isaiah 44:3–4, she read aloud:

FIGURE 3.3 Rahel and her son in front of a pineapple field outside their home. Photo by author.

> For I will pour water on the thirsty land,
>   and streams on the dry ground;
> I will pour out my Spirit on your offspring,
>   and my blessing on your descendants.
> They will spring up like grass in a meadow,
>   like poplar trees by flowing streams.

Annamma Joseph

Annamma Joseph and her ninety-seven-year-old husband lived with their journalist son and his family in a government-owned Dalit colony that was more tightly packed than Rahel's. Welcomed out front by her son and his two teenage daughters, Jestin, Haley, Paige, and I were ushered to their sitting room. From here, we could see Annamma slowly making her way with a cane from the next room. Warmly beaming a nearly toothless smile, she joined us in our circle of chairs. Noticing her leaning in to see us better, we huddled more closely. As we were introducing ourselves, neighborhood children squeezed into the doorways. Fidgety at first, they quieted when Annamma started telling her stories, punctuated by a raspy cough and the crowing of a nearby rooster.

Like Rahel, Annamma's early memories started with her father's death, leaving her mother to raise her five children on her own. She recalled how their precarious existence was suspended by her mother's intense faith. After doling out food for her children, for example, she would disappear. "I remember how we would be there, wondering where our mother was. Looking around for her, we'd find her praying, on her knees, and crying." Annamma shook her head, "She would give us our food and go inside to pray—with tears."

The highlight of the week for Annamma's family was Sunday services. "The night before, we would take a special bath with coconut oil," she recalled. "And in the morning, we would clean our teeth and wash our faces to get ready." Living in Kerala's maze of backwater streams, the route to church required several crossings that were especially harrowing during the monsoon season. When the priest's assistant was able, he would ferry the family in a canoe. Otherwise, Annamma told us, lifting her hands over her head to demonstrate, "we would have to walk across, holding our clothes up like this. We would have to go into the water and swim across two streams." Pausing, she said, "But even in this way, we would still go." At the church, those who had nothing to eat at home, as was often the case for Annamma's family, were given food and coffee.

Like Rahel, a turning point in Annamma's life was when, at age ten, she and some of her siblings were filled with the Holy Spirit at a Wednesday evening prayer meeting. After this, "we gave our lives to Jesus," she explained. "I am still going on in my faith like this. I've been going to church and won't stop going now. Any problem that comes up, we still go to church and pray." Repeating these last words, Annamma said, "And *pray*."

As our conversation wound down, we asked Annamma if she wanted to add anything. With a smile, she reflected on her life as a series of blessings. Where she once had to swim across streams to get to church, her son now took her in his car. "This is because I have continued in the faith that my mother taught me." Describing for us again how her mother had prayed with tears, she said, "She taught me to pray."

Another group of women whose life stories brimmed with difficulties were those we met at an elder daycare center in the village of Kothadu. Leading us there was Sosa, the daughter of our first interviewee, Mary. Following in her mother's footsteps, Sosa taught sewing and embroidery to disadvantaged women in the community. She suggested we visit the elder center Christmas party to see if, after the festivities, some of the women might be willing to talk to us. At the party, we enjoyed song and dance numbers performed by local students as well as by some of the older women, followed by lunch. As lunch was finishing up, the event organizer took to the microphone and called for volunteers to share their stories with us.

At Sosa's suggestion, we set up a circle of plastic chairs just outside the building to catch a breeze that had kicked up. For three hours we interviewed four women—two Hindu and two Christian—all of whom shared stories of enduring sorrow and faith. Judging from the steady flow of women who joined in to listen and add side comments, it's likely that, with more time, we would have heard from more.

Kunjamma

Kunjamma was the last to join our circle, just as someone, to our relief, turned down the blaring piped-in music. A tiny woman whose hair had yet to turn gray, she looked intently at each of us as she spoke. Her childhood memories began with the drowning of her oldest brother followed by the death of her father three months later. With her mother forced to return to work in the paddy fields, Kunjamma was left to care for her two younger siblings. Similar to the other women we met in Kothadu, Kunjamma's troubles continued unabated, her whole life sustained only by God. "When I arrived here in Kothadu I had no parents. I married a husband who was a drunkard and a gambler," she explained. "So, then I realized there was no other way to move forward in life than to call on God. All the time I am praying. That's the only thing I have in my life. I still have a lot of sorrows, so I keep praying and praying." She added softly, more to herself than to us, "Sometimes I get tired of praying."

Raised in a Hindu family, Kunjamma grew up praying to a variety of deities. Yet after working as a sweeper at the nearby Shiva temple, she'd grown especially close to Lord Shiva. As is common among Kerala Hindus, she also sought "peace and comfort" wherever she could find it, which included churches known for their special blessings. Now that walking had become difficult, Kunjamma visited these churches only on special occasions.

Jaya

This Kerala-style blending of traditions brings us to Jaya. Her daughter, Bindu, a friend of my friend Sujatha, arranged for us to meet her mother followed by lunch at their Ernakulam home. When Haley, Paige, and I announced our arrival through their slightly opened front door, we could see colorful art pieces lining their light-filled entryway. Wafting heavenly aromas from the kitchen, Bindu emerged to show us to her family's dining table where Sujatha, her husband Anil, and a visitor from Portugal were seated. Jaya arrived soon after, her right arm in a sling from a recent fracture. Spotting Anil, whom she'd known since he was a boy, she started teasing him straightaway.

Jaya's story, like Grace's, featured a devotional shift sparked by a crisis. She had grown up in a Brahman household where her faith in the family goddess was absolute. "I knew that if I really fell at her feet, I would get whatever I wanted," she told us. But after five years of marriage with no children, she began to wonder whether the goddess was listening. Deciding to appeal to Vishnu at his powerful Thirupati temple in the neighboring state of Tamil Nadu, Jaya and her husband stopped on their way to visit an uncle who lived in Chennai. Here they learned he'd become a devotee of the Velankanni Virgin Mary and had built a small shrine in her honor in front of his house. The uncle convinced the couple not to go to Thirupati but to pray to Mary instead. He told them, Jaya recalled, "to simply put down ten rupees, or whatever you have in your hand" at his shrine. He promised that Mary would grant their hearts' desire, and when she did, they could bring the baby to Velankanni, located down the coast, to offer their thanks.

Jaya and her husband prayed as instructed and headed home. Soon after, they learned that she was pregnant with their first child, a son. Owing this to Mary, Jaya and her husband, eventually with two children in tow, visited Velankanni every year on her son's birthday. As her health declined, Jaya had continued to make offerings to Velankanni Mary at a roadside shrine in Ernakulam.

Since her first pregnancy, Jaya's devotion was solely focused on Mary. Her daily prayer routine, as she described it, centered on the Hail Mary prayer: "There are four prayers: for happiness, sadness, in praise, and for your light. Each of these I say fifty times. Early in the morning, I wake up and pray an hour or an hour and a half. But during the daytime it's about forty-five minutes." Aware that Kerala Hindus often see Mary as part of a larger Goddess tradition, I asked if she shared this view. Jaya was adamant, "They are two different things. They are not the same. I only believe in Jesus and Mary now. Until I die, I will follow Mother Mary."

Although Bindu and her older brother grew up making annual pilgrimages to Velankanni, they eventually followed more traditional Hindu paths. Near the end of our interview, Bindu's husband arrived with honey *prasadam*, liquid blessings from his morning visit to the Shiva temple. Putting dabs of the sweet mixture onto the outstretched hands of those of us around the table, he skipped over his mother-in-law. She explained, "For me, God is Jesus, son of God. I pray to him and he takes my sorrows away." Acknowledging her family's divergent paths, she said, "Everybody is different. Like the five fingers of a hand, we come with different behaviors."

As with all the women we met, we asked Jaya if she had a poem, a song, or a special object she'd like to share. Like nearly everyone in Kerala, she offered a song. While almost all the other women chose devotional hymns, Jaya's choice, "Manushyan Mathangale," a film song, is anything but.[9] After softly singing a few bars, Sujatha humming along, Jaya told us, "It's a song sung by Yesudas that says that man created religion. God is not Hindu or Christian. There is only humanity and these other things are not really relevant."

The lyrics cut deeper still. They sing of how religion, drawing lines between Hindus, Muslims, and Christians, has made us into strangers and enemies. Ripping apart humanity, religion leaves God behind as well.

The world has become a lunatic asylum
Thousands and thousands of human hearts

Become the battleground.
While God is dying in the streets,
Satan is smiling.

The Relevance of Relationship

Written in 1972, one year after John Lennon's similarly envisioned "Imagine," "Manushyan Mathangale" strikes an even harsher tone. It seems a strange hit song for an Indian state known for its peaceful pluralism. It was also an odd, perhaps incriminating choice for Jaya given her determination to stay true to Mary and Jesus, drawing a line in the sand by declining her son-in-law's blessed offerings from Shiva.

On the other hand, we could view Jaya's unwavering loyalty to Mary and Jesus as less about a need to set religious boundaries than about an ethic of reciprocity. This we repeatedly heard from women in Kerala whose extensive devotional routines held up their end of the deal in exchange for heavenly assurance and blessings. In this light, Jaya's loyalty to Velankanni Mary is not so much about her allegiance to a particular religion as to the one who, at last, granted her desperate desire for children. For her, religious dogma and division were beside the point or, as she put it, "not really relevant."

"Manushyan Mathangale" furthermore fits a cultural logic in Kerala when it's heard not so much as an antireligious tirade but as a jab at religious fundamentalism. Its enduring popularity serves as a warning as Kerala continues to stave off the rampant religious nationalism currently on the rise elsewhere in India. The fact that adherents of different religions have coexisted amicably in the state for thousands of years, "like the five fingers of a hand," has long been a point of pride for Malayalis.

After lunch, Bindu took us on a house tour where this dynamic played out in microcosm. The focus of our tour was the artwork hanging throughout the house, most of which, we learned, was painted by Jaya. Stopping to admire each image, we saw that nearly all were of Hindu deities, beautifully crafted by the Mary-and-Jesus-loving matriarch for her family to enjoy.

4

On Their Own Terms

●●●●●●●●●●●●●

The Sisters of St. Joseph

Most of my conversations with the Sisters of St. Joseph (SSJs) took place in their Motherhouse, built in 2002. It's a bright and airy building with endless windows that look out onto fields, marshes, and gardens. It's also around the corner from Nazareth University where I teach, founded by the same SSJs. The original Motherhouse built in 1927 has since been taken over by the campus, renovated to create classrooms. What were once sisters' bedrooms are now offices, like mine.

The new Motherhouse chapel, a high-ceilinged space ringed by colorful stained-glass windows, is where mass is celebrated throughout the week. In a community whose median age is currently eighty-four, it also hosts a steady stream of funerals. The night before each funeral mass, the sisters keep a vigil, a time for swapping stories of the deceased who lies in state near the altar. In April 2023 I attended Barbara O's vigil. She had spent over forty years of her sisterly career in Itaguaçu, a small town in the Brazilian interior, so most of her tales were set there. Barbara was best known for founding the town's first medical clinic, where she worked as a physician's assistant and trained local women to be nurses. She was also the parish administrator, assuming priestly roles in a region where clergy are spread thin. At the vigil, two of the sisters who also had lived in Brazil translated emails off their phones from those who

FIGURE 4.1 Sister Barbara Oczyk checks a patient's blood pressure. Photo credit: Archives of the Sisters of St. Joseph of Rochester.

knew Barbara well. Referring to Irmã (Sister) Barbara as friend and confidant, mother figure and warrior, they recalled how she had stood by them through life's challenges and victories.

Near the end of the vigil, I shared a story, too—one I'd heard Barbara tell several times. She always began by explaining how, when critically ill patients came to their clinic with needs beyond their capacity, getting them to the nearest hospital in time wasn't always possible. Troubled by this, Barbara seized an opportunity during one of the governor's official visits to Itaguaçu. On such occasions the town would pitch a platform in the center square where the visiting dignitary would sit alongside town leaders. Barbara would laughingly say that, "as the only nun in town," she'd be invited onto the platform, as well. This time, when it came her turn to speak, Barbara boldly turned to the governor and told him that he *must* find an ambulance for their clinic. One week later, the town had its new ambulance. Perpetually amazed by this, Barbara would conclude by saying, "And to think this happened because I was a sister!" It was a punchline that always made her laugh. When I shared her story at the vigil, the sisters burst out laughing as well. Her audacity for the greater good was familiar to, if not shared by, many in the chapel.

At the next morning's funeral mass, Sister Mary Anne greeted us from the lectern. She had joined the convent the same year as Barbara and had also lived many decades in Brazil. She had saved a story for the occasion, this one about a rattlesnake that Barbara discovered riding along with her in her Volkswagen Bug. Barbara had pulled over, banged on the car door to coax the snake out, and killed it with a shovel. But that's not all, Mary Anne explained. Using the shovel's edge, she sliced off the snake's rattles and mailed them to her nieces in Rochester. As laughter erupted around the chapel, all eyes on a row of Barbara's nieces sitting up front, the funeral opened with "Here I Am, Lord," its stately tune and lyrics reflecting well Barbara's life approach.

I, the Lord of wind and flame.
I will tend the poor and lame.
I will set a feast for them,
My hand will save

Finest bread I will provide
Till their hearts be satisfied.
I will give my life to them.
Whom shall I send?

Here I am, Lord.
Is it I, Lord?
I have heard you calling in the night.
I will go, Lord. if you lead me.
I will hold your people in my heart.

Hearing the chapel swell with song, it seemed not just a tribute to Barbara but to the many sisters among and before them who had dedicated their lives to remarkable service. Surrounded by bodies straight and stooped, voices clear and quavery, I was moved by a sense of both power and loss. Barbara was almost eighty-three when she died and had entered the SSJs in 1956, when women did so in droves. With vocations fizzled now almost entirely, she belonged, as my SSJ colleague Susan put it, to a once robust "dying breed."

This chapter's title, "On Their Own Terms," is a nod to how the SSJs of this generation ventured beyond expectations of their day, pursuing extraordinary lives that would have been nearly impossible if they hadn't joined the convent. Yet this era in which women entered in large "bands" was also one in which convent authorities steered women's futures with a heavy hand, sometimes against their will. The lives of the SSJ sisters, especially at that time, weren't therefore lived entirely on their own terms, nor were they meant to be. We return to this tug-of-war between opportunity and obedience in a later chapter.

What I mean here by "their own terms" has more to do with entering the convent in the first place. While women described being drawn for a variety of reasons, most faced resistance at home. Very unlike their migratory California peers, the sisters were deeply rooted geographically and religiously. All grew up not far from the convent they joined, and all but one was raised Catholic. Complicating matters, however, was that most were raised in religiously relaxed households. Prayer routines like in Kerala were nearly nonexistent, and even bedtime prayers common among nonchurchy Icelanders were rare. About half the sisters reported growing up with one parent who wasn't Catholic. The fact that most were not groomed to be nuns meant that breaking the news to family was often excruciating. Learning that your teenage daughter would leave home straight out of high school, trade her birth name for a another, and be available for one-hour visits only once a month understandably came as a blow to religiously lukewarm or non-Catholic parents.[1]

The following accounts feature this interplay between young adult determination and parental responses. Stirring up strong emotions among many of the women who shared them, they are tales of audacity and courage not normally told at vigils.

The Stories

Sr. Anne Michelle

Anne Michelle, my very first SSJ interviewee, was also the first to share such a story. Opting to meet in her dormitory-style bedroom, she offered me her stuffed beige armchair and sat facing me in her rocking chair. She spoke animatedly about her childhood, her sparkly blue eyes at times brimming over. Clear from the start was her admiration for her "very, very Christian" Episcopalian father. Offering examples of his goodness, she told me how he'd give lifts to strangers, bringing them home for a meal or to stay for weeks or even months at a time. Her father had been divorced before marrying her Catholic mother, which barred her evermore from receiving communion. "When she married my father, the Church stepped in and went pshhhooo," Anne Michelle said, making a sweeping gesture of dismissal. Yet her mother stayed the course, bringing her children to church every Sunday and enrolling them in Catholic schools.

Anne Michelle's path to the SSJs began with an eighth grade rebellion against her Mercy Sister schoolteachers who, she felt, were coercing the girls to attend Mercy High School. The final straw, she recalled, was when "one sister was going up and down the aisle one day, asking, 'What school are you going to?' I had already registered at Mercy. I'd chosen my subject. But when she got to me, I don't know why—I think God was in there somewhere, I said, 'Nazareth!' I don't know why I did it, why it came out of my mouth. And she went *up* and *down* me, and said the only reason I wanted to go there is because *I* wanted to ride on the bus with the *boys*!"

Laughing at the reenactment, aware that Nazareth Academy run by the SSJs was the competing all-girls Catholic high school in town, I said, "So, she did not like that answer."

Anne Michelle shook her head. "I got so angry at her. So, when I got home, I was still sputtering and my dad said, 'Now what's the matter?' So, I told him. He said, 'What do you want to do?' I had already registered at Mercy, paid the twenty-five bucks or whatever. He said, 'Honey, where do you want to go?' I said, 'Nazareth.' So, he got me into Nazareth Academy."

Anne Michelle flourished at Nazareth, where her SSJ teachers instilled a desire to join the order. This came as a disappointment to both parents, especially her father. At this point in her story, Anne Michelle went to fetch a large scrapbook from across the room. Sitting back down in her rocker, thumbing through the book, she said, "My dad was a printer, and a poem he wrote is in here." Hoping to get the poem recorded, I asked if she could recite it for me. Without making eye contact, she cheerfully said, "Nope!" and handed me the book. Pointing to the page with the poem, she explained that her father had written it a few months after she entered. It was around Christmastime. Before I began, I asked why her father didn't want her to enter. Letting out a long sigh, she said, "He thought he was losing a daughter."

With Anne Michelle listening intently, I read,

God blessed us with children,
But little did we know
That he would call one back to him
The light of life to show.

He sent us a blessed bundle
On fire cracker day. [Anne Michelle interjected that her birthday was the Fourth of July.]

We hoped we were deserving
What more can parents say?

Now first there was a carriage
And then there were the bikes
And then there were the school days
With long and pleasant hikes.

Remember at the sand pits
You went against our wish?
We nearly lost your life, my dear
And then I couldn't have written this.

I looked up, "Oh no!" Anne Michelle laughed and nodded. The poem continued with more childhood snapshots. Nearing the end, fighting to keep my composure, I understood why she didn't want to be the one to read out loud.

Now when your school was over
With those that you held dear,
You decided that our Maker
Would be your life's career.

So, at the Nazareth Convent
You decided you would stay,
But mother, dad, and brother
Couldn't see it just that way.

We never can forget you
As you marched down as a bride,
That awful wounded feeling
That we all felt inside.

Our many trips to Nazareth
Knowing all your friends so gay,
Gave us a different feeling
In a bright and clearer way.

Now as we say our prayers to God
Who gave his only son,

> We are very proud to tell the world
> We are parents of a nun.

I whispered, "Yeah." Anne Michelle, eyes misting, nodded and smiled.

Sr. Marie Michael

Marie Michael had a similar story to tell. An avid gardener, agile and physically fit at ninety-three, she wore a white shirt with lightly sketched flowers that matched the soft curls of her white hair. She had chosen for us to meet in a small common room next to her bedroom where, on the coffee table between us, she had set out a vase of pink roses.

Marie Michael came prepared with two pages of handwritten reflections on the questions I'd sent before our meeting. Recalling her childhood, she described herself as deeply religious despite the fact that her Baptist mother, who had agreed to raise her children Catholic, didn't join them for Sunday mass and didn't always agree with Church teachings. "I actually wasn't baptized until I was three, probably because my mother wasn't quite ready." Her mother nonetheless helped her children with their catechism lessons, Marie Michael explained, reminding them to go to confession on Saturdays and attending major events like first communion and confirmation. "She was always a friend to me. But the one thing that I missed was having her as a mother who I could share my spiritual experiences with."

Marie Michael couldn't remember saying mealtime grace or bedtime prayers at home. But she did recall loving everything about going to church. Along with Saturday confession and Sunday mass, she went to mass daily, an extra effort that, "as a skinny and not-too-healthy child," even the school sisters questioned. When I asked if her siblings went with her, Marie Michael had to think. She recalled pulling her little brother on a sled on her way to church. But she would leave him at her aunt's house, and she didn't remember anyone sitting next to her on the pew. Taking stock, she said, "Isn't that interesting? I just remember that they were different from me."

Marie Michael wanted to join a convent right out of high school, but waited for her mother's sake. It was during her fourth year of college as a nursing student that she decided to join the SSJs. Given her childhood piety, I guessed that her parents weren't surprised. Marie Michael shook her head and recalled her mother's response: "She said she would never come to see me."

I gasped. "That's heartbreaking."

Marie Michael teared up. "It was . . . She was there the next weekend." Looking up at each other, we both laughed. "Yeah. I think that my staying home for another three years—she maybe thought that I wouldn't do it. And when I made my final profession, she cried." Marie Michael teared up again. "She said, 'I didn't think it would ever happen.'" Brightening, she added, "But in her final years, she said, 'It's you who took care of me.'" Having heard this from several sisters, that aging parents often came to realize that the daughter they thought they'd lost was the one who could take care of them in later life, I mentioned this to Marie Michael. She nodded. "At the very end, my mother would say, 'You are the one who has really been with me,' things like that. So, I think she really accepted my vocation at the end." With a sigh she said, "But it was not easy."

Sr. Barbara G.

Barbara G. was one of the several sisters I met who lived outside the Motherhouse. Our conversation took place in a simply furnished sitting room of an SSJ residence attached to a church. Wearing a dark blue and white batik blouse over a yellow top, Barbara had a thoughtful demeanor, often pausing before responding to my questions.

She began her childhood recollections by describing her Sicilian immigrant parents. Catholic in name only, they were not churchgoers. Her father, "a strong Italian male," thought church was for the women. "That's what the women do: they go to church, they take care of the kids, they cook." Barbara laughed. Her mother, on the other hand, "just didn't understand it. That's what she would say. But she grew to." Despite their disinterest, her parents enrolled both of their daughters in Catholic schools. At first Barbara attended Sunday mass alone, joined later by her younger sister. The reason they went, she explained, was because the school sisters expected this of them.

Barbara didn't remember her family saying grace before meals or prayers at bedtime but she did recall seeing rosaries around the house. Her father's mother, Grandmother Gulino, had an especially impressive set. "It was wooden, made with big wooden beads. That was fascinating to me." When I suggested that she must have said the rosary, Barbara laughed. "No, it was hanging on the wall!" Yet Grandmother Gulino was the one whose religiosity made a lasting impact. Widowed while in her thirties, she had managed to bring all five of her children to the United States from Sicily. She had endured hardships that, as Barbara saw it, must have created in her a powerful faith. This she witnessed on Sundays after family supper gatherings at her grandmother's home. After the meal, Grandma would walk to the church behind her house, grandchildren in tow, to visit to the saints. "That was really where my faith was seeded. We would go from statue to statue to statue. And she would talk to all the statues in Italian—and we would listen!"

"Did you understand any of it?"

"No. We didn't understand a word. But we knew that she had some sort of connection." I told Barbara how special I imagined this must have been for the grandchildren, visiting a quiet, cavernous church after hours. She agreed. "Oh, this is what we did! I don't think anyone thought not to do it. She wanted to do it, and we loved her. So, we followed her."

Barbara had no intention of joining the convent until the end of her senior year in high school, sparked by a spiritual experience she didn't see coming. She knew that breaking the news wouldn't be easy. Her mother, while not happy, accepted it. Her father, however, lashed out a litany of dissent: "'You're going into the army! You're shutting yourself away! You're taking yourself away from the family! You're not going to have children!'" After that, he refused to speak to her for almost two years. Barbara sighed, "He was very upset. It was very hard for me." Because her mother didn't drive, her father would shuttle her and Barbara's sister to their monthly visits to the convent. While they went inside, he would wait in the car or go for a walk. A sister who worked with the novices would often go out to talk to her father, and over time, they became friends. Their friendship became a bridge, as Barbara saw it, that eventually brought him around.

Sr. Loretta

Loretta met with me in the parlor near the Motherhouse entrance, a notepad in hand filled with reflections. She began her childhood memories by telling me how her father had died when she was nine, leaving her and her younger sister with an intensely distraught mother. "I think that was the most significant first influence. Because when the parish priest came to tell us about our father's death, what he said to me was, 'You're the oldest. You're responsible for taking care of your mother.'" Adding to this weighty situation was the "loud and clear" message from their mother "that we'd better be good kids." Enrolling her daughters in parochial school, Loretta recalled her mother saying, "When you get to Catholic school, the nuns are going to take care of you!"

Not sure how to interpret Loretta's singsong tone, I asked, "Take care of you in what way? Straighten you out?"

Loretta nodded. "Discipline you."

The school nuns who taught Loretta were indeed severe. At times, she was so frightened by them that she became ill. As mandated by the sisters, Loretta started attending daily mass but "only up to a point," as she put it, "until I didn't go at all. My mother didn't know I was skipping church and going to a friend's house." Wanting nothing more to do with Catholic schooling after eighth grade, Loretta convinced her mother to allow her to transfer to the public high school.

After high school the SSJ sisters came back into view. Loretta joined a Girl Scout troop that, as was often the case in those days, was led by nuns, one of whom was Marie Michael. These sisters seemed nothing like her stern schoolteachers. "You see, they were *young*. I didn't realize it at the time, but when I look back, I realize that there was less than ten years difference in our ages. So, I saw them as a joyful, joyful people. And I think that's how I got on the track of changing my view." When I asked how her mother and sister felt about this, Loretta explained that her sister who had stayed in the Catholic school system, going on to Mercy High School, became a Sister of Mercy. When Loretta entered the SSJs, her mother was delighted. "Because we were going to be safe. She wouldn't have to worry about us anymore. So even though I left her alone and, essentially, was the last one to go, she was very happy about it."

"That's what she cared about. You being safe."

"Yeah."

"Aww, your poor mom."

"I know it. I know it." Loretta laughed lightly.

Sr. Jamesine

In Jamesine's Motherhouse room, a pink pillow embroidered with the name "Mary Anne" sat on her bed. This, I learned, was her baptismal name, replaced by the name the Mother Superior chose for her: Jamesine. As was custom, Jamesine heard her new name for the first time a year after she entered, when the bishop called her up to receive her habit. Most of the sisters I interviewed had since reclaimed their given names, but Jamesine decided to keep to this commitment. As for wearing the habit, nearly every SSJs alive today has long given this up.

Jamesine and her two older brothers were raised in Rochester by a Catholic mother and a Protestant father. Her father didn't join the family at Sunday mass, but, Jamesine was quick to add, sounding like Anne Michelle, "He didn't need to do all that. He was just a really good Christian man." Jamesine's mother had a special devotion to the Virgin Mary, naming her only daughter after Mary and Mary's mother, Anne.

Jamesine told me how her draw to religious life began with a crisis at age twelve. She had been babysitting her brother's two young children and had slept overnight at his house. The next morning as her brother drove her back home, his car collided with a milk truck. Jamesine recalled watching her brother get out of the car to bend back his damaged fender while the milk truck driver goaded him into a fight. Opening the car door to throw his glasses onto the front seat, he went back out. "Then the two of them started to tussle. And this was in January, and there was a lot of ice on the road where they were tussling. Anyway, the milk truck driver came down on top of him and broke his neck." I gasped. Jamesine nodded. "He lived about six days after that. And I was in the seventh grade at the time. And I remember my father coming and picking me up at school. And he had to tell me that my brother died. And of course, it was *impossible*. My brother. This big strong man."

Jamesine took a breath. "So anyway, I remember kneeling at his casket and thinking, 'What's this all about?' And I always say that it was at that point that my vocation was born. It was at that time I thought, 'If life is this fleeting, you'd better *do* something with your life.' You know? I think that, from then on, this was what I was going to do. But it was due to his death." Jamesine recalled how her admiration for her SSJ schoolteachers also steered her desire to become a nun, but it was her brother's death that sealed it. "It was the only thing I thought about from that time on."

When Jamesine told her parents that she wanted to enter the convent right after high school, her father wanted her to wait a year. But she insisted. She worried that if she waited, she might not go through with it. Although her mother didn't resist, Jamesine knew they were both brokenhearted. "I was the baby of the family and when I left home it was an empty nest."

"But they must have known, if you'd had that determination for so long," I said.

"True. But I think they missed me a lot. It was strict in those days, you know? You didn't see your parents that much."

Sr. Joan Margaret

Joan Margaret, a retired theology professor who once taught in what is now the religious studies department at Nazareth, is one of the few sisters I knew before our interview. Lively, warm, and sharp-minded at ninety-two, she was also the only sister who described her childhood in ways I had expected, rivaling the deep religiosity of women in Kerala. Raised by devout Catholic parents, she recalled how her family would recite mealtime and bedtime prayers, attend daily mass, go to Saturday confession, and gather to say the rosary in the evenings. She also recounted in vivid detail the religious imagery that filled their home.

Joan Margaret, taught by the SSJ sisters from kindergarten through college, found school to be an unmitigated joy. She recalled with a laugh how, early on, she even cherished the smell of the nuns' wool habits, hoping to catch a waft as they walked the aisles. Seeing my surprise, she said, "I just loved that smell! Just inhaling it made me feel so good."

Joan Margaret grew up with uncles, aunts, and cousins who were nuns and priests. When her two older sisters joined the SSJs, she at first felt that this was enough for one family. But during her senior year in high school she changed her mind, a decision that was met with full parental support. To underline this point, she had brought to our interview excerpts from letters that her parents had written to her and her sisters after they'd entered. Joan Margaret still read these excerpts daily, as they expressed for her "a real school of spirituality." The passage she chose to share was from a letter her father had written in 1940 after her sister Dorothea had entered: "Your choice of a spiritual life is far greater than anything else. Therefore, we all hope and pray for your success in the sisterhood, a life I always felt you could live."

Looking up, Joan Margaret said, "So it's the positive support. Today you don't get that. Parents usually say, 'Don't go off, wait a few years, you'll miss giving us grandchildren.'"

"Right, right," I nodded, aware that this was not just a recent phenomenon.

"But there was none of that."

Sr. Barbara O.

Barbara O., whose vigil and funeral began this chapter, was raised with her three younger brothers by Polish-speaking parents. "My mom was the holy one," Barbara explained. "But my father did not feel the need to go to church. He would say to us, 'I haven't killed anybody!'"

"But your mother could have said the same thing," I teased. "Or you kids could all have said, 'I'm a good person, I haven't killed anyone, so I'm gonna stay home.'"

"Oh *no*." Barbara was emphatic. "We were going to St. Stanislaus School. And we had mass at nine o'clock. And you *had* to *be* there. We had to be there with our teachers."

"So, you just went, no questions."

Barbara's face was stern. "You didn't *ask* questions."

Barbara's mother was "always in church," as she put it. She was the leader of a women's group, all of whom "were very religious. They were *holy*, I'm telling you." At home, this translated to running a tight ship: "We had to go to confession on Saturdays, *every Saturday*, with our mother. So, I'd have to go to my mother and say, you know, 'Is there something we did that we shouldn't have done?' And she told us stuff that we did."

"Oh! She gave you things to confess!"

Laughing, Barbara said, "Oh, she did! She did!"

Barbara traced her desire to become a sister to an eighth grade teacher who collected pennies to support Maryknoll mission priests. During the priests' trips back home, they would often visit the class to thank the children and share stories of their work. Barbara was enthralled. "It was a simple thing, but that stuck with me. So much. Right then and there, I wanted to be a missionary." Barbara's initial plan was to become a Maryknoll sister, but she was talked into joining the SSJs by a high school sister who suggested she could work in the Deep South, at the hospital the sisters ran in Alabama. Soon after Barbara entered, Brazil became an option as well.

Near the end of our conversation, I asked Barbara, as I did everyone, if she could identify a moment, a place, or a life pattern that felt most sacred to her, outside church. Without hesitation, she said it was the times she felt she could bring solace to people in Itaguaçu. "This is why I loved Brazil so much. People would come to you and tell you these awful stories; they would ask you questions and you'd be there for them. You'd be there for them, helping them out physically, mentally." Barbara paused. "You were there for them and you spoke to them as equals. It's not, 'I'm better than you, because I'm a sister.'" Reflecting further, she said, "I am like this because of my mom. That's a part of my mom that's also a part of me. I feel like my mother was working in the mix." Her mother, who had always wanted to be a nun, had lived vicariously through her, Barbara explained. "When I told her I wanted to go into the convent, she was thrilled. My mom gave me full support. She was just so happy."

After Barbara's story-filled vigil, I walked to the front of the chapel where some of her "band," the sisters who'd entered the same year, were gathered around her open casket. Together we admired the blue crystal rosary beads threaded through Barbara's fingers, originally her mother's. The bulky wooden cross propped up by her hands, they explained, was her missionary cross, given to her when she left for Itaguaçu. The sisters especially wanted me to see that Barbara wasn't wearing her SSJ cross necklace, as was custom, as no one could find it among her belongings. Instead, she wore the St. Barbara medal that she'd always worn, given to her by her proud and thrilled mother. When she entered, her baptismal name, Barbara, was replaced by Paulissa. Arriving in Brazil, however, learning that "Paulissa" rattled people because it sounded a lot like *polícia* in Portuguese (another story that made Barbara laugh), she took back her name. Buried in the medal that bore her baptismal name, both name and medal given by her mother, it appears Barbara's mother was indeed "working in the mix" from the very start to finish.

Part 2

The Real

● ● ● ● ● ● ● ● ● ● ● ●

5

Where Does It Hurt?

● ● ● ● ● ● ● ● ● ● ● ● ●

Rejecting and Revising
God and Religion

> I carry a torch in one hand
> And a bucket of water in the other:
> With these things I am going to set fire
>   to heaven
> And put out the flames of hell
> So that voyagers to God can rip the veils
> And see the real goal.
>
> **RABI'A AL 'ADAWIYYA,** "I Carry a Torch
> in One Hand"

Introductions out of the way, we enter the heart of the book. Moving from orientations rooted in particular places to themes threaded throughout, we now bring to light what really matters to older women across contexts. Enlivening the conversation is a steady strain of resistance, a tendency within later adulthood to defy everyday conventions that constrain and diminish us: gifts conferred from life's edge.

In part II, "The Real," this resistance translates to a regular refusal to cordon off joy from sorrow, victory from disappointment, heavenly glory from earthly drudgery. Calling to task social, cultural, and religious norms that artificially obscure or sanitize life's difficulties, older women's stories and opinions convey a realism that refuses standards of perfection and invincibility. They defy expectations that keep us vainly scrambling after the impossible.

We begin part II with reflections on formal religiosity. Experienced in vastly different ways across contexts as hurtful, helpful, and sometimes both, they reach a consensus of sorts. Like the eighth-century Sufi mystic Rabi'a for whom heaven and hell blocked the goal of divine union, women commonly expressed frustration with scenarios in which divinity reigned in judgment from on high. In California, in Iceland, and among the SSJs, women regularly described deposing or reenvisioning this remote, perfectionistic God over time. In Kerala, where divinity was experienced as earthbound from the start, no need for adjustment, women appeared to be one step ahead.

God as Problem and Solution

As we've seen, Californian women distinguished themselves through their religious departures. Digging deeper, we find that many who cleanly broke from childhood traditions did so in response to a God who didn't hold up well under the weight of painful reality. Rather than finding solace in this divinity, they felt abandoned. In chapter 1, for instance, we heard how Paddy left the family's Pentecostal faith after her beloved mother had disappeared for three years to a tuberculosis sanitorium. It wasn't until our second conversation that she connected the dots. With incredulity ringing in her voice, Paddy recalled her thirteen-year-old thoughts: "Y'know, I'd think about it going to bed. I'd wonder about why that happened, why my mother ever had to go away when she was such a wonderful person. And God was there, supposedly, to heal her. And how come my mother had to go through three years of this? And have a lung taken out of her?" Paddy's voice softened, "What a wonderful person she was to me. So, 'What's it all about Alfie?' Y'know?"

"So, the religious questioning that you mentioned last time, that really started when your mom went away?"

"Oh yeah." Paddy repeated, barely above a whisper, "Yeah." She continued, "I just think, if there is this superpower up there—and it's hard to imagine and I guess we're not supposed to be able to imagine . . . If he's up there, I don't understand why sick children aren't healed. That's just a question that comes to me. Why are some people starving and other people allowed to make more and more and more money and not do good with it? And still expect to be up in heaven?" Paddy looked over at me. "I can't get it. I just can't get that one."

Ann sketched a similar story of shifting religiosity. Sitting side by side on her couch, her new kitten bouncing between us, she described herself as *"very religious"* growing up in Yonkers, attending daily mass and even toying with becoming a nun well into her twenties. Yet the God Ann came to know as a child, like Paddy's, "always let me down," as she put it. "I never had the feeling that God would help me." Laughing lightly, she added, "He didn't help me. I was all by myself." The final straw for Ann was when her ceaseless prayers for her son with schizophrenia had no effect. "There are so many things that I wanted and I prayed for and—*nada*." Lightening her voice, she added, "I think, well, of course not. God isn't messing around with all of my wishes . . . if there is a God anyway."

In Iceland, where formal religion carried less weight to begin with, such stories of rupture were rare. Margrét, an exception, began by describing her "very religious" (although non-churchgoing) grandmother. As a Spiritualist, she'd claimed a "direct link" to a loving and all-powerful God. Margrét recalled learning prayers from her, taking comfort in this divinity until, at age six, her mother died. "Then, everything she had told me about the very good God collapsed. So, it took me many years to accept that loss. And that betrayal." Margrét's disillusionment deepened while working as an international correspondent, where she saw firsthand how religion could be so instrumental to human suffering. Acknowledging that religion could also be "healthy and helpful," she felt it was too often used as "a terrible weapon that can destroy everything that is good and nice." Margrét reflected, "So this was me losing my religion—which is also quite healthy, I think. I don't believe in an afterlife. I don't believe in waking up in heaven. I will have my body burned. And when life is finished, it's finished."

Although SSJ sisters also described growing up with a God who bestowed blessings from on high, their troubles had more to do with the other side of the equation, with divine judgment. When the topic came up, women uniformly recalled learning about this severity not at home but at school, channeled at times by the school sisters themselves.

Among those with daunting nun stories, Sr. Josepha shared several. She began by explaining that she and her sister Marilynn, who had started out at a public elementary school, were in for a shock when they transferred to the new Catholic middle school run by SSJs. "My sister was in the classroom right across from me and she had a teacher who used to *yell*," Josepha said, with a smile. "She was a sister who used to *scream* at them!" One evening over dinner, as Josepha recalled, Marilynn told the family how mad sister had been in class that day. "My father asked, 'What time was it, Marilynn?' And she said, 'Probably around one o'clock, Daddy.' And my father said, 'Oh! I heard her at the prison!'" Josepha explained, as an aside, that her father worked at a prison four miles from the school. As I burst out laughing, she concluded, "And Marilynn actually believed him! Because she could really *yell*."

With a change in tone, Josepha shared some stories of her own. One involved a boy in her class whose eyes were hurting from the sun's reflection on his polished desk. Josepha recalled how he had asked the sister if he could put down the window shade. Her response: "The sun is not on your desk, the sun is in the sky! Leave the shade right where it is!" Josepha nodded when she heard me gasp. "That went right through the top of my head! It just made no sense to me that somebody would say that. And I thought, 'If I ever teach school, I'm not going to talk to the children in that way!' I was furious." Sr. Josepha not only ended up teaching but joined the same order as her middle school teachers. The reason, she explained, was that the frightening middle-school nuns were eventually replaced by loving and capable SSJ high school teachers whom she deeply admired.

Sisters who managed to avoid this severity in childhood were often introduced during novitiate training. Growing up Catholic, Sr. Kay told me, "I never had that image that God was going to *get you* or punish you." Discovering this punishing God upon entering religious life, Kay was further exposed when she began working in parishes. Amazed by the durability of this judgmental God, one that Vatican II reforms later swept away, she told me, "In fact, some of the older sisters still aren't sure they're even going to heaven." Seeing my reaction, she explained, "Because they think maybe God doesn't love them."

In Sr. Mary Ann's words, the God of her childhood was "sort of difficult person." This, she felt, was a standard view not only for Catholics in the 1940s and 1950s, but for society at large. "See, at that time, you obeyed your elders," she explained. "You *obeyed* this and that. It's nothing like it is now. So, God was somebody that 'you'd better watch out for,' kind of thing." Mary Ann recalled how, before Vatican II, she believed in a God, but "didn't know what this God was. It was certainly not a personal God. So, my ideas have expanded. And I don't see God as judgmental at all anymore. To me, God is a loving, merciful..." she laughed, "*very* merciful when dealing with me." This reminded Mary Ann that she'd brought a passage to share. Pulling out a folded sheet of paper from her jeans pocket, she explained that it was written by a Benedictine sister, Joan Chittister, passed on by her friend Sr. Marie Michael. Settling back in her chair, she read,

> God is not in the whirlwind, not in blustering and show, Scripture teaches us. God is in the breeze, in the very atmosphere around us, in the little things that shape our lives. God is in the contradictions that assail us, in the circumstances that challenge us, in the attitudes that impel us. God in the motives that drive us, in the life goals that demonstrate our real aspirations. God is in the burdens that wear us down, in the actions that give witness to the values in our hearts. God is in the stuff of life. God is where we are, including in the very weaknesses that vie for our souls. God is not a mystery to be sought in strange places and in arcane ways. God is a mystery to be discovered within us and around us and savored.[1]

Watching Mary Ann lower the paper onto her lap, I enthused, "How beautiful. It's an ode to an immanent, nonpunitive God, even in our weaknesses."

Mary Ann nodded. "And I've said this probably a thousand times: God is in the middle of the mess."

Listening to the SSJs describe the harsh God of their childhoods, it occurred to me that I'd heard nothing of the sort in Kerala. Returning for our second round of interviews, I decided to check. When I asked Annamma C, as traditional a Catholic as could be, if the American sisters' pre–Vatican II God sounded familiar, she was startled. Normally light and lively, she quickly set me straight: "God is very kind. *Very*, very kind. He helps us. That's all. We are filled with miracles all around us. Healing and miracles and all of this. So why would we see God in this way?" Other Catholic women in Kerala, including the five Carmelite nuns we met, shared this view. In full habit and clearly more conventional than the Rochester SSJs, the Carmelite sisters uniformly envisioned God as a loving force in their lives. When reflecting on their deaths, all were quite certain they were headed to heaven.

Helping to make sense of this cultural difference, Robert Orsi describes how the valorization of pain and diminishment within mid-twentieth-century U.S. Catholicism coincided with a cultural moment in which the children and grandchildren of European Catholic immigrants were moving out of ethnic neighborhoods and into middle-class modernity. Resentful of their neighbor's success or guilt-ridden at their own, the elevation of suffering at the hands of a stern God became a grand leveler. "Pain purged and disciplined the ego, stripping it of pride and self-love; it disclosed the emptiness of the world."[2] Easing this generation's entrance into the mainstream, it also helped keep Catholics at a safe remove. In Kerala, where only one woman I met recalled her childhood God as a disciplinarian, there also seemed little interest in casting life's difficulties as a badge of honor or as leverage for redemption.[3]

Marginalized women in Kerala whose lives brimmed with challenges also did not, unlike their peers in California and Iceland, give up on a divinity who wasn't holding up their end of the deal. More like the post–Vatican II SSJs, they envisioned God as abiding in the middle of life's messes. With no bargains to strike, there was little room for betrayal. They were not swept up, as Dorothee Soelle words it, "in the pattern of the powerful and the powerless, who make a deal with one another, a deal that is called 'religion.'"[4] Those living under dire circumstances, enveloped by divinity, did not see giving up on God as an option. As Elliyamma from the Dalit community put it, "God is with us whenever we suffer illness or when our hearts are broken. There have been many troubles, like hard work in the paddy fields and other kinds of hardships. These are a part of life. And in all those troubled places, God is there, as well. So, whenever the problems come, I know God will support me."

The women we met at the Kothadu elder day center expressed this view most vividly. Seythu, who had just moments before belted out Malayalam film songs to a rapt Christmas party audience, laughingly told us how she felt Lord Krishna's presence whenever she sang. Becoming serious, she said, "Whenever I am feeling down about all the difficulties in my life, I think of Krishna and start praying to him. Then things go smoothly." Losing her mother at age seven, enduring a lifetime of family upheaval and poverty, Seythu had learned that "only God can give us what we need. I know that God will *never* leave me. God will always take care of me." Speaking in a sweet, lilting voice, Celine described life's harsh realities that were startling to hear. Raised in poverty, she had worked in coconut husking from the time she was eight. At eleven, her father was paralyzed in an accident, sending the family into destitution. Married to a man who refused to work, she now lived with her son and his wife who treated her in shockingly disrespectful ways. Yet Celine was clear: "I don't get anything from my family, so I have to hold onto God very tightly. God is everything to me, holding me by my right hand and a part of everything I do."

Liberation theologian Leonardo Boff reflects on how, in scenarios of utter despair, divine presence can be felt as pervasively as troubles themselves. He relates an exchange with a Brazilian woman whose only son, a fifteen-year-old, was shot by the police while scavenging through the city's garbage heap. Boff asked the woman if this made her question God's existence. He recalls her startled response: "She looked at me and said, 'Me? Why would I not believe in God? For is God not my father? To whom else would I cling if not to God—and if I could not feel myself in his hand?'" Boff concludes, "Marx is mistaken. On this final stage, faith is no opiate but radiating liberation, a light that drives away darkness; it is life beyond death."[5]

Religion as Problem and Solution to the Problem of Religion

Also complicating Marx's prognosis are instances when women described formal religion as a force for both liberation and oppression. This mixed messaging emerged in conversations with Dalit women for whom formal religion both supported and stymied their struggles against caste oppression, and with the SSJs whose convent structures designed to rein in egos also opened up unthinkable opportunities. Finding footholds in systems that affirmed their worth, women gained leverage to question authorities who insisted otherwise.

The Dalit Context

Winding our way through a maze of narrow lanes in a Dalit colony just outside Kottayam, no road signs in sight, we arrived at Thankachikkuttan's home. Greeting us out front, she led Jestin, who had arranged our meeting, my two students, and me to her front room. Settling in around a long metal table covered by a floral tablecloth, we found ourselves in the company of Dalit luminaries. Lining the main wall were framed images of Ayyankali (1863–1941), who helped Kerala Dalits win the right to education and to walk the main roads; B. R. Ambedkar (1891–1956), a national Dalit icon; and Kumari Mayawati, a North Indian politician currently working on behalf of marginalized groups.[6]

Thankachikkuttan began by telling us what it was like to grow up under Kerala's *kudikidappu* system, where once-enslaved Dalits who continued to live and work on their landowners' property also continued to live under submission. "Everything that had to do with us, whether school or marriage, the landowners would decide," she explained. "When a new baby was born, they would tell us what name to give them. We were not allowed to even cook our food as we liked. There was total non-freedom at that time."

Thankachikkuttan then moved on to share her story of resistance. She told us how, at age fifteen, a friend of hers was discovered to be pregnant. Aiming to shame her, a schoolteacher dragged the girl into every classroom to announce her state. Furious, Thankachikkuttan confronted him: "I asked him, 'If this child were Ezhava or Nair [non-Dalit Hindu castes], or Christian or Muslim, would you have done this to her?'" In response, Thankachikkuttan was sent to her family's landlord for questioning, where she unapologetically defended herself. Garnering the support of two younger members of the landlord's family, she was spared punishment. With a smirk, she added, "But one of the older people reasoned that, if I am behaving like this, if I am educated more, what will happen in the future? So, the landlord decided I would not continue my studies. Instead, he got me married." As for her pregnant friend, Thankachikkuttan added, barely above a whisper, that she ended up taking her own life.

On a side wall next to the kitchen doorway were framed images of Mary and Jesus, indications of Thankachikkuttan's adult conversion to Christianity. She told us how, as a child, she'd been disturbed by her family's daily readings from Hindu scripture. "I learned that Lord Rama came here to give the land to brahmins. Why should I praise this Rama, when he gave the land to brahmins?" She also recalled being bothered by how Rama entered a dispute between two brothers, aiming his arrow and killing the unarmed elder brother from a hiding place. "Daily we are praying this at home, reading this, and it occurred to me that it wasn't fair."

The final straw was after Thankachikkuttan's husband died and she was left to raise her children on her own. "I had to completely depend on the landlord," she explained. "One time, when I took some things from there, just to eat, just to survive, they treated me like I was a criminal." Called in for questioning, she again stood up for her rights. "I told them that they cannot stop me from doing this because all they have—their house and the property—has been built on the blood and sweat of my ancestors." With nowhere to turn, feeling the Hindu gods would help her only if she gave offerings to temple brahmins, Thankachikkuttan decided to take refuge in Jesus. Yet she was also aware that no religion was above caste discrimination. While her landowners happened to have been high-caste Hindus, high-caste Christians benefited from the same system.

As was more typical of the Dalit women we met, Annamma Joseph's parents had converted before she was born. Her strongest childhood memory, as was mentioned in chapter 3, was the intensity of her mother's prayer throughout life's difficulties. Annamma also recalled her parents' and grandparents' stories about British missionaries who campaigned for Dalit rights. She explained, for instance, how they supported their struggle for the right to walk on the main roads. "Our forefathers banded together and would walk with long sticks, swinging them in front of them. My mother told us about this. When they started doing that, people would get injured if they got in their way. That's how they got the freedom to walk in the street." Struck by a thought, Annamma leaned in and, taking both my hands, lowered her voice: "The white people also started giving us white clothing to wear." Seeing my confusion, she clarified, "The foreigners who came and preached enabled us to wear white clothes."

Still unsure of what she meant, I looked over at Jestin, who explained, "It was the foreigners who humanized us."

Moved by Annamma's intensity, squirming at the idea that colonizers could be humanizing, I said, "It's the story of colonialism from a very different perspective, isn't it? Because there was also dehumanization."

Jestin nodded. "Yeah. It's a very different narrative of colonialism."[7]

Still leaning in and holding her grip, Annamma emphasized, "If you pray, whatever you are asking for, God will do it for you. *Anything*." Giving my hands a squeeze, she let go and sat back.

Prohibitions against Dalits wearing clean white clothing lingered into the 1940s in some parts of Kerala, rooted in high-caste Hindu and Christian insistence that sartorial signs of purity and privilege be reserved for them. Working to lift the ban, missionaries encouraged Dalit converts to wear clean white clothing at Sunday services, but stealthily at first. Walking to church in their dirty rags, they would change once they arrived.[8] Just as there are two sides to colonialism, as Jestin put it, Christianity in Kerala has served to both uphold and disassemble caste discrimination.

It shouldn't therefore be surprising that even the Church of South India (CSI), champion of Dalit rights, can fall prey to corruption. When visiting Kunjamol Mary's home, we heard about her recently deceased husband, T. J. Peter, who in 1983 founded the People's Movement of Faith for Liberation that aimed at breaking casteism within the CSI ranks. Gathered in the main room of their home, Jestin described T. J. Peter's work. As a church catechist, he had used his position along with his biblical knowledge to bring other Dalit members into the movement. Kunjamol Mary told us that the church had suspended her husband twice due to his activism, threatening their livelihood. Yet the work paid off, with policies now in place to stem further corruption.

Those formally involved in Dalit struggles in Kerala, especially among the older generations, tend to be men. When women described standing up for their rights, like Thankachikkuttan, these were typically on-the-spot responses to particular incidents. Such was the case for Anitha. One of the quieter women we met, she would often defer to her son who, sitting on his motorcycle next to her porch where we gathered, regularly interjected his opinions. It was only after our interview, after we'd started down the dirt path away from Anitha's home, that her story of resistance came to mind. Calling us back, we returned to our circle of porch chairs. Anitha began by telling us about her eldest son, a diligent student, who had earned high test scores in secondary school that more than qualified him for entrance to a prestigious Catholic college. Yet his application was rejected without any explanation. Jestin clarified that this was common practice, that Dalit rejections often had to do not with a student's qualifications but with the family's inability to offer bribes or, as he put it, "additional donations."

A Catholic herself, Anitha was furious that this college was being run in crooked ways that, she knew, contradicted its teachings. With bus fare lent by a neighbor, she traveled to campus to speak directly to the priest in charge of admissions. Once in his office, she questioned him about her son. Hearing his vague nondefense, she called out the greed and hypocrisy that led his college to deny admission to Dalits. Concluding her tirade in the way of Sojourner Truth, she asked, "Am I not a daughter of God?" Leaving him speechless, Anitha returned home. Knowing she couldn't beat the system, she vowed that her son would be educated elsewhere, which he was. She proudly told us how, ending up at a less prestigious government college, he had worked hard and, by the grace of God, had done well for himself.

Sisters of St. Joseph

The SSJs I met had entered religious life five to twenty years before Vatican II reforms radically changed convent culture, starting in the late 1960s. Many recalled the severity of novitiate training during pre–Vatican II times, aimed at forging humility in the new recruits. As described by Sr. Helen Prejean, a Louisiana SSJ of the same generation, convents gave "top value to the virtues of obedience and submission" for entering sisters. "Bolstered by the novice mistress's public reprimands," sealed by "limited social contacts and relationships with everybody else in the world," the process was, to put it mildly, "detrimental to healthy personal development."[9]

When recalling their early convent years, the challenge sisters mentioned most often had to do with the commandeering of future careers by convent authorities. Some entered with the understanding that they would be trained for a particular occupation, only to find this plan to have been inexplicably switched. Some recalled being asked for job placement preferences only to be given their last choice, for reasons unknown. Those who pursued graduate degrees to fill faculty positions at Nazareth were often sent according to the needs of the college without consideration for their own interests. A few sisters felt that this heavy-handed approach helped to explain the existence of terrifying school nuns, as some women may have resented taking up work as teachers, a role they hadn't chosen nor were cut out for to begin with.

Regardless of how career paths were decided, the enduring charism of the SSJs, traced to their seventeenth-century founding in LePuy, France, centers on work among society's marginalized. Embedded within the stark Catholicism of mid-twentieth-century America, the work served to discipline and keep women from the temptations of the world, yet opened opportunities that would have otherwise been unimaginable. This irony was lost on no one. Listening to Sr. Virginia describe the vast and varied positions she'd held over the decades and across the globe, I mentioned how I was repeatedly astounded to hear all that the sisters of her generation had accomplished. With a twinkle in her eye, Virginia said, "Oh, I can't *tell* you! I'd never have had the experiences I had here if I 'stayed out in the world,' as they say."[10]

Sr. Barbara O. was emphatic about both sides of the convent coin. From the time she was a teenager she had wanted to travel the world and joined the SSJs with this in mind. Although she eventually spent over forty years of her life in Brazil, Barbara was stationed not only nearby for her first teaching post but at her home parish where her younger brother was still a student. She knew at the time that this kind of placement was unheard of, a deliberate attempt to cull her adventuresome spirit. Looking back, she laughed at how furious this had made her.

Eventually arriving in the Brazilian town of Itaguaçu, Barbara worked first as a teacher and parish administrator who became increasingly concerned about the lack of access to medical care. She recalled a particularly horrifying instance involving a woman whose baby was having trouble breathing. Rushing them in her car to the nearest clinic a half hour away, Barbara didn't notice that the panicking mother was holding her baby against her chest. Realizing what had happened, I gasped. Shaking her head, Barbara said, "She killed it. When we got there, the baby was dead."

"Because the baby had suffocated against her."

"Yeah. She was just holding it so tight. I never realized she was doing that." Barbara set her jaw. "But let me tell you. After that, Barbara was very, very, very careful."

In 1976, Barbara returned to Rochester to be with her dying father. During this time, a sister administrator approached her and said, "'I'd like you to go with me to the hospital in Elmira.'" Barbara made a confused face. "I said, 'I don't really have any problems.' And she said, 'Oh no, no, no. I want you to meet somebody.' So, she wanted me to meet this PA who studied in Stonybrook."

Realizing this led to her work as a physician's assistant, I said, "That's wonderful!"

"It really is. But she didn't even ask me. Do you know what I mean?"

Seeing her serious expression, I heard what she was saying. "Well, yes! That's par for the course." Barbara nodded.

After three years' study at Stonybrook, Barbara returned to Itaguaçu as a PA. Setting up the town's first clinic, she helped train local women to be nurses who have, ever since, kept the clinic running. "That was one of the big reasons we went to the country," Barbara insisted, "not to take work from them but get them into the work."

Sr. Barb L. worked at the Good Samaritan Hospital in Selma, Alabama, founded by the Rochester SSJs, where she also trained local women to be nurses. Arriving in 1959, Barb's time in Selma coincided with the rise of the Civil Rights Movement. She recalled the 1965 voting-rights march in Marion, Alabama, where state troopers beat and shot at unarmed marchers, one of whom was Jimmie Lee Jackson. "This young man, with his grandfather and his mother, ran into a café to get away. One of the troopers was beating his mother and, as he tried to turn around to help her, another trooper shot him in the stomach." Although Marion is thirty miles from Selma, Jackson was brought to Good Samaritan because it was the only hospital within a nine-county radius to treat African Americans. Barb explained that one other hospital had twelve beds in the basement reserved for Black patients, but because Good Samaritan was open to everyone, "nobody came who wasn't Black." Jackson underwent emergency surgery and survived for eight days. Barb told me how, during her morning rounds, "He would take my hand and say, 'Sister, don't you think this is a high price to pay for freedom?'" Barbara turned to me. "And what you answer to that, I have no idea. What to say?"

Jackson's death spurred on other marches including the crossing of Edmund Pettus Bridge in Montgomery that came to be known as Bloody Sunday. Again, unarmed marchers assaulted by state troopers were rushed to Good Samaritan. Although fifty miles away, it was still the closest hospital to treat African Americans. Among them was civil rights leader and future

FIGURE 5.1 Sisters Josepha Twomey (holding baby Synethia Perkins), Dorothy Quinn, Mary Weaver, Margaret Isabel Tracy, and Mary Paul Geck greet Dr. Martin Luther King Jr. at Good Samaritan Hospital in Selma, Alabama, 1965. Photo credit: Society of Saint Edmund Archives.

senator John Lewis. I had heard that Lewis credited Barb for saving his life, but when I mentioned this, she laughed. "Yeah. He thinks I did. But I tell him, 'You know what? When I saw you, you were already taken care of!' He was on a stretcher in the emergency room." Barb paused. "But we were there. That's what I tell him. That's the point. We were there."

In 1968 Barb returned to Rochester where, like many SSJs at the time, she was encouraged into further study. Earning two master's degrees with work toward a doctorate, she taught at the University of Rochester for twenty-six years until, just before her eightieth birthday, she "retired." When we met, Barb was volunteering at an SSJ center for medically fragile babies and was on the board for St. Joseph's Northside, a drop-in center founded by the SSJs. Near the end of our interview, I mentioned Sr. Virginia's statement about the worlds opened to the sisters of their generation who had "left the world." Quick to respond, Barb said, "I think about that so often, that I never would have had any of these experiences and met these people. And it just feels like such a blessing."

Sr. Josepha, who famously appears in a black-and-white photograph with Martin Luther King Jr., taught at a school in Selma in the early 1960s. When her father died and her mother fell ill, Josepha returned to western New York for good. Teaching in local city schools until 1986, she followed in her father's footsteps by working in prisons, as a chaplain, until her retirement seventeen years later. An effusive storyteller, Josepha especially relished sharing memories of her prison days, the sweet toughness of the inmates, and her role as the nun who championed their humanity.

One of Josepha's stories involved three inmates dying of AIDS: one in a coma, another in a deep mental fog, and the third very sick but still conscious. All three were sent to the prison hospital in chains. When she arrived to visit the one who could still speak, she was appalled not only to find him in chains but to learn that no one had explained to him his condition. "So, we talked for a while," Josepha said. "He didn't know what was ahead of him. And you can't help but think, 'My gosh, what can I tell him?' I mean, what would a doctor tell the young man? I didn't know. I was right in the middle of it." Josepha decided to get down to basics: "I asked him, 'Honey, do you have any clean underwear?' He said, 'No S'ter.'" This, Josepha explained, was how the men from Brooklyn talked. She continued,

> So I said, "That's okay. I'll get some. I'll either get it at the prison or I can go right across the hall and take some of the underwear that I gave Peter [another inmate in chains] yesterday. I'll go and rip it off!" And he's lying there—he's so, so sick, he died shortly after that—and he started laughing. And I said, "What is the matter with you?" And he said, "I don't think sisters are supposed to rip things off." And he started laughing all over again. I said, "Let me tell you something. You have met the sister who's going to rip things off of Peter!"

After gathering clean shorts, a shirt, and socks, Josepha tackled the next pressing issue: his chains. She painted the picture: "He's got leg irons on his ankles. Those leg irons are like handcuffs. And they're rubbing on his legs." Josepha described marching into the superintendent's office and telling him, "'You have three men over there who are going to be dead in the next three days.'" She shrugged, "I have no business saying that. I have no idea if they're going to be dead." Josepha continued, "I said to the superintendent, 'We have three men out there. They are wearing *leg* irons. And they will each be dead in the next few days!'"

I whispered, mostly to myself, "Why the heck are they wearing leg irons?"

Nodding, Josepha told me that the superintendent ordered a guard to fetch his phone. He called the prison hospital and demanded the leg irons be removed immediately.

Near the end of our conversation, I told Josepha how I was struck by the ways her stories so often involved a fight for the dignity of these imprisoned men. She responded, "Oh, and they *knew* that. They knew that. That's one of the reasons they took such good care of me." I also admitted that I couldn't imagine facing such desperate conditions every day, year in and year out. To this she shook her head, "I loved it. They were *wonderful* to me. The young men were wonderful to me. In some cases, much more so than the officers. But who cares?" Josepha shrugged. "I don't care!"

Sr. Jamesine also began her career as a teacher. Eventually earning a master's in education administration, she also served as a school principal and two terms as the SSJ congregation president. Retired from SSJ leadership, Jamesine earned a law degree so she could realize her long-held dream of opening a law firm for the working poor. For ten years, she met with clients, raised funds, and built up the firm. She told me that although she loved working with clients, she was consistently frustrated by a system of male entitlement that, "to be honest with you," she said, "was a lot like the Church." She painted a typical scenario: a female client who earns minimum wage files for divorce. Her husband with a high-paying job hires an attorney who keeps the case going, despite Jamesine's pleas to settle. "As long as the attorney kept the case going, he'd get big money coming in. So that's the part of the work that got me. It was that injustice and the unequal status of these two clients."

"Between the men and women."

"Yes, men and women. That's why, as I say, there are many things about this that are like the Church."

Jackie, who spent most of her nursing career caring for older adults, also expressed frustrations with the ways the Church marginalizes certain groups of people. This, she noted, flies in the face of theologies that portray God as inclusive and all-loving founded on the teachings of Jesus himself. "I know God is there for me and for everybody. *Everybody*," she insisted. Also resonant for Jackie are mystical approaches that envision divinity as a spark residing within each of us, without exception. With a sigh, she added, "But you know, I've had to come to grips, and I guess everybody does, with the fact that there is evil in the world." By this Jackie was alluding to clerical abuse, her greatest disappointment with the Church, enabled by its top-down structures and dualistic theologies. "See, when the Church teaches that God's up here," Jackie raised one hand up high, "and God's going to take care of us, down here," she lowered the other by the seat of her chair, "I'm thinking, 'Well what? What? A man is down here abusing a kid and God does nothing? What's that all about?'"

Jamesine and Jackie were among the handful of SSJs who shared their dismay over practices of exclusion and worse, buoyed nonetheless by their sister peers, select priests and theologians, and even a pope whose social vision largely matched their own. For nearly every sister I met, however, one resentment settled so close to the surface that it was often too obvious to mention. This had to do with how their institution, while opening otherwise unthinkable avenues for them, continued to close its doors to women's ordination. Such resentments were no doubt fueled by a certainty, based on the stunning accomplishments of their SSJ peers, that many of them could do better.

Minding and Narrowing the Gap: Divinity, Self, and Other

Anitha's rhetorical rebuke to the college priest, "Am I not a daughter of God?" encapsulates frustrations at religious inconsistencies shared by both Dalit and SSJ women. While they embraced theologies that supported their full humanity, their religious institutions often fell painfully short, denying their potential as humans while undercutting divinity's reach as well. We conclude with scenarios that skew the other direction in Kerala and for the SSJs, where divine power is understood not only to be less removed and less conditional but as reliant on humanity to activate earthly blessings. Here we find an intimately involved divinity of which the mystic Rabi'a, whose epigraph starts off this chapter, would no doubt approve.

In Kerala, I regularly heard women across traditions describe divine action as entwined with their own. Ananda Lakshmi explained how her family temple in northern Kerala distributed food, money, and clothing to the poor, founded on the belief that "this universe belongs to everybody, so we shouldn't focus on 'mine, mine.'" Since everything we have is Goddess-given, she explained, "our job is to simply participate in the flow of divine blessings." In so doing, blessings circle back. "Do your duty, share, and live happily. Because I think like that, the Goddess has given me health, every blessing. So, sharing is important and we should never think, 'my child, my husband.' It should be everybody's." Waiting for the sounds of approval around the room to subside, she concluded, "When you give to others, the Goddess gives to you. If you do service to others, the Goddess will take care of you."

Teresa, a Latin Catholic, followed a similar line of logic when sharing her story about the time she fell while crossing a busy road on her way to mass. This was a double-miracle story. First, she wasn't run over by a bus and, second, someone in the crowd that formed around her returned the gold chain that had flown off her neck. Entering into the flow of blessings, Teresa decided she would give the chain away as a wedding gift to a poor, motherless woman she knew. Recalling her family's astonishment, making us laugh, she told us how her children waited five years before buying her a new chain, worried she might give another one away. Holding out her new chain for us to see, she defended herself: "But I had decided that, since God had given back to me the one I lost, I was going to give it to someone more deserving."

When we asked Mary, a Syrian Catholic woman, if she had a life lesson to share, she responded, smiling wide, that "without God, there is nothing in the world for me. All is given by God. Everything is God's gift!" Invoking a system of human-divine infusion, she continued, "And I believe, I believe *fully*, that you do not harm anybody, not even an ant. *Then* God is with us. Of that I am very sure. Very, very sure." Savitri from the Hindu Nair community echoed this sentiment: "When I do something right, helping someone in distress or giving to people in need, I feel close to God. If you keep God in your mind and act, you will always do the right things."

Annamma C., a well-to-do Syrian Catholic who had dedicated her life to serving the poor, told us that her most treasured work involved teaching embroidery to disadvantaged girls. With eyes sparkling, she told us how some of these women still visited her with daughters and granddaughters in tow. Her role model growing up was her hardworking, generous mother, yet Annamma's enduring inspiration had always been Jesus. Letting that sink in, she backed up. Seemingly worried that she may have placed herself on equal footing, she turned to me intently, insisting that it is only through Jesus that her work was possible.

"Yes." I nodded in agreement.

"Jesus said, 'You must love others as you love yourself.' And when you see someone feeling upset, you must try and help them. When they are sick you must go and visit them. Love and affection, that you must do." After pausing, she added, "And if you do, you will be very, very happy."

Still nodding, I said, "It's true."

Annamma rephrased: "Peace and happiness you will get when you help others."

In agreement, we moved on to other topics. Yet when wrapping up our interview, Annamma's unease returned. Taking my hand, she assured me, "I'm only telling you these things because you are asking."

Chuckling, I said, "Oh, I know! Absolutely. And I so appreciate your telling me."

"I just want to help the poor. I always just want to help people. That is my peace and happiness."

"And by telling me about your work, you are helping me." Patting her hand, I repeated, "You're helping *me*." Seemingly satisfied, Annamma smiled and patted my hand back.

Squirming within a paradox, walking with humility in the footsteps of divinity, Annamma saw herself, like so many of the women we met in Kerala, as part of a human-divine cycle of blessings. Divinity dwelled within women's outreach to others. The SSJs have a term for this: "mysticism of relationship." Envisioned as a human-divine cycle of activity on earth, this is how many of the sisters today frame their work. Unlike their Kerala peers, however, they came late to this understanding, and only after putting aside their pre–Vatican II training that stressed selfless work as a way to please a faraway, judgmental God.

It turns out this "new" mystical framework is not so new. Embedded in the SSJ's founding principles, it is central to the seventeenth-century writings of Fr. Jean Pierre Médaille, a Jesuit priest whose support gave legitimacy to the six founders of their order. Buried for centuries, Médaille's writings were retrieved and translated in the early 1970s when Vatican II reforms encouraged religious orders to do just that, to recover founding documents and to read them in light of the signs of the times.

As part of this ongoing retrieval process, the SSJ sisters hosted a monthly Zoom series, "Roots Alive!" during the winter and spring of 2021–2022. Attendees were mostly sisters from across North America and beyond with over two hundred faces filling our computer screens during each two-hour-long session. Each began with a prayer, followed by presentations from Sr. Patricia Byrne, a historian, and Sr. Marcia Allen, a theologian, both of whom had spent most of their careers studying the founding documents. Sessions concluded with small breakout groups and a final discussion.

Listening to Sr. Pat describe the lives of the founding sisters during the second session, I was reminded of the SSJs I had interviewed. Sidestepping societal expectations of their day, the French founders were some of the first nuns to work outside cloister walls. Because young women were not allowed to walk freely without male accompaniment, they dressed in widows' garb that later became the nun's habit. Propelled by society's urgent needs during a time when marauding armies pillaged and spread diseases across the region, these women served in hospitals, at orphanages, and in prisons.

Also enflaming the region at the time were mystical movements that also influenced sisterly formation. During one of our Zoom sessions, Sr. Marcia described the founders' mystical view of God as an all-encompassing love expressed through the Trinity in which God the Father is an inclusive love, Jesus is love outpoured, and the Holy Spirit is love's connective tissue.[11] Bringing this to life through their interactions with society's forgotten, the early sisters saw themselves, as Sr. Marcia put it, "in God and God in all things." They participated "in a love that does what it is and is what it does," where divisions between subject and verb, essence and action—between self, other, and God—melt away.

At one of our breakout sessions, sisters in our small Zoom group talked about how these "Roots Alive!" presentations reinvigorated their vocational purpose. A few also expressed their dismay at how far their early convent training had strayed from these founding ideals. At the wrap-up session that followed, Sr. Pat likewise commented on the distance they'd traveled since their founding. She recalled being told upon entering, for instance, that the SSJs had a special devotion to the Holy Trinity. Yet this conception floated loftily above earthly affairs, a radical departure from the order's founding view of the Trinity as "dynamically at work in us and among us." Sr. Pat also marveled at how today's sisters "found fire" in their founding charism once it was recovered, in spite of their early training. She reasoned that now, fifty years later, they wouldn't still be saying "yes" to this dynamism "unless it was already in them."

Based on my conversations with women across cultures, an earthbound divinity "at work in us and among us" clearly has broad appeal, far more worthy of devotion than one who reigns from on high, a divinity that Icelanders and Californians saw fit to reject and that the SSJs gladly dethroned. Yet rarely did I hear women in Kerala describe the need to abandon or alter divinity in this way—which is not to say that they didn't question the hypocrisies of formal religion. Far from blindly adhering or lagging behind as colonizing mindsets might assume, they appear to have been ahead of the game, religiously speaking.

Bringing home this point was a trip to Bangalore that a group of SSJ sisters took in 2009. During one of our "Roots Alive!" sessions, Sr. Marcia, a member of the delegation, described the visit's aim, which was to introduce and discuss their founding documents with some of the Indian sisters who worked there. Marcia recalled how, when she shared Fr. Médaille's mysticism of relationship, portraying divinity as a force of love that worked within and among them, the Indian sisters embraced this concept with an enthusiasm equal to that of their American counterparts. "I was so struck by the fact that we were there, Westerners, dealing with women who came from a totally different culture, and it was the same experience." Marcia beamed at the memory. Their response to the documents, she recalled, was that "they leapt to them." Shaking her head, she repeated, "They leapt to them."

Sr. Marcia may have been surprised, but, based on my conversations in Kerala, I'm not. Rabi'a, I'm guessing, would have seen this coming all along:

DOOR NEVER CLOSED
A man not knowing
said to God:
"O God at long last
open a door for me."

Rabi'a was there:
"You fool!
The door's never been closed."[12]

6

Critical Junctures

• • • • • • • • • • • • • •

Love and Loss

> There is nothing so whole as a broken heart.
>
> **RABBI MENACHEM MENDEL**

When Olla and I visited Margrét's home, we spent most of our time in her living room, all three of us facing wide windows that looked out over a sparkling fjord and onto the city of Akureyri. As we neared the end of the formal portion of what was a lively, rollicking interview, I asked, "What would you say life has taught you?"

"Oof." Margrét made a face.

Olla and I laughed. "I know," I said. "It's a hard question."

"Life has taught me so much. I can't give a concise answer to this."

A good sport, Margrét pressed on. She told us how grateful she was for her nonconformist life as a journalist. She then reflected on how she'd learned to be more patient, "to be more open, to understand other people better, not to condemn." After a moment's thought she added, "Of course, if you experience good and bad things in life, it's bound to teach you to value the good things. If you don't have bad things happen in life, you don't value the good things. You don't realize how good the good things are." As Olla and I nodded enthusiastically, Margrét backed down. "But like I say, I can't give you a single answer."

"Right," I assured her. "So, you've given us many."

"Just don't make me sound like somebody who thinks she has found the one and only answer."

"I think you've been very clear about that."

"Okay." Margrét looked half convinced.

As far as I can recall, Margrét is the only woman to have expressed this idea outright, that hardships can teach us the value of the good things. Yet this sentiment was implicitly repeated across conversations, in the ways women framed their life stories. It's a confluence of opposites that emerged in one of two ways: through tales of catastrophe that culminated in gratitude or through reflections on life's treasures bound up in scarcity and loss. Such accounts spoke to how, as Arthur Kleinman puts it, "love and hope are not negated by loss and threat; if anything, they become better understood and more deeply cherished."[1] Anthropologist Michael Jackson concurs that "the most terrible and the most beautiful are often married in life, like light and shadow." These "critical junctures" are scenarios where we find ourselves "most alive to what one might call the real or the religious." For Jackson, "the real" in this context refers to how critical junctures can wrest us from habitual beliefs and behaviors, while "the religious" represents the "epiphanies, breakthroughs, conversions and revelations" that follow such disruptions.

Jackson also reminds us of how critical junctures often form the paradoxical backbone of religions, in which, for instance, the new life of Easter is impossible without Good Friday death.[2] The lotus, a sacred symbol across Asian traditions, would be another example: blooming clean and pure above the muck, it relies on the same for its existence. So it goes with the muck of life. While potentially making us "callous, bitter, insensitive, mute," as Dorothee Soelle words it, suffering has the potential to transform—as long as we don't try to blunt or forget our pain.[3] Rebecca Solnit likewise warns against blunting. In her critique of social activists who believe human rights to be "total and permanent" once they're achieved, she counters that this is as good as saying that victory is impossible, as real victories are always incomplete, incremental, and ongoing. The wish to bypass pain, she writes, is the "secular equivalent of paradise, where all the problems are solved and there's nothing to do, a fairly boring place."[4]

In the previous chapter, we explored critical junctures of sorts, where divinity worthy of devotion did not float above earthly pains and imperfections but resided within them. Continuing the course set by part II, "The Real," we now consider the life stories that older women chose to share that sturdily braided love and loss, light and shadow, rejecting the impulse to bypass life's difficulties. Just as their chosen portrayals of divinity regularly refused official constructs of heavenly perfection that demoralized them, the junctures binding their life accounts refused the spruced-up photo album or social media portrayals that so often demean and discourage. The emotional weight of women's stories confirms that scenarios where "all problems are solved" not only are boring and untrue but flatten the potential for epiphanies and breakthroughs.

The tendency to hold joy and sorrow in tension and in ways that further joy is, it turns out, a late-life specialty.[5] Often referred to as poignancy, it arises when life's fragility can no longer be ignored. Coming to grips with the fleeting nature of all that we love, people often move past a flat sense of sorrow to engage more deeply with beauty and meaning. Pronounced in older adults as well as in those living with terminal illnesses, poignancy is less indebted to the number of years lived than with their dwindling.[6] It is a preference for the positive that cuts through at the most definitive periods of loss imaginable. Dismantling conventional habits of thought and behavior, it is among the gifts conferred upon us at life's edge, a critical juncture in itself.[7]

The stories that follow draw from each of the four locations. Yet missing from the mix are accounts from Kerala's most marginalized women, who described disappointments and losses as permeating entire lifetimes, for whom divinity was the singular source of solidity and support. Such lifetimes could be considered critical junctures in themselves, with God set in blinding relief against a backdrop of incessant sorrow.

The Other Side of Catastrophe

An isolatable crisis, on the other hand, makes for a good story. For many women, such an event was a defining life feature, a lasting lesson in appreciation for the things we normally take for granted. With new eyes to see, these stories often culminated in gratitude for catastrophe itself.

In California, Judy and I met in her retirement community apartment that she shared with her husband. Their furnishings were unusually spare and simple, something I didn't notice until I'd asked our final question about life lessons. "Basically, one big life lesson was when we were burned out by the fire," Judy responded. Referring to the Los Alamos fire of 2000, she assured me that, thanks to early evacuation, no lives were lost. The Red Cross had turned the high school gymnasium into a shelter, providing meals, cots to sleep on, and medical support. Recalling the sense of communal loss and sustenance, she quipped, "If you've got to lose your home it's best to do it in the company of a lot of other people."

Moving on to specifics, Judy told me about her first material possession after the fire destroyed everything: a plastic mug from State Farm Insurance. With eyes glistening, she recalled her excitement when she was given the mug. "I said, 'I've got a mug! I now finally have a possession!'" Turning to the small refrigerator behind her, she said, "I'll show it to you! I still use it." Pulling out an insulated mug faded from red to pink, she placed it on the table in front of us. "There it is. I put my tomato juice in it now." As I leaned in for a closer look, noting the barely visible State Farm logo, she proclaimed, "So you learn the value of life: that you can lose everything and still be alive."

Hearing her thrill over this old plastic mug, I added, "And still find joy in things."

"Yes. I was so excited. 'I've got a possession!' So, I learned that life goes on. And you get through it. No matter. Now that's a fairly earth-shaking thing and we got through it okay." Hearing her story, I couldn't help thinking about the California fires raging around us that summer. I asked if this was triggering memories of Los Alamos. Judy nodded and emphasized the importance of early evacuation. "But you can always replace things." Holding up her pink plastic mug, she said, "State Farm might give you another coffee mug!"

Sr. Jamesine's catastrophe was a near-fatal car crash that happened about a decade earlier in Florida. She listed for me her injuries: two broken ankles, a broken pelvis, broken ribs, a punctured lung, and a broken neck. "I should have died," she said. "I was really banged up." She recalled how the EMT first responder who worked to pry open the car door suspected she'd broken her neck. When he told her not to move, Jamesine responded, "Oh great. My brother died of a broken neck." As this was in late December, the stunned EMT worker simply said, "Oh. Merry Christmas." Arriving at the hospital, Jamesine was "given up for dead," as she put it. But after a two-month stay, an angel flight back to Rochester, and a seven-month recovery period at the

Motherhouse health care unit, she was back on her feet. Recalling the long haul, she said, "I didn't think I'd ever be able to walk again." Switching gears, she added, "But actually, I'm very fortunate. I always say to people, 'Well, I got up today and I'm fairly functional!'" With two rods now holding her neck together, she demonstrated how she could slightly and slowly turn her head from left to right.

Later, as we moved on to my final question about what life had taught her, I said I suspected this might be related to her accident. Jamesine nodded,

> I think it is. I think it is. I learned a lot of lessons when I was recuperating from the accident, you know.... Every ounce of energy within me went into trying to get well. And then to be able to come out of that, being able to read, being able to pray, being able to see, and to walk. All of that. I think of it all the time. One of my favorite expressions is that I have no complaints whatsoever. I'm grateful for everything. It's exactly how I feel. And although I have a lot of pain, of discomfort, every day, it's okay. It reminds me of what I'm able to do, of what I couldn't do for a long time. As I say, I'm grateful for everything.

Jamesine motioned around her spare Motherhouse room. "We live in a palace, you know? Private room, private bathroom, meals prepared for us. I cannot imagine why anyone would feel entitled to this." She shook her head, "We are not entitled to anything. I'm just grateful for life."

Kay in California had started using a walker to steady her gait when she was in her seventies, when a case of bronchitis morphed into Guillain-Barré. When we met, Kay first brought up her illness in response to my question about what she considered sacred in her life: "I was just thinking, with this part," Kay motioned to her walker, "how it led me into complementary medicine." She explained that because the standard medical world doesn't know how to treat her condition, her turn to alternative modes introduced her to the "beautiful energies" surrounding us. If not for her illness, she wouldn't have known about such wonders that, for her, were sacred.

Later, when asked about her life lessons, Kay again pointed to her walker. She told me how her condition continues to deteriorate. She could no longer cook because of her shaky hands, and her feet won't allow her to do the things she used to love, like hiking in the mountains. "It's been a growth process," she said. Soon after her diagnosis, she signed up for a warm-water exercise class. "And that was an eye-opener because I'd never really been around handicapped or 'weird,' sick people. So, my circle of compassion just grew. A lot. So that was a real, major lesson."

Impressed by her honesty, I said, "Yeah, I'll bet."

"At one point someone asked, 'Where would you rather be, where you were before, or now?' And I don't think I'd give up this experience. With the disability. Because I think I'm a different person. I've had a lot of learning, you know? About acceptance and appreciation for things. So, it's okay." Admitting that it was still hard to run into people returning from mountain hikes, hearing about all the wildflowers they'd seen, Kay listed all that life had given her, her travels, and the children she raised. She summed up her life lesson: "It's to never take things for granted. You know, to try every day to be grateful for all the gifts that I do have."

In Kerala, Grace's catastrophe story was a crisis of her own making, delivered in luscious detail to my students and me. She was fourteen at the time, a student at a boarding school run by Belgian nuns. One morning in painting class, she told us, their teacher, Mother Lucinthia, announced that they had just received a beautiful painting from Belgium. It would soon be exhibited for all to see but for now, she told the girls, it must be kept in a special room. Grace recalled her words: "So, don't enter the room. Because if you enter, you may do something and it will fall down and break. So, don't enter until I tell you to come into the room." Grace paused for effect. "So, we all went away. But I became curious. And everyone was sleeping in the afternoon..."

Guessing where this was headed, my students and I inhaled.

"So, I went into that room. And the moment I went into the room I touched something so that it fell and broke."

As I sat back, hand over my mouth, Haley and Paige uttered sounds of horror. Grace continued, "And you can imagine at the age of fourteen what my feelings were! And I'd been told by many people that Europeans are such people that they will tie you up to the top and beat you up. I was so scared!" With this running through her mind, Grace retreated to her room and hid under her bed. Then she began to think, as she put it, "This was not the right thing to do."

We chimed in, "That's right!"

"But I was thinking, my father will beat me up, the nuns will also beat me up, what will I do? I cannot *tell* you the feelings that I had. So finally, what I did was, at four o'clock, Mother comes and rings the bell for all the girls to come and play. So, before it was four o'clock, I went and stood—there was a huge pillar in front of that room—I went and stood there like this." Grace hung her head and scrunched up her face. "*Frightened*. I was so frightened." From where she stood, Grace told us, she could see Mother Constantia, the head mistress, looking at her. "I ran down to her and hugged her. I said, 'Mother, I broke that painting!' I told her like this." Grace paused. "You know what she did?" We shook our heads. "She hugged me back and said, 'Grace, that's okay. You broke the painting, but you told me the truth.'"

Through the sounds of our relief, Grace concluded, "That was a great lesson for me. I can never forget it. I will always remember that, the particular thing she told me, where I was thinking there would be beating and shouting. Instead, she's hugging me and saying, 'Grace, you broke a painting but you told me the truth.'"

My students and I met Elizabeth at the home she shared with her son and daughter-in-law in a village outside Ernakulam. Joining us was Faxon, Elizabeth's neighbor, and Jenena, his fiancée at the time. The life crisis Elizabeth related, also set in childhood, she didn't realize she was having until she was nearly grown. Seated in front of a large framed image of Jesus, closely surrounded by our inquiring group, she began by telling us that she was raised by a stepmother. She then backed up to explain how, when she was a baby, the youngest of five, her birth mother died. At her dying mother's insistence, her father remarried someone they both knew and with whom he had two more children. When she was five, Elizabeth told us, her father died as well, leaving his second wife to raise seven children on her own. This, she assured us, her stepmother did lovingly. All were well cared for and educated.

At this point, we moved on to other topics. After we'd worked our way through the other questions, Elizabeth's daughter-in-law wanted to bring us back to the subject of the stepmother. Gesturing toward Elizabeth, she said, "She had a very good childhood, because her stepmother looked after her very well. Until she came to the college, she didn't know that she was her stepmother."

Not grasping what she meant, I nodded and said, "Okay."

Rephrasing, she said, "Until she was a graduate, only at that time did she come to know. Some child told her."

Not sure I understood, I said, "Explain that. I am sorry. So, she didn't know that..."

"She thought she was her own mother."

Finally getting it, the room went silent, eyes misting behind our smiles. The daughter-in-law nodded. "She thought she was her own mother. She never knew it was her stepmother until she was almost seventeen."

"Oh!" I looked over at Elizabeth, who met my gaze.

Jenena said, "She was given so much love that she didn't realize..."

Faxon said, "So, when she was in college, someone told her..."

Elizabeth's daughter-in-law finished, "told her that that was her stepmother."

"Otherwise, she would have never known," Faxon said.

"Never known," Jenena echoed.

Smiling as she watched the revelation unfold, Elizabeth confirmed, "I was very lucky."

I've since wondered what she meant by this. Was she lucky for being so well loved by a stepmother? Lucky that she never suspected she wasn't her birth mother? Lucky for not knowing her birth mother had died? Regardless, Elizabeth's take-home point, which could have justifiably been a sense of loss, betrayal, or anger, was gratitude. The same could be said for so many of the other catastrophe stories I heard, of which these are just a sampling. Women were lucky to be the owner of a new plastic mug; to be able to get out of bed in morning to read, to pray, to walk; to experience loving forgiveness rather than get clobbered by a nun. They were grateful to have learned gratitude. Narrowly escaping paralysis and death, Sr. Jamesine insisted that no one, in the end, is entitled to anything. Everything is gift. In catastrophe's wake, gratitude simply made sense.

The same could be said about late life, a slowly unfolding crisis in itself.[8] For the women I met, unsolicited expressions of gratitude permeated our exchanges. Shaped in different ways, this was most often expressed in gratefulness for life itself. Certain contexts also lent themselves to particular types of gratitude.[9] Most notably, nearly every SSJ sister expressed her appreciation for how her vocation opened up otherwise impossible opportunities, and in Kerala, women of means with advanced degrees or who pursued public professions were thankful for fathers and husbands who encouraged them to buck convention. Across cultural differences, women's appreciation consistently emerged when they knew things could easily have been—or would soon be—different. In other words, gratitude partnered with precarity.

Childhood Love and Loss

Contexts for hearing out Margrét's point, that the bad things in life help us "realize how good the good things are," include inversions of catastrophe stories. Most often recalled from childhood, these stories that focus in on the people and places that women most deeply treasured were consistently steeped in situations of loss and scarcity.

Faxon and Jenena, who had introduced us to Elizabeth, also brought us to meet with three sisters at a Carmelite convent down the road. Greeted at a side entrance, we were led to a vacant convent bedroom set up with a small table and several chairs. The first to meet with us was Sr. Sapientia who, arriving with the help of a walker, warmly held my hand during our introductions. As we took our seats, she began by reflecting on her childhood, where it became immediately clear that the shining star of her early life was her father. The youngest of nine, Sapientia had been his faithful companion, and he in turn doted on her. She told us how the two of them would rise early every morning and, leaving the busy household behind, walk hand in hand to mass. When he learned of her intention to join the convent, knowing this meant she'd move away for good, he at first forbade her. But eventually, with cajoling from the parish priest, he gave his blessing. Helping to ease the transition, Sapientia spent her first two pre-novitiate years at a boarding school that allowed weekend visits home.

At age twenty-two, Sapientia moved into the convent for good. With eyes brimming, she told us that, six days after she entered, her father died. The family had sung hymns and said their evening prayers as usual that night, but after her father had gone to bed he was awakened by a sudden pain. Suffering through the night, he began vomiting by early morning and, soon after, passed away. Pausing to collect herself, Sapientia told us how, after his death, one of the sisters spoke her worst fears, wondering whether her father had died of a broken heart. This possibility still haunted her. "I still think back at that incident, of my father dying in six days' time, because I was so close to him." With a small smile, she added, "I pray for my father every day. And I know that, up there in heaven, he is happy to hear from me."

Welling up with her, I said, "I'm so sorry you had to go through this."

Sapientia nodded. She admitted that, realistically speaking, her father's death probably had nothing to do with her leaving. But then again, she said, "letting me go must have made him feel very bad." Thinking a moment, she said, "He was like Abraham offering his son." This stopped me. In Abraham's story, his son was spared. Everyone survives. Later it occurred to me that Sapientia was comparing the great faith of these two men, both willing to let go of a beloved child, for God's sake. For this, her father was eternally blessed. Assuredly hearing her prayers from heaven, Sapientia took comfort.

Sr. Lorraine met with me in a parish house in downtown Rochester where she and several other SSJ sisters lived. She had been the middle child among seven siblings where, like in Sapientia's family, parental affections were stretched thin. "There wasn't time for our parents to give to each one of us. We sort of were . . . a *group*." Laughing at her choice of words, Lorraine explained how financial struggles further strained family dynamics. "So, I never felt that warm cozy feeling with my mother. She was just too busy. She was either having another baby or just trying to make ends meet. My father had a very small paycheck."

The light of Lorraine's childhood was John, the oldest sibling and eight years her senior. Dearly loved by all, he filled the void left by her busy parents. "He was our big brother and we sort of idolized him because he was such a good guy." Lorraine recalled instances when, to her delight, she felt singled out by his attention. One time, when John bought the family's first telephone from his earnings playing clarinet and saxophone, he assigned Lorraine a special role. She remembered bursting with pride when, pulling her aside, he told her, "'Now, I want you to be my secretary. If anybody calls, write it down.' So, I felt sort of . . ." Lorraine shuffled her shoulders with self-satisfaction. Another time was on a summer day as Lorraine wandered aimlessly through their empty house. On his way to go swimming with friends, John took pity on his little sister and, to her amazement, invited her to come along.

Graduating from high school near the end of World War II, John enlisted to play in the army band. Lorraine described how, as the war was winding down, they received a telegram from the Philippines with news of his death. Although he was saved from enemy fire by playing in the band, "they just didn't know how to treat pneumonia or kidney failure—or whatever it was—in the jungle," Lorraine explained. "What did they know? It was a field hospital. Like *M*A*S*H*." Tearing up, she recalled how she had prayed every night for John's safe return while he was away, figuring that her entire family must have been doing the same. "So that was huge for us, a *huge*, huge sorrow for my parents. I don't think my mother ever recovered." For Lorraine, the loss deepened the imprint of the one who had validated her sense of worth, made all the more meaningful in a context where parental attention and affirmation were hard to come by.

For Lolly in California, a hectic childhood created a special yearning for her mother. When asked about early memories that stood out, Lolly's quick response was, "My mother's smell. I *loved* my mother's smell." She explained how their two-family flat in Utica generated endless work for her mother. "She was raising *all* the children, doing *all* the housework, washing the clothes, buying the clothes not only for her children—she had four, my aunt had three. So, she raised seven children." Lolly marveled, "Her energy was amazing. She just did everything. And she didn't ask for help. She just felt she had to do it.

Who else was going to do it? She just knew that her sister was not a good mother." As the oldest, Lolly held the prized position of being her mother's helper. This had a double benefit. It gave her not only access to her preoccupied mother but a sense of self-worth when performing tasks reserved just for her.

Interested in her initial response to my question, I asked Lolly if she could say more about why her mother's smell stayed so strong in her memory. "She was my anchor in so many ways—and I used to love to go into her closet and . . ." Lolly breathed in. "And I'd look at her clothes, and smell her clothes." Laughing lightly, she added, "I think it was that love, that joining, that bringing in everything about that person. I would go into her closet and just smell her clothes, wanting that closeness with her."

As Jenný was an only child raised by older parents, the backdrop against which her childhood love shone had nothing to do with scarcity of attention. The three of them, as she put it, were inseparable. When Jenný was fifteen, however, her mother died, and one year later so did her father. Without close relatives to care for her, she was left to fend for herself with the help of close friends. This she explained in a rather matter-of-fact way during our first meeting. Our conversation then moved in other directions.

Returning to Jenný's home eight months later, we mostly caught up on life updates. Near the end of our time together, when we asked if she had a poem, a song, or an object of significance to share, Jenný got up from the kitchen table and walked into her nearby sunroom. She reemerged, beaming, with a large pair of metal clippers in her hands. Raising them up for us to see, she told us that they were once her mother's, used in her work as a rattan furniture maker. She proudly explained that her mother had traveled alone to Norway in 1925 to learn the craft, becoming the first woman to join what was then a booming industry. Returning to her seat, Jenný placed her mother's clippers on the table in front of her.

After a moment, I asked if she had more to say about what the clippers meant to her. Hesitating slightly, Jenný told us how she had lost her parents during a time when "you just didn't talk about those things." With a sigh, she said, "So I put a really thick lid on my emotions. It was something that I didn't speak of for a long time." She admitted that, as the years rolled by and she continued to keep quiet about her losses, she no longer felt entitled to speak of them. "I felt like they shouldn't matter anymore." Patting the clippers in front of her, she said, "But today I feel that I am advanced enough that I can talk about it." As Olla and I nodded in support, Jenný explained how the clippers that she now used to tend her garden "connect me to both my

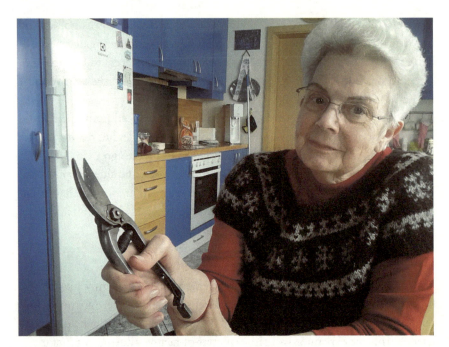

FIGURE 6.1 Jenný with her mother's clippers. Photo by author.

parents as individuals, but also to those memories, and to the love, which I feel is still there."

As the three of us continued to eye the worn, slightly rusted clippers, Olla noted the contrast between their humble appearance and the exquisite products that Jenný, a fine craftswoman, and her parents, both furniture makers, created. We agreed that they were in some ways like a sacred object whose exterior only hinted at a deeper efficacy. At this, Jenný became adamant. "There are so many things today that people consider beautiful—collectors' items and things like that. But it's all so superficial. It's just scratching the surface." Putting her hand on her clippers, she said, "But then we have something like this, with a connection that goes deep. When you grow older, you get this stronger knowledge of things. It's a stronger connection to the nature of things, to the core of how things work." Noting how people are so often attracted to "how things look, not how they feel," Jenný asserted, "I think that I am now more connected to the core of things. This sharpens as you get older. And these," she held up her clippers, "touch the core of things that I love."

Dísa's childhood loves were amplified not only by scarcity and loss but by neglect. When Olla and I met with her in her assisted living quarters, we had barely settled into our chairs when she was off and running, stories of growing up on a northern Icelandic farm tumbling out of her, her laugh bubbling up as she conjured memories both light and heavy. Dísa opened with joy, recalling how she loved rolling up round hay bales in the summers, keeping sweet company with the farm animals, and soaking in the beauty of the now-famous salmon river that ran through the property. She recalled the magic of her school route: a winding cow path that led to a *kláfur*, a flat wooden platform that she pulled by rope to ferry herself across the river.

After reveling, Dísa explained that she actually didn't move to the farm until she was five. Born of an extramarital affair, she was raised by her grandmother until, as she put it, "my mother wanted to take revenge on my father, so she gave me away to these people." As was common at that time, her adoptive parents who had long been trying to conceive children of their own hoped that by adopting Dísa their luck might change.

Moving on to other subjects, Dísa returned to her childhood when we asked her what she considered to be sacred in her life. "A holy moment for me was when my first stepbrother was born," she said. "I think it's because of me that my brothers were born. It's because of me that they were alive." Despite this, Dísa recalled how her adoptive parents had treated her without affection from the start, forcing her to work long hours on the farm. Yet her brothers, who validated her existence, became nurturing presences for Dísa over time. "They were wonderful to me. Their mother was always very tired at the end of the day, with sore feet from burrs. So, when they were very small, they started to share a bed with me." Recalling how she would sing to them the songs her grandmother taught her before she was sent to the farm, she reflected, "I cared for them when they needed someone. They were very special to me." Searching for a better word, Dísa said, "They were magnificent."

Likely deepening Dísa's love for the farm itself was that her connection was tenuous. Ensuring that nothing of his would be passed on to her, Dísa's adoptive father never legally changed her birth name. She recalled how his send-off to her when she left to get married hammered home this point: "He slammed his hand against the wall and said, 'You will get nothing from me! My boys will get everything!'" Dísa laughed. "That was the gratitude I got for all my slavery, for all those years I lived there."

Near the end of our time together, Dísa gave us a tour of her photos—of her deceased husband and their children, grandchildren, and great-grandchildren—that filled a large book case set against a wall. When we asked if she had a song, poem, or object to share, she motioned to an intricately carved wooden shelf hanging on an adjacent wall. This, she explained, was made by Guðmunder, the elder brother. Above it hung a framed black-and-white photograph taken by Ásmundur, the younger. Treasured items, both depicted the family farmhouse, reminders of a place she loved and those who loved her through her sorrows. Dísa sighed, "I wish you could see the farm." With slight satisfaction in her voice, she informed us that neither brother married or had children. Both had died early. With no heir, the farm had been turned over to the government.

In Kerala, Ammini also spoke of her deep affection for her childhood home, rooted in the purpose and worth it gave her as a child, heightened by the knowledge that it was never hers to keep. Speaking to us from a home in Ernakulam that she shared with her daughter, Rachel, and Rachel's husband, Ammini recalled how she loved playing out in nature as a child, how she felt protected by her surroundings, and was never afraid to stay at home alone. She also recalled her disappointment upon learning that her life would take a different course than the boys in her family, that she would be married off and would have to leave. From an early age, she saw clearly that "the stress was given—the property, the affection, everything—more to the boys than to the girls."

Rachel clarified, "We are a patriarchal society."

Ammini nodded. "As a custom, as a culture, men, the boys, are given everything."

Rachel elaborated, "Mommy's cousin who stayed with them and studied at a school close by, even extra manuals were kept for him. You know? To write in."

Ammini laughed. "My brother also, he may be given three packs of these a day. But I may not even be given one. How can I not see this? But I never took offense at it because . . . I think that it was ingrained in me. I understood that this was the way things worked. Although I knew it was happening, I didn't think it was incorrect. As I grew, of course, I started thinking, 'Ah!'"

"What made you start thinking, 'Ah?'" I asked.

"I knew, you know, that I have an equal brain."

Rachel nodded. "She is very smart."

Ammini went on to tell us how, as a teenager, she would participate in her family's agricultural work such as measuring the paddy fields, typically a man's job. The sense of accomplishment this gave her deepened her love for the land, as did the sting of injustice. She described how she once overheard her father and grandfather deliberating over whether or not to continue the girls' education since they would be married off anyhow. "With all this talk about

FIGURE 6.2 Ammini shows us a miniature pineapple in her Ernakulam city garden. Photo by Haley Saba.

sending me off and my brother staying there, every time I started hearing this . . . I would really hate this kind of talk. Why should I be sent off? So, then I started to, you know . . ."

"To rebel!" Rachel inserted.

Ammini's face brightened. "Yes. I wanted to be home, more than anything else. I didn't want them to think that I should be sent away. You see?" We all nodded. "When somebody comes to talk about dowry, I would think, 'Ah, are they selling me?' You know? I used to have those kinds of thoughts."

When my students and I returned to Ammini and Rachel's house two years later, the subject of Ammini's beloved home came up near the end of our visit, when we asked if she had an object, poem, or song of significance to share.

Thinking for a few seconds, Ammini asked, "An object means what?"

"Anything," I replied.

Beaming, she announced, "An object is my home!" Drawing out her words, she said, "My *home*. It means everything to me." Gesturing around her, Ammini said, "My home is not this home, but the home that I was born to. That is my home. That is something I can never forget. My parents. Everything." She reflected, "Anywhere else, even when I meet my people—my children, my husband—it's different. But this is my . . ." Ammini teared up and sighed. "Oh, there's everything in that. Everything in that. How can I explain it? Even the butterflies I see there, or the snakes, or whatever. Everything there is so *fine* for me."

I conclude this sampling of stories in which love and self-worth are heightened by scarcity and loss with reflections from ninety-six-year-old Pennamma, whose account was set in early adulthood. This was not something she set out to tell us but was brought to light by her daughter-in-law, Reeni. Reeni did this throughout our visit, gently drawing out her quiet mother-in-law, filling in the gaps when her memory lagged.

When I asked Pennamma if there was anything outside formal religion that felt sacred to her, she drew a blank. Casting about, she finally said, "In my life, I had to do whatever my husband said. There was no freedom to think on my own." Seeing my surprise, Reeni clarified, "She never had the freedom to think otherwise. What she was told by her elders is what she continued to believe. Again, in her married life, whatever her husband said, she obeyed. Beyond that, there was nothing. She never had a mind of her own."

Although I was familiar with how traditional gender roles in Kerala could be especially confining for women of Pennamma's generation, class, and Syrian Christian background, many of those we interviewed found ways to work around the system. Some earned higher degrees, started businesses, or organized outreach services with the blessings of fathers or husbands. That Pennamma had little say even in household affairs kind of stopped me in my tracks. I turned to Reeni. "I wish I could think of a follow-up question. What would you ask?" Reeni, whose life was very different than her mother-in-law's, suggested, "How did she *live* like that?"

Trying another angle, I asked Pennamma what brought her joy. She told us how she used to enjoy playing the piano, but because her husband didn't encourage her, she stopped. Reeni added that she and her husband, Pennamma's son, were trying to get her to play again. Thinking further, she told us how, until about two years ago, Pennamma used to harvest, shell, and remove the mace from nutmeg that grew on the surrounding trees. This was her hobby, as she put it. As my students and I responded with enthusiasm, I suggested, "So that must have made you happy, to be able to do that." Pennamma smiled warmly. Reeni then remembered how her mother-in-law also used to care for the chickens that were kept in the coop during the day, letting them out every evening. "She would enjoy calling them and just enjoy having them around." We laughed together at the image and Pennamma again smiled at the memory. Seemingly exhausting the topic of joy, we moved on.

Before we finished our formal interview, I asked Pennamma if there was anything she'd like to add. As she shook her head, Reeni sat upright, remembering another source of joy. She reminded us of two portraits we'd passed while walking through their entryway, stationed on either side of a clock. One was of Pennamma's husband and the other—a smaller, smiling figure—was of his brother. This man, as Reeni put it, was "born challenged and Ammachi was the one who took him on. By this I mean that she saw to it that he was really looked after well." Stirred by the memory, Pennamma perked up. "He only had the brain of a five-year-old. I had to take care of him like a little baby. I had to feed him." Placing a hand on her mother-in-law's shoulder, Reeni was emphatic: "But she *really* looked after him. Gave him dignity. She was such a caregiver. She enjoyed doing this. So that was a *major* thing in her life." Reeni went on to explain how, before moving into their current home, Pennamma had lived in an extended family household where she could see how her brother-in-law was being neglected. With no way to help him at the time, once they moved to their own house, she made sure he had proper care. "He used to love being here. He used to go very reluctantly to the other houses, to my father-in-law's brother's houses. Even though she was his sister-in-law, she looked after him so well that, in the end, he used to call her 'Mother.'"

Pennamma listened intently as Reeni described the care and dignity she had given her brother-in-law who, in return, gave her a sense of purpose and love. It was a joy that shone all the brighter in a setting where agency was in such short supply. Hearing Reeni's final point, Pennamma's smile broadened. "In the end," she repeated, "he called me *Amma*." Mother.

Gilded Sorrows

In his *Book of Delights*, poet Ross Gay describes true joy as precarious. He spells out a false etymology in the word "de-light" that suggests both "of light" and "without light," intrinsic to the experience itself. An appreciation for this interplay, he submits, is something we learn over time. This Gay refers to as "grown up joy."[10] Zadie Smith likewise distinguishes between pleasure that is mundane and joy that is more complex and complete. For instance, while food and people's faces give her pleasure, her young daughter, also a pleasure, offers "that strange admixture of terror, pain, and delight that I have come to recognize as joy, and now must find some way to live with daily." This is "a new problem," she writes, as children who give joy, if lost, "would mean nothing less than your total annihilation . . . Joy is such human madness."[11]

This chapter's stories of fulsome, realistic joy—where catastrophe instills gratitude and love is magnified by lack and loss—bring to mind a ceramic bowl. The bowl entered a conversation in California when Pat was describing to me a spiritual approach that fascinated her, one that portrays all things, animate and inanimate, as worthy of our respect. To illustrate, she fetched a small, shallow bowl from across the room, off-white with delicate brown stripes and blue green swirls floating at either end. Placing it on the coffee table before us, she explained that it was a Japanese antique that, when it was given to her in 1984, had white chips circling its rim. Wanting to fix the piece properly, Pat brought it to a repair shop that specialized in the Japanese *kintsugi* method. Fascinated by the philosophy behind the method, she had kept the brochure in her work desk. Locating the brochure, she read aloud an excerpt: "In the Orient, one does not seek to repair by creating the illusion that the break never happened. Rather, one attempts to incorporate the mending itself as simply another facet of the piece's unique character and living." Holding up the bowl, Pat showed me how its once white chinks gleamed with eighteen karat gold. Returning to the text, she read what for her was the crowning point: "It would be a violation of the spirit to fake a covering up. So, to honor the *ki*, the ongoing energy given by the creator, is the real and lasting measure of the piece's value."

The philosophy behind kintsugi repair, of embellishing rather than hiding the time-worn, draws from the Zen concept of *wabi sabi*. Rooted in the Buddhist teaching of *anicca*, reminding us that all things, in truth, are bound to decay, wabi sabi also underlies the Japanese art of finding beauty in imperfection. So-called defects are intrinsic to wholeness.[12]

Exquisite antiques—pottery and people—are bound to get knocked about during long lifetimes. For the older women I met, this seemed a reasonable assumption. Choosing and shaping their life stories as they did, they seemed little interested in concealing life's chinks and cracks, in blunting pain and creating the illusion of perfection. Quite the opposite. Like Jený's beloved rusty clippers that connected her "to the core of how things work," to what really matters often found within sorrow and decay, women's complex appreciations revealed a poignancy that appears to ripen near life's edge. To "fake a covering up" of one's troubles and travails not only shortchanges life's fulsomeness but diminishes the potential for joy—not to mention a good story.[13] A "violation of the spirit," it would only conceal jagged edges fit for gilding.

7

Lost and Found

• • • • • • • • • • • • •

The Fruits of Letting Go

> The only choice we have as we mature is how we inhabit our vulnerability, how we become larger and more courageous and more compassionate through our intimacy with disappearance.
>
> **DAVID WHYTE,** "Vulnerability"

What has life taught you? More than any other question, this one tended to stop women in their tracks. To be honest, I was impressed when someone volleyed an answer right back, and I sympathized with those who balked. Given a moment, however, everyone had something to offer, and across time and space, two broad lesson themes emerged: (1) to let go of expectations and (2) to trust in an enduring goodness. While letting go and trusting might at first appear to pull in opposite directions, they can also serve as interlocking puzzle pieces, forming a logic that takes shape over long lifetimes.

One way to tease out this logic is through the core Buddhist teaching of *anicca*, the truth of impermanence, mentioned at the close of the last chapter. The importance of this truth is that, once realized, it exposes the futility of our desirous grasping and, upon letting go, our suffering lightens. Mahayana Buddhism adds that, by letting go of self-serving desires and expectations, we discover our true nature: an infinite source of wisdom and compassion known as *bodhichitta*. Put another way, by submitting to certain uncertainty, our hearts can unclench and an inexhaustible goodness can rise to awareness. The crowning text for Mahayana Buddhism, *The Heart Sutra*, takes this teaching and runs with it. Narrated by the thousand-armed Bodhisattva of Compassion, it is a litany to anicca, negating all concepts that we hold to be solid and true. Its middle stanza states, for instance, that "there is no body, no feeling, no thought, no will, no consciousness. There are no eyes, no ears, no nose, no tongue, no body, no mind."[1]

While some women described letting go or trusting in goodness as singular, separate lessons, they were often entangled. Defying normative structures and inclinations that keep us vainly chasing after control, these lessons keep to the course set by this book, in which the clarifying view at life's edge is discovered to be countercultural. Arriving at the final installment of part II, "The Real," where women have so far described divinity as most powerfully present within messy reality and life's treasures as amplified by sorrows and losses, lessons in letting-go-as-gaining convey the paradoxical "real" more explicitly. Women expressed their life lessons, earlier embedded within theologies and narrative frameworks, directly and often emphatically, even if it took a moment to gather them.

Hanging On for Dear Life

Speaking of reality, let me first state the obvious: people are less likely to deliberately let go of their futile desires in order to awaken bodhichitta than to be dragged into such awakenings. As Pema Chödrön puts it, we tend to discover our true goodness and wisdom "when we can no longer shield ourselves from the vulnerability of our condition, from the basic fragility of existence."[2] This is no doubt what late life can feel like, an excruciating version of *The Heart Sutra* in which, over time, there are indeed "no eyes, no ears, no nose, no tongue, no body, no mind." Few greet diminishment willingly, nor do they, when it comes, necessarily recognize its fruits.

In this spirit, I want to first acknowledge that recognizing a life lesson is not the same as mastering it. Like Margrét, who I quoted at the start of the last chapter as not wanting to be portrayed as "somebody who thinks she has found the one and only answer," some women wanted to be clear that older age does not necessarily confer wisdom. While life at its edge may open vistas worthy of our attention, putting insights into action is also, to be fair, another matter. Having arrived, holding on for dear life may feel like the only reasonable option.

This I learned during my first round of interviews in California. Prompted by the literature I was reading on older age and spirituality, I began asking what turned out to be a confusing question. The literature, which framed late-life decline and loss as a kind of enforced spiritual exercise, suggested that older adults tended to refashion their worldviews in ways that helped them let go.[3] This made sense to me. So during my first six conversations, I introduced these findings and asked women if it made sense to them too. Most were baffled. Five of the six insisted that, far from letting go, old-age decline meant hanging on mightily to the faculties and abilities they still possessed. Far from gaining spiritual wisdom, they obsessed over the minutia of what was being lost. Frustrated by the theories I offered that seemed to romanticize older age, some wondered if these were perhaps composed by younger people who, not there yet, feared what lay ahead.

In her soft, straightforward way, Paddy puzzled over this idea that older age could be a type of spiritual exercise. So she asked me to say more. I explained how the authors suggested that because aging brings about loss, it can be a time of learning and wisdom. Listening carefully, she interjected, "I would call it 'thought' rather than 'wisdom.'"

Surprised that she would reject "wisdom," I said, "All right, then!" Paddy chuckled. I continued on, adopting her wording, "So I'm asking people if this stage in life has given you something to think about—or broadened your thinking in a way." Seeing her frown, I diluted the question. "Or invites you to broaden in any way?"

Determined not to sugarcoat, Paddy said, "It's not broadening my thinking. It's not broadening my activities. When you lose half your sight, that doesn't make you feel very good. And it can make you feel very frightened. And that certainly affects your life to some extent. I don't know how it would broaden you." Thinking for a moment, she became definitive. "No, there's no broadening to that. There's a narrowing. You have to realize that you've been full of energy and full of fun and all those wonderful things, and you now have to pull back in. You can't travel as far. So, you have to ask yourself, 'What's it all about, Alfie?'"

Worried I was annoying her, I sheepishly explained, "The reason I ask this, is that so many spiritual traditions, like Christianity and Buddhism, have this discipline . . ."

"To become closer to God, is that what you mean?"

"Yeah, you give up things in order to connect more deeply to your spirituality."

"Oh, I don't look at it that way! I look at it, if anything, that God will give me patience to go through what I'm going through. Physically, all over, you're losing something—the way you walk, the way you talk, the way you look. Everything is narrowing. So, you need the patience to go through that." I told Paddy that I couldn't agree more, and we moved on to other topics.

Posing the question to Marge, I watched her ponder. After a moment of silence, I added, unhelpfully, "So I was wondering about this. Aging is a humbling process, kind of a 'wake-up call' to the fact that life is impermanent." Letting out a low laugh, Marge said, "If you don't know that by now, you're not living."

Aware of Marge's spiritual bent, I tried asking, "So do you see a lesson in that? Something that enhances or changes or deepens your sense of spirituality?"

"You have life experiences, you learn from them, you grow from them—hopefully," Marge said. "You lose parts. 'Parts wear out,' is a phrase I often use. Skills you had, memories you had, wear out. And so, it's just part of life. You're dying all the way along. It's just that it hasn't come to the crashing point yet. So, I think you want to be as giving and helping and compassionate as you can with those that you love. Do what you can while you're alive, until your neurons are all shot and then there's not much you can do after that. But I don't know. I haven't gotten there yet."

By the time I met with Eleanor, my fourth interviewee, my wording had become nearly apologetic. I explained, "These are just theories I've read about, where some people are saying that the aging process, for some, can be an exercise in knowing that everything changes and in coming to grips with that."

Eleanor deftly responded, "Knowing that things change and coming to grips with it are two very different things. They're different. Yeah, accepting it—why should I worry because I can't do anything about it anyway? It's just the way it is."

"Right."

"But it doesn't mean that you don't wrestle. Sometimes there are circumstances in my own life that I wrestle with, but I also know it's just the way it is. Can I change it? No. Age you can't change. I know that my health is in a declining state. And I *hate* that. But I can't change this. I mean, I do what I can, but it's just the way it is. I think if you can accept things, that's much more peaceful than endlessly trying to rail against..."

As Eleanor searched for the word, I suggested, "You don't 'win.'"

With a nod, she continued. "Okay. It's just the way it is. And I'm just not going to beat myself up trying to make it different anymore. But it doesn't mean that you don't go on trying. Somehow." Eleanor chuckled. "I think it's just the nature of the beast. Just go on trying and trying. I think: 'If I work a little harder, I can make it better.'"

Helen came closest to responding as I'd anticipated. Listening to her, I was reminded of books she'd written where she unflinchingly describes her father and husband's dying processes. When I told her I imagined that thinking deeply about loss wasn't new for her, Helen agreed. She described the retirement community she'd moved into seven months earlier as "a marvelous university of the self." It was already impacting her own attitude about aging. "I'm uneasy with certain physical aspects that I see every day in very old people," she admitted. "I think, 'I don't want to be like that. I hope I die before I get that way.' I have all those sorts of things going on in my head. I see everybody bent over and stooped. My own posture has improved because," Helen sat up, "'I'm not going to be like that!'" Describing these voices in her head as "interesting and informative and useful," she reflected,

> They bring me down to size and wake me up and open my heart and my compassion enormously. And I know it's going to keep on going. This is a place to learn about yourself. And we're all just a body over which we do not have all that much control. And it's going to do all sorts of whacky, terrible, distressing things. And we're going to have pain and discomfort and get all cuckoo and everything. And we just have to take it in and be okay with it when it happens to the people we see, and be okay with it when it happens to ourselves and our dearly beloved others. This is a very big deal.

The connection Helen drew between accepting impermanence and finding compassion echoes how the realization of anicca opens into bodhichitta. Yet Helen insisted that, for her, the process had nothing to do with spirituality.

Let's just call it a path to more humanity and more connection to yourself and one another. Because all that I was just running on about, you see it here every day and in every way. You know what's coming. We all know, we always have since we were little, that we're going to die. But it's highlighted here. And it's an opportunity for growth in compassion. It's a huge opportunity. And when I moved in here, I was completely aware that I was doing the right thing for many reasons. But I didn't realize this one. So, it's a huge, new gift.

Everything Passes: The Benefits of Letting Go

After my first round of California interviews, I stopped asking people if they saw advancing age as a spiritual exercise in letting go. Instead, the subject often came up on its own, including during subsequent California conversations. Usually embedded in life lessons, it wasn't so much related to the losses of older age as to long-life perspectives. For many, letting go was viewed not as a spiritual goal as much as a key to living well, "a path to humanity" as Helen worded it, amid life's uncertainties.

When I asked Sr. Mary Ann about her life lessons, she read off four items that she'd earlier jotted down on a piece of paper. She prefaced the second item by saying, "I've learned this over and over and over again." She recalled how a boy she'd taught in high school once said, "I hate change," which prompted her to think, "Kid, you are going to have a hard life." Looking down at her notes, she said, "So I think you learn that change is just a constant." With a smile, she added, "That sounds like an oxymoron . . . but anyway." I told her that this made good sense to me and she elaborated, "There's always change, you know?" Pointing to a recently treated precancerous spot on her nose, she said, "It could be change in you—like on my nose. It's change in the weather. You think everything's going along fine and then all of a sudden something happens. I think change is a constant."

"And that's a life lesson, to recognize that?"

"Yeah, I don't think you can say, 'It's going to be this way.' You can't. Because if you do, you're going to be very frustrated all the time."

Sr. Jackie's biggest life lesson, as she put it, was learning that "letting go is okay." Here she referred to letting go of negative emotions. Particularly hard for her had been the guilt she carried into the convent after leaving her younger siblings behind with their alcoholic father. "But that's just one example. It applies to people I don't like. And I struggle to let go of that dislike, or whatever it is, and I try to understand them instead. And if I can envision a thread between me and them, I snip it. It works miracles. It does. So that's a lifetime lesson." This led Jackie to another lesson: "And the other thing is to know that you only have one day at a time, and to try and make the very best of that, and to love in that day, and to be happy with it. And that's been a struggle too." Connecting the two, she concluded, "I think they sort of go together, don't they? Because if you can get rid of those things that are causing you discomfort, things you need to let go of, then you're free."

Seythu at the Kothadu elder daycare center made a similar connection. She described how, by letting go of past regrets and future expectations, she could find freedom and peace in today. When we asked about her life lessons, she had just finished describing the manual labor and dire poverty she had endured throughout her life. After a life like that, she reasoned, "What's there to learn?" Recounting as well her children's continued unkindness, she threw up her right hand as though tossing her troubles to the wind. "So, for them, at least let them be calm and peaceful. Let them lead a happy life. That is good enough for me." As her circle of listeners nodded in support, Seythu said, "Let them not take care of me. It's good enough that I have legs to bring me here. Today I may go for a function here or there. Or I might go to a wedding. All that I have is the day."

"One day at a time," I said.

Seythu agreed. "One day at a time."

Along similar lines, Chödrön writes, "If we're willing to give up hope that insecurity and pain can be exterminated, then we can have the courage to relax with the groundlessness of our situation."[4] Because hope ultimately "robs us of the present moment," Chödrön advises that we embrace a state of non-expectation, an "utter hopelessness" that allows us to live for the day.

Ann in California shared this view. After relating some of her life challenges, she reflected: "A big theme in Christianity is hope. You know: faith, *hope*, and charity." Looking at me intently, she said, "I don't believe in hope." Settling back, she explained,

> I believe what the Buddhists say, that when you hope, it means that you're not thinking of what's going on now. And you may well not be. And I think, for me, I have to learn to be at peace with wherever I am. I don't want to be hoping for something tomorrow, or that things change, or that my son gets better. They're all there, of course, but to be thinking about how, on another day, things will turn around . . . I would rather just be here now, and think that, however it is now, I'm able to deal with that.

When we met again a year later, I asked Ann if she had a life lesson to share. This returned her to this earlier point. She told me how her life had taught her to value satisfaction and gratitude rather than needing "to have all your dreams come true," as she put it. "I've studied Buddhism and I think they're so right in that the more you want, the less you have."

I chimed in, "That's so true!"

"This applies to people who are always grasping for something, who want a different outcome. Of course, we all *want* a good outcome. But to hang your flag on that and say, 'I have to have that outcome,' I don't feel that. I feel much more like I'll do what I can and what happens, happens." Looking back on the arc of her life, Ann contrasted this view with her earlier inclination to call on God. Believing this God would lift away her troubles only set her up for disappointment.

This brought to my mind the conversations I'd had in Kerala that winter, where women's reliance on God seemed to deepen during times of utter despair. I mentioned this to Ann, telling her that it sounded like the opposite of what she was saying. At first, she agreed. Then she changed her mind: "But there's acceptance in both of them. There's acceptance in the idea that either God will take care of it or it won't be taken care of and that's all right."

This rings true to me. As we saw in chapter 5, life's disappointments often prompted women to either do away with an ineffective heavenly deity in whom they'd placed their hopes, like Ann, or bring God down to earth (if not already there) as a source of comfort within suffering itself. This latter approach applied to Seythu, who gave up hope on family support and yet, in the midst of her troubles, trusted that God, as she put it, "will *never* leave me. God will always take care of me." Through faith, not in spite of it, she discovered, as Chödrön words it, the courage to relax into groundlessness that, for her, was a free fall into God's loving presence.

Naninga in Iceland described this exactly. The first time Olla and I met with her, our conversation was tender and tearful, as it had been only three weeks since her husband Jón had died rather unexpectedly. Visiting eight months later, she told us that although she still missed Jón, she was doing surprisingly well. Only a few months earlier, she explained, her unbearable sorrow was making her feel as though she was dangling off a ledge, holding on for dear life. During such times, as she put it, "People around you are telling you that you need to let go. But you keep hanging on even though you're exhausted and it hurts." Thanks to her faith, she explained, she eventually loosened her grip. "Faith is like being able to let go and let God take care of things," she told us. "And when we hang on and don't let go, we are only making things harder for ourselves."

Fr. Bill Shannon, a longtime theology professor at Nazareth who liked to refer to himself as "an honorary SSJ," presided at Motherhouse funerals for decades. His eulogies often described the sisters as studies in letting go, their death being the final release into God. When reflecting on the life of his colleague and friend, Sr. Dorothy Agnes, a math and German professor, he referred to her as "one of the freest persons I have ever known. She knew that true freedom came not with hanging on but with being willing to let go." To illustrate, Bill read a prayer by Teilhard de Chardin that he found tucked into Dorothy Agnes's prayer book, penned, as he put it, in her "tiny but elegant handwriting."

> When the signs of age begin to mark my body (and still more when they touch my mind); when the ill that is to diminish me or carry me off strikes from without or is born within me; when the painful moment comes in which I suddenly awaken to the fact that I am ill or growing old; and above all at that last moment when I feel I am losing hold of myself and am absolutely passive within the great unknown forces that have formed me—in all those dark moments, O God, grant that I may understand that it is You . . . who are painfully parting the fibers of my being in order to penetrate to the very marrow of my substance and bear me away with Yourself.

The prayer's conclusion, Bill told the assembly, Dorothy Agnes had written on a separate line: "Teach me to treat my death as an act of communion."[5]

As Naninga and the women cited at the start of this chapter remind us, the prospect of letting go in the face of suffering and loss goes against every impulse. The urge to scramble for solid footing, especially "when the rug's been pulled out and we can't find anywhere to land," as Chödrön puts it, is powerful.[6] Yet this, she argues, is how we become free to live in the moment, to discover our full humanity. As described by Arthur Kleinman, this impulse to bypass uncertainty and suffering, especially strong in mainstream North America, is revealed in our tendency to diagnose and medicalize ordinary unhappiness as clinical depression or existential angst as anxiety disorder. Our resistance to "genuine reality," as he puts it, produces a challenge-free approach to life based on "a superficial and soulless model of the person."[7]

When I asked Ann if she had any advice to help others let go of expectations, she shook her head. This, she told me, she had to learn the hard way. "I think I've developed resilience through all of the sufferings I've experienced, both physical and emotional. I've learned that you can't let a trauma dictate the course of your life. It has to be isolated. It was separate. It was awful. You experienced it and got through it somehow. And you can look at the bright side." Shaking her head again she added, "That sounds *so* shallow. But, as I say, deep down we're all shallow." As I burst out laughing, she concluded, "Protecting yourself from pain causes you to miss out—if you protect yourself too much. So, I think letting down that protection and being open to pain makes it easier to deal with it."

Taking It Up a Notch: Inviting Pain

In *To Be Cared For*, anthropologist Nathaniel Roberts writes about Dalit Christians in Chennai who not only accept life's hardships but see in them a path to holiness, that "just as Christ's suffering served a purpose, so did theirs."[8] This was not something I heard in the Dalit colonies in Kerala nor at the Kothadu elder center. While these women were confident that divinity was seeing them through their difficulties, no one assigned virtue or sanctity to suffering itself. Those who did, albeit subtly, tended to be middle-class and well-to-do Catholics for whom hardships were isolated, as Ann put it, not a lifelong condition.[9]

Suffering as a path to holiness is nothing new. Well-worn within both Hindu and Christian traditions, it is also a path in which women have historically excelled.[10] Fitting the bill was St. Alphonsa (1910–1946), a Clarist nun from Kerala who became the first native-born Indian saint in 2008, and was the focus of my dissertation in the 1990s. Hagiographers describe Alphonsa's short adult life as wracked by agonizing pain and illness that she welcomed as gifts from Jesus. In a letter to her confessor retrieved after her death, she wrote that it is "in giving crosses that Jesus shows His love." Grateful for the privilege, she prayed for her pain to increase: "O Lord, give me more to suffer silently. I would drink deep of the chalice Thou hast given me—drain it to the very dregs."[11]

Born just one week after Alphonsa, Mother Teresa wrote similar letters to her priest-confessors. For her, suffering arrived in the form of spiritual desolation that spanned nearly a half century. Initially buoyed by a vital sense of God's presence, spiritual aridity became her constant "traveling companion" from the time she began working with the poor in Calcutta in 1949 until her death in 1997. She eventually framed her agony as a privilege, her sense of

FIGURE 7.1 Annamma, Haley, and Paige with photo of Mother Teresa. Photo by author.

abandonment as a sharing in Christ's abandonment on the cross. Letting go of her struggle, she reveled in divine camaraderie.[12]

Key to saintly suffering is keeping one's pain under wraps. In a 1994 conversation with Sr. Xavier, an eighty-year-old peer and friend of Alphonsa's, she recalled how Alphonsa would say that admitting to pain "would be like a hen laying her eggs and making noise afterwards. If we were to hear the hen making noise, we would come and take away the egg. In that way, if we speak about our pain, Satan will come and take away our merit." In this spirit, Alphonsa and Mother Teresa both requested that their letters to their confessors, those that lay bare their tribulations, be destroyed. Yet in both cases these letters were not only preserved but segments have been published, testimony to the holy agony they both silently bore.

Annamma C. had the honor of hosting Mother Teresa during both of her visits to Kerala. She also shared her theology of suffering. During our first visit to Annamma's home, she told us how Jesus "suffered for us without any complaint." As such, "whenever we suffer, we must not talk about our sufferings, but must offer them to Jesus who suffered out of love for us. Like him, whenever we suffer, we must surrender, offering all our pain and injuries—*everything*—to him." When we returned two years later, she expanded on this theme by telling us how her prayers helped her endure her sufferings. "I ask

Jesus, 'give me the strength to bear these pains in my body, mind, and heart.' I only do this with Jesus's support."

Hoping to lighten the mood, Annamma's granddaughter remarked that she sometimes tells her grandmother, who is constantly praying, "Jesus needs a break! You know?" Annamma smiled while we laughed. Not wanting to appear too demanding, she insisted, "I always say, 'thank you Jesus,' That's my prayer. In our suffering we surrender and, in our happiness, we give thanks." To the sounds of approval around the room, Annamma's granddaughter patted her grandmother's arm. "That's *good*, Ammachi."

Sr. Mechtilde, a force of optimism, also extolled the virtues of silent suffering. Halfway through our interview, when we asked about her life lessons, she offered some advice. Speaking in slow, serious tones, her eyes magnified through thick eyeglasses, she told us that we must always believe in ourselves. Clearly directing this at my two students, she said, "Come what may, let nothing disturb you. Let nothing make you to turn back. And don't repeatedly tell yourself, 'What a thing I've become, I should not be like this! What a thing!' Do not take on this dissatisfaction." Moved by Mechtilde's intensity, I could see Paige's eyes filling and Haley discretely wiping at hers. Mechtilde leaned back and smiled. "No. I am satisfied. I am glad. I am happy that I am able to suffer."

Not sure I heard correctly, I asked, "You're happy that you're able to suffer?"

"For Jesus's sake, I am ready. Anything I will suffer," Mechtilde nodded. "So, there are times when sisters may speak about you, that you're not doing any work or not being up to the mark. But when I hear this, I will say, 'Thank you, Jesus. May the divine features of Jesus be imprinted in my heart, soul, mind, and body. And may I be able to stand the strain of every difficulty.'"

Still casting about, I asked, "He *helps* you through your sufferings. Yes?"

Ignoring my bait, Mechtilde beamed. "This I like! I like suffering without telling anyone, without complaining. I have not told my Superior all my difficulties." We earlier learned that a fractured back keeps Mechtilde in constant pain, yet she insisted that she'd rather take care of things herself, through prayer. "Prayer. It's the best medicine for me."

Annamma C. and Sr. Mechtilde were the only women among the thirty-two we met in Kerala, including four other nuns, who not only spoke of submitting to suffering but extolled its virtues. Yet from what I could tell, neither Annamma nor Sr. Mechtilde came close to embracing this path with the same enthusiasm as midcentury American Catholicism, a gusto for suffering that the older SSJ sisters recalled from their early convent training yet had gladly left behind.[13] When I met with pilgrims at Alphonsa's shrine in the mid- to late 1990s, I regularly heard them describe her silent suffering as a source of sanctity and power. Yet few, if any, aspired to the same. People flocked to her shrine not to emulate her pain but to find relief from the same.[14]

Abiding Goodness

Taking matters back down a notch, we now turn to the fruits of letting go. For many of the women I met, this had to do with accessing a goodness broadly understood as divinity, as abiding within humanity or in nature, or as a continuity to which we all belong. Often realized over time, this goodness could also be jarringly exposed, in a moment. Typically obscured by everyday experiences and expectations, it came to light despite evidence to the contrary. When speaking of how they came to trust in this elusive goodness, women could be insistent. Although cutting against the grain, this trust, at their age, wasn't blind or naive.

By far the most common source of unexpected goodness, circling us back to the first lesson, was the result of letting go of judgment. If you live long enough, I often heard, you learn that everyone has something of value to offer. When asking for life lessons in Iceland, this was nearly the unanimous response, unembellished and to the point. After at first telling me that it was impossible for her to choose a life lesson, Edda had a second thought: "I think perhaps it's that most people are interesting, when you get to know them. We're all different from each other, but most people are interesting. My neighbors are very different from one another, but I like them. Everyone has something, I think." Gathering her thoughts into a lesson, she said, "You shouldn't judge people before you get to know them. And when people are not nice, they are that way for a reason. Something has happened to them. Some people have had difficult lives and have scars on their souls."

I heard similar lessons from the SSJ sisters. Sr. Mary Ann told me how, after teaching high school for many years, meeting students from across economic and cultural backgrounds, she'd learned that "people are basically good." This was further confirmed when she worked in soup kitchens and neighborhood centers where people were often dealing with serious life challenges. "I think that's where I learned that people are people are people. And their needs are the same. Their desires are the same." Californian women offered similar observations. Jan told me how she used to go into San

Francisco's Tenderloin district with other women from her church to visit with people living on the streets. "We'd pack lunches and go in about once a month. And I'd look at those people and think, 'You have a mother somewhere who loved you.' And when you were a little kid, you had a lot of good in you. But you've been hurt along the way." Jan shook her head, "And all you can do is love 'em."

While women most often described discovering human goodness over time, this was sometimes brought home in a single encounter. Such was the case for Judy. When I asked her for a life lesson, she told me she had learned not to judge. This led her to recall an incident from when she was nine. It was during World War II, when German prisoners of war were at times put to work on American farms, filling in for young farmers who were overseas fighting. Living in Massachusetts at the time, she described how, when playing at her best friend's grandfather's house, he told the girls over lunch that, in a field just behind his house, German prisoners of war were harvesting potatoes. Seeing their curiosity, he offered to walk them over to take a look.

Judy recalled the scene. "So, we walked down, one on each side of him." Eyes wide, she added with a laugh, "We were *clinging* to him because it was . . ."

"Scary!"

"Yeah! And as we got closer, we heard singing. And as we got even closer, we saw them." As the daughter of a professor who grew up around college students, Judy remembered her shock. "They were, you know, the same age as the college kids that I knew all my life. And they were throwing potatoes at each other and singing, and having a wonderful time. And I thought," Judy's voice lowered, 'This is the enemy?'"

Jolted by her point, I whispered, "Oh my God." As I unsuccessfully tried to hold back my tears, Judy handed me a tissue. Wanting to get us back on track, I asked, "So how did that affect you?"

"How did it affect me? It affected me all my life."

Holding up my tissue, I said, "It affects me!"

"What I mean," Judy explained, "is that I remember when, many years later when we were in the midst of the Vietnam War, someone was making slurs about the Viet Cong and how bad they were, demonizing them. I said, 'Everybody is somebody's father, somebody's son,'" Judy teared up, "'somebody's brother.' And that came from that experience."

Near the end of our interview, I reflected back on how this story was such a powerful testament to the ways war relies on dehumanizing the enemy. Careful with her words, Judy said, "In war, the enemy must become the Other—not *an* Other, but *the* Other."

Sister Josepha's story also involved a prisoner. Its moral was less about learning human goodness than about her own inability to live up to what she already, deeply knew. When I asked her for a life lesson, she responded, "I suppose it's that people can be good, if they try. And kind." Letting out a long sigh, she said, "And I'm not . . . to particular people, I'm not always nice. Which is terrible. Because I think there is hope for anybody who, you know, is 'ugly.'" Josepha then related an incident from nearly two decades earlier that continued to weigh on her. It was her final story in our three-hour-long interview that brimmed with lively tales, many of which involved the prison inmates she served with deep regard and nonjudgment. This final account hit a different chord.

Josepha began by describing a young inmate who frightened her. She rarely saw him and was never called in to mediate for him or to give him counsel. But when their paths did cross, the anger and hatred she felt from him were palpable. Late one day, when the floor where she worked was emptied of staff and the inmates were in another cellblock being counted before going to the mess hall, Josepha looked up from her desk to see this man, silently staring at her. She recalled the scene: "There's my friend, in the doorway of my office where I'm sitting. He's just looking at me. And I'm thinking, 'I'm in this area all by myself. And there is no one but this man at my door.' And I am in a panic. I really am. I have no idea what to do. I'd been working almost seventeen years in prisons—this was right before retirement—and I'd never thought of this possibility."

Josepha recalled walking toward the doorway and asking, "Is there something I can help you with, honey?" Clearly angry, the inmate said that he'd learned that she had told a guard something that could get him into trouble. She responded that, as chaplain, it was her job to pass on information, to protect people. She replayed the scene: "I said, 'That's part of who I am and what I am and what I do.' And I'm thinking, 'I'm still in this same position,'" which was standing in the doorway, alone, with the inmate. Josepha decided to close the door in the inmate's face. "It's a nice heavy door. And I just slammed it. I just went behind it with my hand and I shoved it. And there was a huge bang and boom." Josepha's voice quieted, "As I was walking back to the chair at the table, I was thinking, 'That was the dumbest thing you have ever done.'" Waiting at her desk for a few minutes, she went back to the door. "I opened it, scared to God that he was still going to be there." The inmate was gone. Moments later, the prison superintendent called to say he had heard that she had slammed a door in this man's face. He wanted to know if this was true. Josepha told him it was. He thanked her and hung up.

This still bothered Josepha terribly. She didn't get the chance to explain herself to the superintendent, and even worse, he didn't seem surprised that she would do such a thing. Bringing us back to her lesson, that everyone has the potential to be good, she wished she had tried to see things from the inmate's perspective. She should have told him, as she put it, "how *dumb* he was being. Because at South Port, as a prisoner, he's free within the prison. Every day he can walk around, he can go to services, he can do what he wants. I should not only have said, 'That's my job.' I should have said, 'And it's going to be worse on you.' He's going to double his time on his sentence because he's threatening me, he's threatening a woman, he's threatening . . ." Josepha trailed off. "But I didn't say it. I didn't say it. It never came to me until a long time afterwards."

Wishing to ease her discomfort, I said, "But he pushed you emotionally. Sometimes we get pushed and we do things we don't normally do."

"Yes. Really." Josepha looked out the window. "I wanted to find his address and write to him. I'd like to explain this." I encouraged her, hoping she could do that, somehow. I'll never know whether she did, as our conversation took place the fall before COVID closed the Motherhouse to visitors. Josepha died soon after it opened back up.

It's worth noting that although Icelandic, Californian, and SSJ women regularly reported discovering an intrinsic human goodness, no one brought this up in Kerala. Although this difference is too complex to tackle here, I wonder if it has something to do with the extent to which abiding goodness was presumed from the start in Kerala. By contrast, as Rutger Bregman describes it, Europeans and Euro-Americans have a deeply ingrained tendency to view humanity cynically and, as he sees it, erroneously so. In *Humankind*, Bregman traces this view across the Western canon, from ancient Greece through the development of Christian theology, reinforced by literature and film, and across academic disciplines. Left largely unchallenged, it is an assumption such that those who think otherwise, that humans are essentially good, are considered naive. Outlining counterevidence from across fields of study, Bregman promotes a subversively optimistic "new realism" about humanity's goodness.[15] It's a realism that, it seems, can emerge naturally if you live long enough.

Another type of goodness that women described as abiding beneath life's "ugly" veneer was found in nature. We follow this theme more fully in the next chapter, yet I mention my mother's story here since she framed it as a lesson and as something that arrived when the rug was pulled out from beneath her. When I asked for a song, poem, or object of significance, she took a book of Mary Oliver's poems from her bookshelf. Opening to "Wild Geese," she read it aloud. Although my mother was not easily reduced to tears (unlike her daughter), the reading moved her. Wiping her eyes, she explained that this poem had come to her mind after the fall of the Twin Towers on September 11, 2001. Called to jury duty earlier that morning, she sat in a large hall filled with people waiting for their assignments. Together they watched the horror unfold on television monitors mounted around the room. "All we could see is what was happening, over and over and over. And people falling, and . . . oh God, it was awful."

Arriving home that afternoon, Mom went for a walk down our street. At the end is a single chain-linked divider that looks out onto redwood trees and wilderness. "I stood there as you get past the post and looked into that beauty." Whispering, she repeated, "That *beauty*. The trees and the ferns, all of it. And I watched the squirrels and an occasional bird and I thought, 'yeah, the world is continuing. The world's continuing.'" Returning to the poem, she reread,

> Tell me about your despair, yours, and I will tell you mine.
> Meanwhile, the world goes on.

Setting the open book on the coffee table in front of us, she said, "Yup. The mountains, all of it. Everything is there. And the wild geese are coming home."

Picking up the book, I reread the poem's final lines in which Oliver's geese, on their way home high in the sky, remind us "over and over" of a deeper belonging.

Shaken by a world irreparably shattered, my mother's encounter with nature further stunned her. Oliver likens such realizations to a homecoming, to a recollection that we all, in fact, belong. The TV loop Mom described, playing the horror "over and over and over," was drowned out by a truer call, "over and over," to remember our place in the family of things, prompted and promised by nature's abiding beauty. Chödrön similarly describes bodhichitta that is discovered within despair, "in the genuine heart of sadness," as a "coming home. It's as if we had amnesia for a very long time and awaken to remember who we really are."[16]

In Iceland, I sometimes heard women use the phrase *Ég trúi á það góða*, "I believe in the good." When I asked Olla to elaborate, she felt the saying implied a keeping of faith despite evidence to the contrary. It could refer to a belief in human goodness despite our shortcomings or in the goodness of nature despite its dark and dangerous seasons. It also seemed to point to a spiritual force that permeates and connects humanity and nature, an alternative to the standard Christian belief in God as a separate, heavenly figure. When older Icelandic people used the phrase, it sounded to Olla like a holdover from Old Norse beliefs in nature's sanctity.

When we asked Dísa for a life lesson, we had just heard her describe the cruelty and neglect of her adoptive parents. She told us that, after all she'd been through, she had learned "to believe in the good." She explained, "I don't believe in this God anymore, the guy with the long white beard. I believe in the good. And that is what life has given me. I still believe in the good. I don't really use the prayers today in the same way that I was taught. I don't really believe as I used to. But I do believe in the good in the universe. Today I believe that, if you believe in God, it means you believe in the good."

Svala used this phrase when describing her beloved great-grandfather who cared for her in early childhood. With eyes glistening, she said, "He taught me to believe in the good. And that is the main part of my religion." For Svala, faith in goodness was linked to her faith in the power of love, "in God's love for human beings and in love between human beings." This, she in turn applied to the natural world: "When we tend to things, they grow. When we tend to our flowers, we care for them like everything we must tend to." Svala insisted, "We have the ability to make things better. With our goodness, life can be better."

Helen in California related a similar faith in our chain of influence. After explaining how death was, for her, "the great unknown," she went on to assert, "But what I do know without a shadow of a doubt and am daily influenced by and moved by and reminded of is the ripple effect of everyone who lives. We are so profoundly influenced by everything that we read, hear, notice, grasp, from others. And it stays." Circling back, she said, "So, the person dies physically. . . . You never see them again physically. But I believe in the ripple effect."

The next morning, Helen elaborated in an email. She wrote that if we could only commit ourselves "to choosing stones to throw that are smooth and good to handle," we can create "fine and far-reaching ripples." Like Svala, she envisioned love as the engine driving this positive, connective force:

> For me, connectedness, a sense of continuum, and the making of good effort are all at the heart of human potential, of spirituality, and are encompassed in that other great, all-important word: love. Love is in everything I write here, love is in all the striving to and hope of mending hurt people, love is in work and coping and art. I need to stop here before I sound verbose, repetitive,

mundane, and trite—any of the awful things that can happen so easily when trying to write about these wonderfully large subjects. Thank you again, Corinne, for the conversations, love, Helen.

This reminds me of the founding Sisters of St. Joseph whose God, we learned in chapter 5, was far from being "the guy with the long white beard." Rather, divinity was an all-encompassing force of love, binding them to one another and to the poor and forgotten whom they accompanied. Enlivened through their work, this divinity-as-love resided within their "striving to and hope of mending hurt people," of repairing a broken world. Placing their trust in this vast divine goodness, they also, by founding a new religious order, trusted in ripples.

Hope at the Edge

For Chödrön and for Ann in California, hope is a problem. They rightly argue that by holding tight to expectations and outcomes that (we hope) will shield us from suffering, we set ourselves up for disappointment. Buffered by hope, we shut ourselves off from the abundance surrounding us, from the bodhichitta that is our true nature. Supporting this idea were the lessons women learned while in the depths of despair. Blindsided by goodness, they finally gave up on impossible longings. Letting go from a ledge that hurt to hang onto, they fell into divine embrace.

Yet Ann conceded possibilities for hope. This is not so much a contradiction as a different use of the word, one with which Chödrön, while adamantly antihope, would likely agree. Rather than unrealistically anticipating sudden and complete delivery from suffering, it is a clear-eyed hope in a goodness that abides within life's turmoil itself. It is like the divinity that women across cultures described as worthy of devotion, one that doesn't so much rescue as accompany people through their tribulations. Different than denial, it fuels the capacity to persevere. It helps us muddle on. It is a kind of hope that enables an unclenching during difficulties that in some ways puts the Mahayana Buddhist cart before the horse. It is a hope in an enduring goodness that helps us to let go.

This is what Rebecca Solnit refers to as "hope in the dark." In her book by the same name, she portrays this hope as lying outside expectations, beyond particular coordinates and control, as resisting the certitudes of both cynicism and naivete. "To hope is to gamble," Solnit writes. It is to bet "on the possibility that an open heart and uncertainty is better than gloom and safety. To hope is dangerous, and yet it is the opposite of fear, for to live is to risk."[17]

This insistence on hope might sound naive if it weren't so often hitched to older women's hard-won, long-life lessons. Resonating with Richard Rohr's reflections on life's second naivete, we could call it a mature hope. As Rohr frames it, during the first naivete that typically steers life's first half, we tend to follow established rules and religiosities. The second naivete, arriving after we've weathered some of life's confusions and pain, is where we find ourselves living more comfortably with doubt, uncertainty, and mystery.[18] As certainty loosens its grip, hope gains traction.

Hope that finds footing at life's precarious edge, like the heart of bodhichitta awakened within the depths of despair, is paradoxical.[19] While it's understandable that women in California were confused by the suggestion that late-life losses necessarily spur on spiritual growth, we might consider more modest ways of framing this paradox. Sr. Joan Chittister describes a "something more" that she discovers within diminishment. When letting go of "the cosmetics of the self, like the titles, the privileges, the symbols, and the signs," she finds she is "something more than I was—and at the same time less than I was."[20] In the throes of uncertainty in his eighties, Carl Jung also reflects, "I am incapable of determining ultimate worth or worthlessness; I have no judgment about myself and my life. There is nothing I am quite sure about. I have no definite convictions—not about anything, really." And yet, he writes, "it seems to me that I have been carried along. I exist on the foundation of something I do not know. In spite of all uncertainties, I feel a solidity underlying all existence and a continuity in my mode of being."[21]

This unnamed "something more" that imperceptibly sustains us can rise to awareness when bodies and high-rise buildings are crumbling. The subtle hope it engenders, I submit, is realistic. Brought into view through women's experiences of despair and destruction, it serves not to shield or to save but to accompany and carry us along.

Part 3

The More

● ● ● ● ● ● ● ● ● ● ● ● ●

8

Death and Nature

• • • • • • • • • • • • •

Portals into the
Wondrous More

> The beginning of our happiness lies in the understanding that life without wonder is not worth living. What we lack is not a will to believe, but a will to wonder.
>
> **RABBI ABRAHAM HESCHEL,** *God in Search of Man*

Tipped off by the last chapter's parting reflections on a "something more" that abides in the heart of diminishment, part III explores "The More" in earnest.[1] Across contexts and cultures, older women delighted in the wondrous, suggesting a ripening of its significance in older age. A realm that clearly matters, part of what makes life worth living as Heschel suggests, women's encounters with and conceptions of the more defy everyday conventions in multitudinous ways, earning for the wondrous more its own section in this book.[2] Coaxed by mystery yet grounded in earthly structures, it suggests a teetering between what can and cannot be conceived or controlled, like life at the edge itself.

We begin at the outskirts, with death and nature, favorite topics that served as enticing portals to the more. Straining the limits of human knowledge and control, these are also realms that formal religions commonly strive to contain.[3] For the women who shared with me, however, the pull tended to go the opposite way. Death wasn't so much a problem to be solved as a towering unknown that sparked curiosity, and nature's allure often had to do with its unfathomability. The most compelling if not the most sacred aspect of both death and nature for many was how they magnified human insignificance. Rather than stoking fear, the prospect of disappearance and diminishment invited questions that didn't necessarily call for answers. As will be seen, older women's ease with wonder, seemingly a specialty at life's humbling edge, is something that, in our current climate of hardening certainties, we could sorely use more of.

Death Is Fun to Talk About!

In the beginning death was a problem, or so I thought. Wanting to spare women from the elephant in the room, I didn't broach the subject during my early interviews in California. Yet death came up about half the time anyway, as women recalled experiences with family members and spouses and, in some cases, reflected on their own mortality.

Heading to Iceland the following summer, trying to be a good guest, I steadied my resolve. This lasted for one interview. While wrapping up our second, Olla, unable to contain herself, asked if she could pose a question of her own. We were visiting ninety-year-old Aðalheiður in her skilled nursing quarters. A frail woman, she looked tired by the end of our conversation. But trusting Olla's instincts, I encouraged her. Listening to the two of them speaking in Icelandic, I was certain they were talking about death. As my stomach dropped, I could see Aðalheiður's face brighten. Olla's question was positively perking her up. After they had finished their animated exchange, I admitted my surprise (actually, shock). Olla and Aðalheiður were shocked right back. Death was easy and fun to talk about! It was a topic that came up naturally in Iceland, they told me, especially among older people.

From then on, Olla and I inserted a question about death near the end of each interview, finishing our exchanges on a high note. Marveling at the enthusiasm, I sometimes admitted to my earlier surprise. While most were confused to learn that death was a taboo topic in the United States, for Ásdís this sounded familiar. She told us how her children also tried to avoid the topic, yet she was adamant. "We should talk about it *more*. We should also talk more about how life works around children. Of course, we have to be careful that we don't make them afraid, but this is a natural part of life. This is the only thing we know when we start life, that it's going to end."

Returning to California later that summer, I invited the women I'd interviewed so far to a parlor gathering. Skyping Olla into the room on my laptop, she and I regaled them with stories from Akureyri, including about women's eagerness to talk about death. As Olla saw it, the harsh living conditions and low health standards that held forth in Iceland until the 1970s normalized death. It arrived at all ages, she explained, not just in late life. With a recent rise in living standards, however, this intimacy with death and dying was starting to wane. While still a natural topic for the older generations to ease into, it was less so for younger Icelanders.

I then admitted to the women in the parlor that I hadn't raised the subject during our interviews because I was trying to be polite. Seeing no particular reaction, I asked for their thoughts. Women responded that of course they'd be happy to talk about death. Feeling sheepish, I asked if they could think back to when they were in their fifties. Would they have felt comfortable asking older women about death? People admitted that they probably wouldn't. A few suggested that, as with most cultural norms, this skittishness reflects the views of younger generations, not theirs. As Eleanor put it, "We've had a lot of time to get used to it. Most of us know it's a reality that's coming . . . and maybe it's sooner than later because we're getting tired of being tired." Hitting a nerve, laughter erupted around the room.

This is when Sue, who was at the doctor for her back pain, arrived through the sliding glass door. Apologizing for being late, she gingerly lowered herself onto one of the couches, assisted by women on either side of her. Once she was settled, I said, "Okay, great that you're here, Sue. We were just talking about *death*." Raising her voice above the laughter, Sue said, "Oh! Let me *tell* you! I planned my funeral last night I was in so much pain!" Lesson learned, I inserted an open-ended question about death into all future California conversations.

Heading to Kerala the following winter, I again wanted to be a good guest. When I asked a friend what she thought about raising the topic, she waffled and then decided I'd better stay clear. So I did. Yet again the subject occasionally came up on its own.[4] Returning two years later for a second round of interviews, encouraged by other friends to raise the subject, I decided to do so as delicately as possible. All fifteen women we met during that round seemed at ease with the subject, their faces often brightening, as in Iceland. Also, like Icelanders, younger family members weren't always so comfortable.

Such was the case with Teresa. When I asked Faxon, who was helping to translate, if he could ask his grandmother her thoughts about death, he winced. "She's really afraid of death. But I'll ask." Before he had the chance, Teresa, who understood English, looked at him crossly and insisted she was *not* afraid. "Even if death comes now, I'm ready! And after my death, I pray that St. Joseph will guide me to heaven." Overhearing us from the kitchen, Faxon's wife Jenena leaned in to say that Teresa looked forward to the Feast of St. Joseph, which is when she wanted to die. Because Joseph died surrounded by family, unlike Jesus and Mary, he's become the patron of a good death. Every year as his feast day nears, she told us, Teresa gives her gold chain to one of Faxon's sisters in anticipation of her demise. His memory jogged, Faxon laughed. "And last year she was saying, 'Okay, only two days till the feast!'"

When we asked Sr. Mechtilde her thoughts on death, her face cracked into a grin. "Oh! Death! Mm *hmm*! It is my special subject!" Relieved at her response, Haley, Paige, and I together said, "Okay! Good!"

"The other Sisters will say, 'Please don't be talking all the time about death.'"

"Good. So, you don't mind," I said.

Mechtilde shook her head. "I always say, 'The more you talk, the more you think, the more you meditate on death, you are getting closer and closer and closer.'" She was ready.

Before I started meeting with the SSJs, I was encouraged to bring up death. As it happened, no one even flinched. Not only were the sisters comfortable talking about their own deaths, many shared the programs they'd prepared for their funeral masses, complete with songs, quotes, and readings. They were also ready.

Clearly, if anyone was being spared by not talking about death, it was me. It stands to reason that by the time people reach their ninth decade, they've "had a lot of time to get used to" the idea. This is consistent with studies that show that, as one adapts to late-life realities, the prospect of death becomes less frightening.[5] A "special subject" for many women, it also regularly invited wonderment about the unearthly unknown.

Wondering about Death

The matter of death, of course, is not the same as dying. Hearing the question asked open-endedly, "What are your thoughts about death?" women sometimes gave a two-part answer. Sr. Justin in Kerala told us, "Now that I'm eighty-four, I'm saying, 'please call me Jesus, I am ready for you to take me.'" Not wanting to sound too demanding, she added, "I say, 'Not at my will. According to your will and time.'" At this, we moved on to other topics. Near the end of our time together, when I asked if she had anything to add, Justin had one further thought about death. "The only thing is, I tell Jesus, 'Don't make me a burden to anybody. Even to myself. Take me soon.' That's what I say. 'You give me an easy going home, not a long time in bed and all.'" Meeting my eyes with a smile, she said, "Really."

Personal death talk regularly turned into conjecture about the great beyond. Only two women, Eleanor in California and Svana in Iceland, were completely certain about how things would turn out.[6] When I asked Eleanor if she imagined anything beyond death, she said, "Nothing. Nothing. When it's over it's over. And there's a part of me that thinks what a relief that will be." Svana smirked, "I'm just going to be a useful plant." Turning serious, she insisted, "And there's nothing more beyond that. I don't want to live forever."

Everyone else left space for uncertainty. At first, Margrét told us, "I don't believe in an afterlife. I don't believe in waking up in heaven. I will have my body burned. And when life is finished, it's finished." Later in our conversation, Margrét use the term "soul" in passing. When I asked what this meant to her, she said, "I don't know. I don't know what the soul is. Because nobody has found it." This brought to mind an article her daughter had recently shared about claims to have isolated the existence of the soul. Olla remembered reading something similar, that we lose 1.41 grams when we die, believed by some to be the weight of the soul.

This reminded Margrét of an old Icelandic play, *Gullnahliðið*.[7] "It's about a man who is a very doubtful character and his wife is very anxious to save him."

Familiar with the play, Olla chimed in, "To save his soul!"

Margrét nodded. "So, she's ready with a bag when he dies." Miming the wife catching her husband's soul with a bag, making us laugh, she continued, "Then she goes to heaven to talk to Peter with the keys and asks him about whether her husband has arrived. Peter says that yes, he has, but he's been rejected because he was such a bad man." The woman then distracts Peter and, while he's looking away, she throws the soul-bag through the open gate and into heaven. Laughing, Margrét concluded, "So that's what I thought of when I read this article." With this cartoonish image in our minds, my initial question still reverberated. Looking over at me, Margrét said, "Yeah, I don't know. Maybe."

Hope, a practicing Buddhist in California who was disinclined to metaphysics, was made to rethink after her husband's death. She told me how, during his final weeks, she had read guided meditations to him at his bedside which seemed to help ease his pain. During his last moments, she recalled, "His breath got fainter and fainter. A nurse came in and wanted to put oxygen into his nose, but he said," Hope waved her hand weakly, "'No. No, no. I'm dying,' he said. 'I'm dying.' So, she left his bedside and, with that, there were some shallow breaths." Hope paused. "And then he said something. My daughter, my middle child, was in the room and I said to her, 'Did you hear what he said?' And she said, 'Yes. He said, 'Push.''" Hope raised her eyebrows. "What are women told to do?"

"Oh! That's what I'm thinking. 'Push.'"

"And that was the last word that he said. If you ever think that there might be another..." Hope trailed off. "He said, 'Push.' And it was as though he were saying, 'Okay, just let me move into this other space.'" Shaking her head, she concluded, "Yeah. So, I'm left with that."

On the other side of the spectrum, religiously committed women in California were often uninterested in and, in some cases, dismissive of formal teachings about the afterlife. A practicing Catholic, Marge shared a story about visiting the deathbed of a friend whose children had gathered to say goodbye. Hearing them speak of their mother as going into the arms of Jesus, she found herself thinking, "I have no idea." When I told Marge I was surprised to hear this, she explained, "I think we may just go into the ground, which is fine. I have no concept of heaven. I just can't even imagine heaven exists, really."

The SSJ sisters I met were certain that some part of them would continue after death. But beyond that, certainties dissolved. A church teaching they were raised with but that they now largely rejected had to do with divine judgment. Sr. Diane told me, "I trust that the afterlife will be there for me. For us. If we're faithful to this life, God will be faithful to us." At this, she quickly doubled back, "God will be faithful to us anyhow. Whether we are or not." Struck by this point, I told her that I had yet to hear a sister describe anything resembling "no salvation outside the Church." Diane shook her head. "Oh no. We are God's children. Who knows what any one person has been given to work with?"

Sr. Jamesine was adamant. "I don't believe in hell and purgatory. But there is something that happens when we die. I do believe there's something. But I don't believe in some of the stuff that we're taught, that God is going to open up a book and tell us what we did, right and wrong, and all that judging stuff. None of that. None of that. And not even that heaven is some place out there." With a smile, she added, "I think the trouble is that nobody comes back and tells us."

"Yeah. It's a black hole, as far as we're concerned."

"Yes. So, I believe in something. And I do believe that something is related to God, to the divine, that there's something of the divine in that. But I don't know what that is. You know?" With a shrug she concluded, "But whatever will be, will be."

On several occasions, sisters wondered about heaven with a sense of humor. Sr. Annette told me how she loved to stew in "holy questions" about the unfathomable workings of the universe. This led her to say, "I have no concept of heaven. I said to God once, 'You know, it would be pretty boring, just looking at you for all eternity.'" As I burst out laughing at her deadpan delivery, Annette nodded. "Yeah. Thank God he's got a sense of humor."

Sr. Marie Michael had similar thoughts. "So, my vision of heaven is a mystery," she told me. "Because, as I say to him, 'I'm a doer, Lord. I can't just sit and praise you all the time.'" Chuckling to herself, she inserted, "Although I don't know if there's time in heaven."

To clarify, I asked, "So, the idea of heaven as eternally praising God is not all that exciting for you because you want to *do* things. Is that right?"

"Right." This led Marie Michael to recall an exchange with a dear friend dying from ALS. As someone who kept a small foothold in traditional ways, Marie Michael was aware that she often saw things differently from her peers. With this in mind, she painted the scene: "So, I asked her," Marie Michael lowered her voice to a wondrous pitch, "'What are you going to *say* when you go to meet *God*?' And she said," Marie Michael mimicked a small, plain voice, "'I'm gonna say, "Hi!"'" After we'd burst out laughing, she explained, "She'd worked with the Down syndrome children and other children, so she had this simplicity. So, I said back to her," Marie Michael dramatically lowered her voice again, "'I'm going to say, "Oh God, be merciful to me, a sinner."'"

I laughed and repeated the tiny voice "And she says, 'I'm gonna say 'Hi!'"

Marie Michael shook her head. "So, you know, I'm always hoping that I can get to that point where I can just say, 'Hi!' But I'm not there yet, by any means. I've always wondered, 'Can we embrace Jesus? Can I give him a hug when I get there?' You don't know, exactly, what this relationship is."

Among the Christian women we met in India, only one expressed her worries about measuring up. None of the five Carmelite Sisters seemed concerned, however. When asked for her thoughts on death, Sr. Aida laughed, "I'm not afraid of death! I'm waiting for God to call me, even today." With a smile she confided, "I talk to Jesus and ask him why he's not calling me. Maybe my house there isn't ready. So, I tell him, 'I don't need a house there. I can just sit at your feet.'" Sr. Sapientia, also ready and unafraid, told us that, after all, "the reason I am here on earth is to go to heaven." Mindful of her flaws, she knew they would be purified when the time came. "So," she said, "I look forward to being with Jesus in heaven"

Despite their tenuous ties to formal religion, most women in Akureyri held lively views of the afterlife, likely influenced by Iceland's spirit-friendly culture. Similar to the convent sisters in Rochester and India, most were certain that life continued after death, but what this entailed, exactly, they left alone.[8] Edda used a phrase I often heard, that dying will be like "coming home." She told me, "I think about it like that. My parents and the people I have loved, my grandparents, will be there to meet me. I don't know how it's going to be exactly, but in my mind, that's what will happen." Many women looked forward to death as an outright adventure. Inga beamed, "I've considered death often. I'm certain that something else will happen, something new, and I think it will be fun!" Jenný envisioned death as "just a little shift." She explained, "We'll just shift over to another dimension. It's something I look forward to more than dread. I just think it will be so much more fun on the other side."

Despite Naninga's more traditional Lutheran faith, she still left room for questions. Reflecting on her husband Jón's death, she entered into the subject easily. She told us that while his passing took her by surprise, she and Jón were certain they would go to be with God. Neither feared death. She then shared her experience at Jón's bedside at the moment of his passing. She had been holding his hand and whispering into his ear about the people who loved him. "Just after that, there was a little vibration in his Adam's apple. Then he stopped breathing." Naninga paused. "It's so strange and fragile, that the spirit... What is a spirit?" Using the Icelandic *andi*, which means both spirit and breath, Naninga asked, "Isn't it strange? You just stop breathing and then you're dead? I don't know. I'm no scientist. You hear that God blew his andi into the chest of man. Then, when it's gone, where does it go? Does it return to God? I don't know. There are so many things we don't understand."

I was surprised that, in her fresh grief, Naninga pressed on with questions rather than settling into the readymade answers provided by her faith.

Oncologist Rachel Remen similarly finds that, in times of loss and pain, mystery has the capacity to strengthen, "to offer hope, and to lend meaning." Questions can be healing when they're shared, not necessarily answered. "An unanswered question is a fine traveling companion. It sharpens your eye for the road."[9]

Nature's Sanctity

At one point during our California parlor gathering with Olla beamed onto my computer, we discussed terminology. I explained how I had been searching for a word that could encompass "religious" ideas and experiences that might also work for nonreligious women. I told them how, after my plan to use "spiritual" had pretty much flopped, Helen had suggested I try out "sacred." In Iceland, Olla and I discovered that the closest word, *heiligur*, or "holy," worked well for most women. Now, before I tried inserting the sacred into Californian conversations, I wanted to hear what came to people's minds when they heard the word.

Definitions bubbled up: Precious. Deep respect. Timeless. Larger, deeper than self. Ann suggested, "It's part of what makes life worth living," prompting a chorus of yesses. Kip added, "Like the national parks!" referring to a recent federal loosening of park protections. This received another round of support.

"Yes!" I chimed in. "Like the national parks, now under fire. I think we could use that word for them. And most of you don't easily throw around the word 'sacred.' At least I don't think you do." Women around the room shook their heads.

"You're careful. Because you don't want to corrupt it," Eleanor suggested.

Sue added, "It is something that you would never want to change. You would put that above everything else."

Eleanor nodded, "Something worth living and dying for, and protecting."

Repeating Eleanor's final word for emphasis, Pat said, "And *protecting*."

I told them how these descriptions were similar to how women in Iceland used the word "heiligur." I asked, "Does anyone want to make a wild guess as to what Icelandic women said that, for them, was holy?"

Almost immediately and unanimously women around the room said, "Nature." Startled at their collective certainty, my eyes misted up. "Exactly." Admitting my misty eyes, we laughed. I then wondered out loud, "In what way is nature sacred?" This provoked a thoughtful silence. I offered, "There were so many ways women in Iceland talked about it. It often involved wonder and awe, a sense of its beauty, and how it nurtures. They also talked about the earth's tremendous energy. And there was also this idea that, through nature, people felt a connection to all things."

Helen suggested, "In the discussion there and in the discussion here, we've talked about nature. We've also mentioned birth. The thing for me that is holy and sacred is death. It's every bit as large as birth." This reminded me of Svala's sermon on the sacred circle of life, quoted in full below, that embeds death. Finding her transcript on my computer, I read out the portion where she describes the circle as nature's holy truth. Impressed, the women in the room felt it made sense that someone who grew up surrounded by Iceland's powerful nature would have this perspective. I then asked whether they thought their American peers living elsewhere might share this view of nature's sanctity. Most seemed to think not. They figured they were a self-selected group since they'd chosen a retirement community close to nature rather than a posh high-rise. Their peers elsewhere, particularly those not on the West Coast, they surmised, would have a more traditionally religious view of the sacred. This sounded right to me, too.

Two years later, the Sisters of St. Joseph in western New York set us straight. Luckily for them, their Motherhouse filled with large windows gave them daily proximity to natural beauty. One entire side of the dining room looks out over wetlands that teem with wildlife year-round. When I asked the sisters what they considered sacred in their lives, the nearly unanimous response was to gesture with a hand or head toward the nearest window. Each would then elaborate on a particular aspect of nature that moved and inspired them most. For each, the natural world was a precious portal into an unfathomable more, synonymous with God.

When Sr. Josepha and I met in the Motherhouse parlor, we had barely settled in when she began recalling her morning's window sightings. She first explained how, as a child, she didn't think much about God. "But now, I see him all over the place." From the moment her day started, she explained, "I want to be outside. I want to be outdoors. I want to see the animals. I want to hear the birds." Bound to an electric wheelchair, she always made sure to face the dining room wall of windows during mealtime. Just the day before, she had spotted a squirrel high up in a tree. "He was coming down from the highest point and all of a sudden, what I'm seeing is, he *slides*, about fifteen feet, down the tree. And my heart jumps!" Laughing at her internal drama while sitting at an otherwise sedate lunch table, she said, "Nobody knows what Josepha is thinking. But I'm terrified that he's going to miss the tree trunk. But he didn't. He didn't. But he went the longest way sssssttt . . . boom!" Josepha demonstrated with her hands the free fall. "And I was thinking, 'Holy God!' I'm thinking, 'Take care of him! Take care of him!'"

When I asked Sr. Barbara G. what she considered sacred outside formal religion, she didn't have an answer. So I reworded, as I sometimes did for the sisters, and asked where or when she felt closest to God. She immediately responded, "In nature." While she felt God's presence in the mountains or at sunsets, her strongest connection was through water. She told me how, even as a child, she would hop a bus to Lake Ontario, "her ocean," and go walking along the beach or the pier. In the summers she'd play at her aunt and uncle's Keuka Lake cottage, following the stream. "I would always wonder where it came from. How did it get here? How is it that it just keeps on flowing and flowing and flowing into the lake? And to me, that was God pouring out grace, abundance, love to us." Whenever Barbara relocated, she always found a body of water where she could connect to God "in the flow," as she put it. "There's something about the flow of the water. It's everlasting. I always think of eternity and God being everlasting. It just keeps flowing in and flowing out. We keep using what we have and then we flow it out, and then use what we have and flow it out."

Watching her hands sway with her words, I whispered, "That's great."

"So, God's constantly flowing through each of us. Those are the kinds of thoughts I have when I'm by water."

Sr. Mary Anne experienced God in waterfalls and gardens but most of all in trees. "I can't tell you how many retreats I've made where my concentration might be on a tree," she said. She recalled one retreat center entrance, "where you pass these huge, huge trees. You walk down this path and . . ." Mary Ann closed her eyes. "I can still feel the awe, the sense of God. And there was sun. I felt so small. I'm not a small person, but I felt so very small. I don't know, it was just a time set apart."

Sr. Mary Brigid experienced God in the skies. Motioning toward her bedroom window, she said, "Just sitting here, and being able to see the sky. The clouds. And then if I sit up further, being able to see the yard out there. You know, in nature . . . I just love sitting here." Turning to me, she admitted, "I never lower my blinds."

Seeing nothing but open space out her window, I said, "You don't have to."

Mary Brigid nodded. "I'm on the second floor. Why should I? Last night, as I was getting into bed, the moon was shining in. I was thinking about Sr.

Loretta who is very much into astronomy. I know she likes the sky. I was thinking that I must tell her to keep her ears open for when I'm moving to another room, like for more care. She should see if she can get over here."

Sr. Loretta's reputation as a nature lover preceded her. When I asked her for a poem, song, or object of significance, she shared a poem she had written over forty years earlier, inspired by a mountainside lake in the Adirondacks. She'd brought a copy to our interview for me to read aloud. The poem begins with praises for the divinely imbued skies.

MORNING COMES ... THE FIRST DAY
Long before dawn, I am tugged by an irresistible call.
The One who was in the beginning goes before me.

Leading me out under a dome of darkness into a profusion of starred brilliance.
SOLITUDE in which I am never alone. Transfixed. The unrippled lake stretches out before me.

One after another, constellations appear. They form a floating ballet on the water's still surface.

When women in Iceland reflected on what they considered heiligur, they invoked similar nature scenes minus the God language. Their descriptions often corresponded with "the good" that, as described in the last chapter, infused all of life. Veering from conventional Christian understandings of divinity, their sense of an earthbound, connective holiness wasn't so different from the SSJ's nature-entrenched God.

Margrét, who had left God behind long ago, had no trouble finding sanctity in nature. With a living room that looked out over the fjord to the west and kitchen and bedroom windows that framed Arctic mountains to the north, she told us, "I've almost always lived where I've had a view of the sea or mountains or both." Motioning to the fjord stretching out in front of us, she said, "That is sacred to me. And if we're talking about the sacred, it's nature." Margrét felt the same about beautiful music, especially Bach. "He brings me to religion ... not religion, but to reverence in something more than just reality." Margrét laughed. "It *is* reality, but it's so amazing."

When I asked Margrét if she could say more about this "something more than just reality," she said, "Yes. There's something more and it's something quite special." She told us how paintings affected her in a similar way, especially "chaotic paintings that evoke people's feelings. Also, storms. Clouds. Something that's very strong, very chaotic, very untamed. Something unattainable and unmanageable." Opposite qualities had a similar effect. "It can be peaceful—a beautiful sky and a beautiful sunny day when the fjord is like a mirror and everything is reflected in the sea. But I also love the great Nordic snow storms, which are chaotic. I love it when the wind is roaring in the hills. And there is snow on all the windows—I can't see out of any windows. *That* is magnificent." Margrét whispered, "*That* is fantastic. I really get a kick out of that." As Olla and I chuckled at her choice of words, she concluded, "So I'm kind of, how do you say? Schizophrenic."

Sigrún wasn't comfortable applying heiligur to her life, so we searched for alternatives. When we asked if she'd had experiences of connecting to something larger, she smiled broadly, recalling how it felt to grow up on a farm in the valley just east of Akureyri.

> When you are constantly working with the animals and with the land, there is a strong sense of connection, one I would never want to break. It just felt so good to be outside in nature. I have often said that I didn't know what was me and what was nature. You just lived with this stirring inside, with being a part of it all. And you knew the flowers and the animals and the land. And the landscape was so alive because everything was filled with names. So, the land itself was so vibrant to you. It was just a part of you.

Returning to our original question, she said, "But other holy powers? I don't know. It's just the way it was."

In California, Helen recalled a similar sense of connection when she lived in Maui. Simply standing on an island beach on "the teeniest, tiniest little rock that is in the middle of this enormous ocean" was, for her, "the deepest most meaningful experience of living in Hawaii. It's what it is to live in the universe. Because this planet is the teeniest, tiniest little speck in the universe and Maui is the polka dot, pinprick—it isn't even that—on the planet. And I just felt so . . . I felt the vastness of everything. It wasn't awesome, it wasn't distant, it was *life*. It was me, standing there on the sand, with the waves splashing up on my legs. And I felt so connected, so connected to the universe, living on that rock."

For my second interview with Marge, we met at her log cabin in the redwoods, her beloved home for most of her adult life. Sitting in her living room surrounded by windows that looked out onto dense forest, her immediate response to my question about the sacred was, "I can sit out here on the porch and watch whatever's happening. There'll be some bird coming from somewhere. There'll be a breeze; there'll be flowers; there'll be fruit. There will be light shining in a certain way. In winter, the sun rises right about to where the split is in that door. And it shines directly into the back of the fireplace. The earth is sacred—its beauty, its nurturingness, its profundity." Marge teared up, "And I am just washed with gratefulness." Considering the impact, she said, "When I can be outside and be quiet, I can be quiet enough to think thoughts that are helpful and positive. And those thoughts are not necessarily my thoughts. I think of them as the Holy Spirit living within me, speaking to me." Backing up, she referred to this last point, with a shrug, as "textbook talk." I asked why. "Because that's the way the Church talks about it. But I experience this when I'm outside. Or when I'm lying in bed looking outside. Because for me, that's the only prayer I pray."

Marge's resolve to stay grounded, to find sanctity in the earth itself, reminds me of the vastness Helen felt in Hawaii that "wasn't awesome, wasn't distant, it was *life*," or Sigrún's insistence that the landscape's vibrancy was "just the way it was." When Margrét described Bach and nature as bringing her to religion, she quickly ratcheted this down to a "reverence in something more than just reality," then further corrected, "It *is* reality, but it's so amazing." The "something more" that enticed many women, including and beyond these examples, was rooted in the power and vastness of earthly life itself. For the SSJ sisters who applied God language to their experiences, divinity's magnificence was no less grounded.

Like Sigrún, Pat in California had trouble applying the word "sacred" to her life. This would have to mean, as she put it, "something so precious that you almost have to worship it and treat it, in a way, different from the rest of your existence." Yet Pat did concede that the closest thing to the sacred for her would be living beings. Asked for a poem, an object, or a song to share, she chose Rilke's "The Panther." She didn't have the poem handy, but recalled how Rilke had lived at the zoo in order to write it. "Around three weeks, apparently, he spent, just becoming one with a panther that paced back and forth in his cage." Tearing up, she paused. "It makes me want to cry. It's *really* powerful."

Later that day, I found "The Panther" online, where Rilke depicts animal magnificence as exhausted, languishing behind a blur of bars. It brought tears to my eyes as well. Its middle stanza reads:

The lithe swinging of that rhythmical easy stride
that slowly circles down to a single point

is like a dance of energy around a hub,
in which a great will stands stunned and numbed.

You might recall how, during our California parlor discussion when women offered definitions of "the sacred," Eleanor suggested "something worth living and dying for and protecting." Pat, for emphasis, echoed her final words, "and *protecting*." Her choice of Rilke's poem fills out, in a heavyhearted way, what she meant by this.

In Praise of Wonder: "A Higher Incomprehension"

We finish with wonder itself, beginning with three especially charged accounts that weave death and nature together.[10]

Helen's story was her response to my question about how she experienced the sacred in her life. Straightening up, she said, "I have something from just the other day!" She told me that her cousin, Susan, had died of leukemia the week before. That morning, Helen saw a text from Susan's sister, written at five thirty, with news of her passing. The rest of the day was filled with "gazillions of texts and emails" from family and friends. At its close, during "the last part of the sunlight," Helen sat in her apartment where she was sitting now, in her red chair. "I wasn't looking outside," she said, "I was just staring into space, which incorporated seeing the outside. And I was thinking to myself," Helen looked over at me, "'I was going to give this day to Susan.'"

"Oh no!"

"That's what I thought in the morning, that I was going to give this whole day to Susan. And here I'd been running around like a squirrel in a cage. And then my eye focused. The sunlight was coming through the petals of that flower." Helen motioned to a potted plant with bright pink flowers on her patio. "And you know what sunlight coming through a petal looks like. I mean, there's nothing . . ." Stopping to catch her emotions, she said, "It's a sacred moment. And then," Helen chuckled softly, "I texted Susan's sister, the cousin that I'm extremely close to. And I said, 'Outside there's this flower,' and I described it to her and said I wished she could see it. And she texted back, 'I just did.'"

"Oh! Because of the way you wrote it."

Helen nodded. "And it was about Susan and it was so important. And interestingly enough, Susan had absolutely no service. No memorial service, no funeral, no nothing. That was her desire so that's of course what we did.

And several people have said to me, 'Is there going to be a memorial service for Susan?' And I just say, 'No, she didn't want one.'" Helen smiled, "And my brain says, when people ask me, 'Yeah, there was one.' And that was it." Thinking back, Helen said, "And it was a *minute* of time. Or three minutes of time." Trying to apply words, Helen said, "It is something we can't put our fingers on. And something else I love about these huge things is that there's sometimes something that is almost funny in the most wonderful way. Now, the sun does shine out here almost every day and that plant is there. And I have seen the sun coming in on that plant over and over again since when that moment happened. And now when I see it, it's like, 'Oh, oh yes! Susan!' And you almost laugh because it's just so right."

Jan added a death-and-flower story at the tail end of our interview, like a giant footnote. I had turned off the digital recorder while she was rummaging through the rocks I'd painted for one to keep. Looking up from the rocks, she said, "I have to tell you one more thing."

Enthralled by Jan's stories, I said, "Yes!" and clicked the recorder back on.

"My daughter died right here in this room."

Shocked, I said, "She did. Oh. I'm so sorry."

"She took an overdose. It was April 19th."

"What year was that?"

"I'm pretty sure it was 2011. Dates escape me, but I know it was April 19th. So, almost a year later, I was watching my garden out here on my patio, with the potted plants. And there was this weed growing up. I thought, 'Wow, that's growing really fast. I'm going to watch it and see what it turns into.' Well, on April 19th, it was a big sunflower. It just opened up. And that was her favorite flower." Jan laughed at my shocked expression. "So, explain those things to me! They aren't just regular things." As Jan and I shook our heads at these irregular things, we marveled at cosmic humor that's "almost funny in the most wonderful way," as Helen put it.

Collisions of sorrow and beauty, Helen and Jan's wondrously poignant stories were bafflements. Their incomprehensibility magnified their importance.

Svala's accounting of life and death in nature, of the circle of life, was more systematic. Yet for her as well, the circle's significance had precisely to do with how it exceeds human understanding and control. The subject came up after our formal interview, as Svala, Olla, and I were sampling the snacks she'd set out on her kitchen table. Thinking back on what she earlier described as nature's holiness, Svala remembered another story. A few months before, her great-granddaughter was nursing a cold, upset at having to miss school the next day. This was to be November 16, Iceland's National Poetry Day, when children brought their favorite poems to recite. Hoping to cheer her up, Svala suggested she read a poem at her senior center instead. Agreeable, her great-granddaughter chose one of Svala's own poems, one where Svala describes meeting her husband on a haddock fishing boat where she worked as a cook.

This sparked questions. Svala's great-granddaughter wanted to know how they caught the fish. Svala told her that they used worms and recalled how, as a little girl, she would dig them up from the sand during low tide and skewer them onto fishing hooks. At first this was hard for her, she told her great-granddaughter, because she felt sorry for the worms. But once she understood the circle of life, it got easier. "You see, the birds and fish eat the worms and we eat the birds and fish. The sheep eat the grass and we eat the sheep. And when we die, we become the earth again, which nurtures new life."

Drawing out her point, Svala insisted, "The circle is *everything*. Without understanding and believing in the circle of life, the Word of God is meaningless. The Word is meaningless if you don't first understand how the circle of life works."

Svala's insistence that nature's circle precedes the Word privileges earthly rhythms over written scripture. Life-and-death cycles lay the foundation for religious constructs that would otherwise be meaningless. In Sr. Loretta's poem excerpted above, she concludes by equating God's Word with an all-encompassing, interconnected universe. Again, eternal Wisdom embedded in nature subsumes what is written:

I experience the presence of Wisdom. The Spirit of God connects me with messages and energies of every molecule within everything in the universe that is now or ever has been since the beginning.

This primal power engulfs me . . . moves me deeply.
These are God's words.   The word is with God.

Svala and Loretta's parallel yet religiously distinct views bring us to Eleanor in California and Sr. Annette at the Motherhouse. Both women thrilled at the complexity of the natural world, and both were indebted to scientific discovery for expanding their sense of wonder. Theologically speaking, Eleanor marveled at a universe completely devoid of divinity, while for Sr. Annette the two were synonymous.

As related in chapter 1, Eleanor spent most of her young adulthood in a quasi-religious organization, traveling the world. During this time, she never felt free to think for herself until, in her mid-thirties, she had an epiphany in the middle of a biology class. Led to seriously consider the vastness of the universe, she realized that her view of God as a singular guiding intelligence was impossible. Rather, as she put it, "there is just this astounding, incredible universe that we live in, that is full of fascinating things." From that point on, Eleanor recalled, "I loved every course in science. Everything that I could study in natural science became absolutely fascinating to me, because it all has absolute purpose. It fits together. It works. There's no sort of directing force." Reflecting on these wonders, she said, "It's just fascinating and marvelous. It's just so intriguing that all of these things exist. Nobody *made* it happen, it just happens."

Sr. Annette used similar language when delighting in "the whole magic of nature." As she put it, "it just . . . it happens. Every year it happens. I prefer a warmer climate. I've never liked winters. But it happens, you know? In a pretty orderly way. Because nature can get pretty bolloxed up. But, strange to say, it happens—unless we humans get in the way. So, that's the wondrous quality of nature: it happens."

"So, you're saying that nature and its laws, for you, are wondrous?"

"Yes," Annette beamed. "In fact, they talk so casually about—like, they've discovered a star out there. I can't remember, but let's say a hundred billion light-years away from us." With a laugh, she mused, "You know, I think, one light-year—*one* light-year—is hard to fathom. And that star system is a hundred billion light-years away."

Reminded of how she had earlier enthused about the view from her bedroom, I said, "And that tree outside your window, it's even wondrous, in a way, too."

Annette nodded. "Yes. The works of nature, the works of God's hands are wonder-full. You know? We can never encompass them, I don't think. If we really take the time, they never cease to be, at least for me. . . ." Annette closed her eyes and shuddered. "Ooph." Later, when I asked if there were parts of her life that she considered sacred, Annette said, "Oh yes. And I think it's in the questions. It's in the wondering, it's in the 'why?' It's in the 'wow!' You know?"

Swept up by nature's unfathomability, Eleanor's circumscribed God no longer made sense while Annette's divinity was glorified by it. Yet both were egged on by science, enticed by how its discoveries uncovered the extraordinary "more" beyond their purview. We hear this in Eleanor's fascination with a universe "beyond any understanding or human comprehension" and in the sanctity Annette saw in "the wonder, the why, and the wow," prompted by nature's enormity. Together they thrilled at how an unimaginably vast web of systems "happens," human hands off the steering wheel.

In *Consecrating Science,* Lisa Sideris distinguishes between Eleanor and Annette's approach to wonder spurred by science, and wonder at scientific discovery itself. The latter she describes as central to scientism that fuels a new cosmology, a movement purportedly poised to respond to today's environmental crisis. Yet as Sideris sees it, this new cosmology fosters pride in scientific accomplishments that, in turn, reinforces an anthropocentrism that's created our crisis to begin with. Valuing certainty over mystery, puffing up rather than decentering the human, new cosmology furthermore claims to generate wonder that, she insists, is a distortion.[11] Missing are wonder's classic ingredients: "compassion, generosity, vulnerability, openness, empathy and respect for otherness, and—most significantly—humility," qualities that are moreover vital, Sideris submits, for realigning our relationship with the planet.[12]

Back at our parlor conversation in California, after I'd read Svala's passage about the circle of life, Olla, speaking from my computer, called our attention to Svala's wording. She noted how, when Svala said, "When we die, we become the earth again, which nurtures new life," she used the old-fashioned Icelandic word *mold* when referring to earth, or dirt. In so doing, she was borrowing from the old burial rite that translates as "from dirt you were born, to dirt you will return, from dirt may you rise up," comparable to the English "from ashes to ashes, dust to dust."

This old-timey Icelandic word *mold*, the hub around which this circle of death and life revolves, moreover translates most accurately as "humus" in English. A thick, dark substance, humus consists of decomposing matter that is, at the same time, ultrarich in nutrients. A paradoxical substance in which death feeds life, humus also shares the Latin root for the word "humility" that, as Sideris points out, empowers genuine wonder.

Many of the older women who described reveling in nature's sanctity marveled at their own diminishment in its presence. Humility stoked their wonder. We saw this in Mary Ann's thrill at the huge trees that made her feel "so very small"; in Helen's recollection of standing on the "polka dot, pinprick" island of Maui as the "deepest, most meaningful" part of living in Hawaii; in Margrét's exhilaration over the "very strong, very chaotic, very untamed" forces of nature. Finding sanctity within nature's immeasurable, untamable forces also returns us to Rilke's poem about a caged animal. A meditation on wildness contained, on "a great will [that] stands stunned and numbed," it presents a desecration. So, might I suggest, do new cosmology's anthropocentric designs to save us from a catastrophe that we've created.

This inclination to wonder that ripens at life's humbling edge is something to which we might all aspire. Not only can wonder serve as antidote to a potentially destructive scientism, it is a counterforce, as Richard Rohr sees it, to the certainties of religious dogmatism that are dangerously on the rise. Authentic spirituality has always been rooted in wonder, Rohr contends. "People who've had any genuine spiritual experience always know they *don't know*. They are utterly humbled before mystery."[13] Abraham Heschel likewise submits that "awareness of the divine begins with wonder. It is the result of what man does with his higher incomprehension." Impeding our progress is our acquiescence "to conventional notions, to mental clichés. Wonder, or radical amazement, the state of maladjustment to words and notions, is therefore a prerequisite for an authentic awareness of that which is."[14]

As this book repeatedly demonstrates, as one's grip on life loosens, so often do conventional notions and convictions. Becoming more comfortable with earthly disappearance, mystery is welcomed more warmly and "higher incomprehension" can take root more easily. Older-age maladjustments, valuable in their own right, become all the more so in our era of hardening, narrowing certainties—scientific, religious, and otherwise. Closing in on decomposition, a view from life's edge, like humus, may well contain some of life's most vital nutrients.

9

Unearthly Entities

● ● ● ● ● ● ● ● ● ● ● ● ●

Angels, Deities, Spirits, and Saints

Some of the liveliest stories I've heard from older women over the years have involved run-ins with ethereal beings. Animated versions of "the more," they were held responsible for a range of wonders, from the more-than-coincidental to the stunningly miraculous. And yet, whether angel or deity, spirit or saint, the unearthly were extraordinarily predictable, dutifully conforming to cultural and religious expectations.

Given this tidy containment, what follows is a fairly straightforward cultural comparison, similar to chapter 5. It also reaches similar conclusions. In the earlier chapter, we saw how women in Kerala were ahead of the game, so to speak, embedding divinity within flawed human existence from the start. Meanwhile, the others caught up over time, eventually recognizing divinity as earth-drenched or, when this didn't seem possible, leaving God behind entirely. In Kerala, where heaven and earth are more securely entwined, ethereal-human relations follow suit, as they tend to be more intimate and reciprocal. Typically engaged in such relationships, the women I met in

Kerala assumed levels of supernatural authority not found elsewhere. In this chapter's cross-cultural exploration, we are thus led again to question conventional, colonizing stereotypes that depict nonwhite, non-Western women as necessarily stifled by formal religiosity.

Angels and Other Strangers

We begin with angels who, it so happens, are decidedly Protestant. No one among the SSJs mentioned them, and in California and India only Protestant women did so. In nominally Lutheran Iceland, angels abounded but mostly as cemetery sentinels or home décor. Distinguishing angels from the other entities was also their clear disinterest in sustained human relationships. Swooping in to assist or avert crises, they arrived uninvited and rarely stuck around for so much as a thank-you.

In California, Susie's angel story took me by surprise. A regular at the local Episcopal church, she made it very clear during our conversation that she was not one to rely on heavenly powers. For her, God was not something or someone who responded to prayer. When she did pray, as she put it, "It's a way of defining a goal for myself." Yet, coincidences could pile up, making Susie doubt her doubt. Near the end of our interview, rather out of the blue, she sighed and said, "So, I should probably tell you also about my parking angel."

Laughing at her sudden suggestion, I said. "Oh, please do!"

"I call her Deedee's Angel. Deedee's a deacon at our church and also one of my best friends. You know Deedee." I did know Deedee, president of the retirement community at the time. "She knows I call it Deedee's Angel." Susie chuckled. "I don't know what she thinks of that. And I don't know why I think I got it from Deedee. But of all my friends that I've ever had for eighty years, she's probably the closest to God." This angel's superpower, Susie told me, is parking. "So, what the parking angel does is astounding. I don't believe in calling upon this angel because I don't believe that God is waiting for me to ask for something. But I know the angel is there. And that's sort of spiritual." This "sort of spiritual" comment made us both laugh.

Not sure how to respond, I asked, "So are you being funny? Or not?"

"No. Well, yes and no. Because how can I be serious about this angel?" Susie looked at me, eyes wide.

"Right. But you also said, 'astounding.'"

Susie nodded, then offered some examples. One had to do with the annual visits she and her daughter made to the Boston Museum of Fine Arts. Here, parking is notoriously tricky, but the perfect space always opened up. "And I always say, 'Oop, Deedee's Angel is here again!' It happens year in and year out, month in and month out." After offering some local examples, Susie reflected, "It's coincidence, yes. But it happens time and time again, so it's easy for me to say, 'Thank you, angel!'"

Still trying to figure out how to take this, I suggested, "So does that halfway or partially give you a sense of the universe being a friendly place?"

"Well, I don't think of it as having a feeling, friendly or unfriendly. And I can't define what Deedee's Angel is. Is it a rock? Is it a spirit? It's just a coincidence that happens over and over and over again. My life is full of coincidences that have nothing to do with angels. I don't say," Susie holds her hands in prayer position, 'Thank you, God, for Deedee's Angel. But there is mystical stuff in the universe. And I don't need to know what it is."

Judy, who attended the same church as Susie, was raised in a Protestant household disinclined to the supernatural. Yet, for her, God had become "very real." This was largely due to uncanny incidents that, as she saw them, involved angels who were humans who appeared "at just the right moment when you need somebody and they offer just what you need."

Among the many angel encounters Judy had experienced, the one she shared happened on pilgrimage at the Camino de Santiago. She recalled how, after a long day of walking, a large blister had swelled across the sole of her foot. Upon reaching their tiny village destination for the night, she hobbled over to the hostel manager's office to ask about buses to a nearby town where she could get her blister treated. While waiting in the busy office, a woman walked in and greeted the hostel manager in Spanish. During their exchange, Judy heard the word *ampolla*, which she knew to mean blister. So, she approached the woman who, it turned out, was the village veterinarian who visited the office in her free time, to see if anybody had blisters. Judy laughed, "So I did!" She described how the woman set her up on a chair, foot propped up on a stool, while people crowded around to watch. "She punctured the blister, sterilized it, bandaged it," Judy beamed. "And she said, 'Okay, you can walk on that tomorrow.'"

"That's awesome! So that's an example of what you're talking about."

"Yeah, that's an example. When someone appears who has just what you need, out of the blue. And that woman fit my definition of an angel."

In India and Iceland, angel stories also featured human strangers who arrived in the nick of time. Grace was one of two women in India, both Protestants, who told such a story. Hers took place on Balanchine Road, a major thoroughfare in Bangalore. At the time, she was shopping for a vase to use for a church flower arrangement and needed to get across the street. Making it as far as the center divider, she recalled how, looking up the road, she could see six buses heading her way. "It was one thirty. And I thought, 'I don't want to stand in the sun.' So, I thought I would just run." Reminding us that she was eighty-two at the time, Grace said, "So, I just ran. I ran and fell flat on the road."

My students and I gasped.

"The only thought in my heart was this: tomorrow's papers will say that this old one fell on the road and buses ran over her because she was careless. And what a shame for my husband. And then I heard the buses screeching to a stop." Over the sounds of our amazement, Grace said, "But I couldn't get up. My handbag was lying there. My glasses were lying on the street, intact. I was lying flat like that." Grace stretched her arms out in front of her. "Then I felt someone picking me up. Four boys, same height, same color—they were brown in color—same wavy hair. Square face. I remember them so well. All of them were about twenty-two or twenty-three in age. They came, picked me up, carried me to the side of the road. They put me there and said, 'Auntie, is it paining you?' And I said, 'No, it's not paining.' They looked at me like this," Grace furrowed her brow. Coming to her senses, Grace rummaged through her purse to find something to give to the boys. Looking up again, they were gone. She went into the nearby shops to ask if people had seen them, but no one had. "From that moment," Grace said, "I am sure it was the angels who picked me up. Because there was no other way for them to go but through the shops. And even now, their figures are so clear in my mind. Same brown face, brown color, not fair or black, and wavy hair, same height, same dress. Everything. So then I was sure it was my angels."

In Iceland, where angel figures abound, real-life angel stories did not. Naninga, the exception, told two. Both involved road rescues, like Grace's, yet these roads were far from bright and busy. One took place when Naninga and her husband were on their way home from a Christian youth camp where Jón had been helping out. Driving deep into the countryside in pitch-black pouring rain, they got a flat tire. When Jón got out to fix the tire, he realized he had lent out their car jack. Naninga recalled her reaction, "I got really mad. I asked God, 'How can this be? Here Jón has been doing your work with this beautiful ceremony. Why are you doing this to us? Why aren't you here?'" The next thing she knew, a man appeared out of nowhere to help change the tire. Once it was fixed, "he just disappeared into the night."

Naninga's angel rescue came with a lesson: "This just shows us that God is always with us. I got mad and God was reminding me that he is always there and will always guide us on." Grace's near-death event proved she was cared for by "her angels" who apparently have their work cut out for them. For Judy and Susie, angel encounters suggested more generally—and for Susie quite subtly—that something "more" was afoot beyond coincidental good fortune.

Divine Interventions

Naninga had another, more dramatic rescue story to tell. Lacking human intervention, she attributed the miracle to God directly. Taking place during the 1969 Linder Storm, so named because it blew the roof off of Akureyri's Linder Chocolate Factory, Naninga was at home with her three young children at the time. By early afternoon, she began to notice small tornados gathering outside their large living room window. Wondering whether the window could withstand the force, she took her newborn and the cradle into a back bedroom. Returning to fetch her other two children, she saw her small son with his nose to the large window that was now bowing back and forth with the wind. Scooping up both children, Naninga rushed to the back bedroom. As soon as she closed the door, the window erupted with a boom. "There was glass everywhere. There were pieces of glass in the wall opposite the window. Our hardwood floors were ruined because of the glass embedded throughout. Our kitchen around the corner from the living room was filled with snow. The wind blew in so strong during the explosion, the roof was lifted slightly." In a house filled with glass and snow, Naninga and her children remained safely in the bedroom until her husband returned home that evening.

Naninga marveled at the miracle. "So this all happened as soon as I closed the door. And there I felt as though I was protected." Shaking her head, she said, "Svavar would not have survived if we hadn't moved."

All the other miracle stories I heard in Iceland were set within contexts of childhood precarity. These were often short vignettes recalling fervent family prayers that safely returned fathers and brothers from stormy seas or revived those with advanced-stage tuberculosis. In California and among the SSJs, such stories were rare. Yet in Kerala, women across religious and economic backgrounds shared them regularly. Unlike Naninga's account, they usually featured the power of a woman's prayer as instigating the intervention.

Ammini's story took place in the Himalayan foothills where her military husband had been stationed for many years and where they had raised their young family. The event happened when her husband was on sick leave and had decided to visit a high mountain station to see off his old unit before they moved on. He assured Ammini he'd be back in eight days, ten at the most. Ammini recalled for us the unfolding: "No news for ten days, twelve days, sixteen days. No news." Watching the winter snow pile up in the distant mountains, at her wit's end, she contacted headquarters to see if they knew of her husband's whereabouts. They told her that, since he was on leave, they weren't keeping track of him.

Imagining her fright, I said, "Oh my gosh, so that was the only news you got?"

Clutching the armrests of her chair, Ammini nodded, "I was so worried!" She described how, in her desperation, she had gathered her children around her and, kneeling together on the floor, fervently prayed. Just then, the colonel's wife walked into their house holding a small jar of jam. Laughing at how they must have looked, Ammini told us that the woman had come not just to deliver jam but to report that her husband was on his way home. At that very moment, in fact, he was in Kashmir buying saris for her.

As Ammini heaved a sigh, Paige blurted out, "Well that's good news!"

Laughing, Ammini shook her head and concluded, "So, such things have happened," suggesting that God had heeded their fervent prayer, even though she was a little embarrassed to have been caught in the act.

Other intervention accounts in Kerala were less restrained, bearing witness not only to divine power but to women's capacity to access that power. Arriving at Anitha's home in a Dalit colony, we had barely finished our introductions when she asked if we wanted to hear a miracle story from when she was a teenager working in the paddy fields. One of their work sites, she explained, was on the far side of the expansive Venbanad Lake. Traveling by two canoe-like boats, the workers would divide themselves between the boats on their way out. On their return with bundled rice paddies stacked onto the bigger boat, the workers would cram together into the smaller one. During the monsoon season, when wind and rain stirred up large waves, this low-floating boat ride could be treacherous.

During one such return trip, waves capsized the boat. Thrown into the water, Anita recalled, "I was just doing my best to hold onto one of the oars. But all during that time, I was praying toward the church." While directing her prayers to a St. George church across the lake, the wind suddenly died down and everyone managed to reach the shore safely. The sheer panic of the group was such that "everyone was thinking we were going to die. One woman soiled herself, she was so afraid." Yet, Anitha assured us that, thanks to her prayers, the waters calmed and everyone survived.

Thankachikkuttan listed several instances when her prayers had saved her children from life-threatening diseases and extended her own life after a heart attack. It was through her experiences with prayer, she explained, that she had come to know God. She had also built a reputation, called upon to pray for the health of children, for marriages to get fixed, and for the childless to conceive. Lest anyone get the wrong idea, Thankachikkuttan explained how she will always tell people, "I'm not a perfect person, but I can ask my God for his blessings." She also felt that because she is a Dalit woman, "caste people" might come to learn that God does not discriminate. What matters, she insisted, is a pure heart. "If you praise God and pray to God with a pure heart and mind, a mind that is not polluted, God will give us things beyond our expectations."

Wrapping up our time together, Thankachikkuttan asked if my students and I wanted her blessing. As always, we were agreeable. Leading us to her home's threshold, an image of Jesus hanging above the doorway, we huddled, heads bowed. With a white cloth draped over her head, eyes closed and hands clasped in prayer, Thankachikkuttan prayed that we be sent back into the world surrounded by divine blessings and protection.

Sr. Mechtilde, hailing from the other side of the socioeconomic spectrum, also told us about the power of her prayer. She reserved a special hour for prayer after morning mass when she would sit in front of the Blessed Sacrament. "At that time, I can talk to Jesus. I can tell him anything I want. Many have asked that I pray for them. For the children I pray. And now in the hospital there are girls, boys, men, women—sick ones. They all have asked me to pray for them. The doctors will tell me that so-and-so is very sick. Then I will pray for them. So, this is my work." Listing examples of prayers granted, Sr. Mechtilde assured us that, before responding to requests, she first asked permission from the Mother Superior to do so.

After we'd finished our interview, the voice recorder switched off, Sr. Mechtilde remembered one more account. Taking place when she was working as a nurse in Germany, the story was about "meeting the pope before he became the pope." At the time, Mechtilde was on a several-day outing to Vatican City with a group of sisters. On their final day, arriving at the agreed-upon meeting place slightly late, she discovered to her horror that their bus had already left. After searching the area in a panic, as Mechtilde recalled, "I stood there and I cried." Showing us how she had stood, slumped over and helpless, she said, "Crying, crying, crying, wanting somebody to come and take me. But, nobody." Eventually, two priests walked by and, noticing her distress, approached her. "One of them did this." Mechtilde leaned over and gently wiped my cheeks with the back of her hand. "And he said, 'Why are you crying? Why are you crying?'"

Moved by the gesture, the three of us sighed. I said, "Oh, wiping your tears!"

Mechtilde nodded, "Wiped nicely. But I didn't say anything. I was very sad. Sad at heart." The priests offered to walk Mechtilde to a nearby convent, but she refused, desperate to find her bus. The kindly priest then asked if she had any money. Mechtilde nodded but, she told us, "I didn't have a paisa." Peeking into her bag to find that she was lying, the priest took some lira from his pocket and stuffed it into her bag. Soon after this, Sr. Cassandra, an American Carmelite Sister whom Mechtilde knew, came along on her bike. Hearing of her predicament, she offered to take her to where they hoped the bus would be waiting. As Mechtilde climbed onto the back of Cassandra's bike, she thanked the priests. In her deep appreciation for the especially kind priest, she blurted, "You will become pope someday!"

In unison, Haley and Paige exclaimed, "No way!" and the four of us burst out laughing.

As they biked away, Cassandra, also surprised, asked why she had said this. Mechtilde replied, "He just looks like that. And he is sympathetic, so affectionate, so loving." Since that day, she told us, she often thought of this priest and his goodness and had prayed for him.

Fast forward several decades and Mechtilde, retired, was back in Kerala. Not yet aware of the news from the Vatican, she received a phone call from Cassandra to let her know that her friend had become pope. Thrilled, Mechtilde wanted to congratulate him somehow. Remembering her nephew, a priest who was living in Rome, she contacted him and told him her story. Promising to get the new pope on the phone, he managed to track him down and reminded him of the Indian sister who, decades ago, had predicted his future. Together they rang Mechtilde's convent. Once on the line with Mechtilde, Pope Francis greeted her warmly and asked for her continued prayers. Completely beside herself, Mechtilde told us, with a burst of laughter, that she answered, "Yes, my Lord Jesus, I congratulate you!" Catching her breath, she said, "Anyway, he understood that I was . . ."

"Flustered?" I suggested.

"Thrilled. And it's difficult to talk. So then. That's the end of it." Digging into a large bag by her side, Mechtilde pulled out a carefully folded white handkerchief secured with a safety pin. Inside were rosary beads blessed by Pope Francis. The color had faded, she explained, so she wrapped them like

FIGURE 9.1 Sr. Mechtilde with Paige, Haley, and Corinne. Selfie photo by Paige Serpe-Miller.

this, to preserve them. Showing us the large flat bead near the end, imprinted with the pope's photo, she passed the beads around and gave us permission to kiss them.

After passing and kissing the blessed beads, Mechtilde said, "Now, I am going to give you the most important gift: my daily prayer." She promised she would have the children pray, too, especially for Haley and Paige, that they find good life companions. With Haley sniffling in the background, she sweetly assured them, "That's all we can do, Baba. Nothing else. Hmm? You also have to look. And choose. Then Jesus will take care of you." Clasping her hands and bowing her head, cueing us to do the same, Mechtilde gave us her on-the-spot prayer as well, another parting gift.

Holy and Unholy Spirits

Angelic and divine interventions, whether averting a crisis in a flash or through prayer, are fairly straightforward. The following accounts of holy and unholy spirits from Kerala and Iceland, mostly taking place within ritual contexts, are a bit more involved. A few Californians related spirit stories as well, yet because these confounded expectations, I've saved them for the final chapter. The SSJs, meanwhile, had no spirit encounters to report.

For the Dalit Christian women, nearly all of whom were members of the Church of South India (CSI), the Holy Spirit loomed large. For them, Spirit encounters mostly took place during evening prayer meetings vital to Dalit CSI Christianity since its mid-nineteenth-century inception. In some ways extensions of pre-Christian spirit ceremonies, these meetings differ from the earlier practices in that they allow for Dalit women's religious leadership, where those skilled at spontaneous prayer, prompted by the Holy Spirit, can shine.[1]

Dalit women also told spirit stories involving parents or grandparents who cleared their lives of ancestor spirits before converting to Christianity. Annamma Joseph described how her grandfather and his brothers, who helped to build the first CSI church in their area, had to first undergo a temple ritual "to settle their ancestors" before they and the rest of their community could formally join. "From that day on," Annamma said, "our relationships with the spirits were broken and we could become Christians. From then on, we started going to our new church." From then on, the way was also cleared for the Holy Spirit, especially at prayer meetings. Annamma recalled how she and her siblings would often walk long distances to these meetings, sometimes returning home as late as four o'clock the next morning. One of her favorite sites they had to reach by canoe, drumming and singing en route. Smiling at the memory, she recalled how these meetings were especially boisterous. "Everyone would get the Holy Spirit there, jumping up and down, up and down. When my brother Mani got the Holy Spirit, he would jump up and hold onto the roof."

Rahel described a ten-day CSI retreat as a life-changing event in which, after extensive prayer and fasting, she was swept up by the Holy Spirit. A teenager at the time, each day began with grueling work as she and her mother would carry and sell sand on a nearby beach from early morning until evening. After they'd finished, they would head to the retreat. On the final day, Rahel told us, "I was deeply praying with my eyes closed when I saw the cross in front of me. At the same time, everyone in the church saw the same cross with a big powerful light. Everyone stood up and started dancing. Everyone got the Holy Spirit, jumping up and down and praying." When the pastor asked people to slow down, Rahel found she couldn't stop dancing and speaking in strange ways. Tearing up, she recalled how the priest came to put his hand on her head. While she worried that he had come to cast off an unwanted spirit, he instead assured her that the Holy Spirit was with her. "God blesses you," he said. From then on, Rahel went to every prayer meeting she possibly could, to praise God and to dance in the Holy Spirit. Chuckling, she told us that a young man who would often dance beside her at these meetings became her husband.

Leaving behind her Syrian Catholic upbringing to join the Pentecostal Church, Grace also cleared her life of spirits in the form of saints. Her conversion began with a chronic illness for which she received charismatic healing from her younger brother, Jose. Before this, she had resisted his help, mostly because his prayer meetings felt beneath her dignity. Waving her hands in the air, making us giggle, she explained, "I just didn't like reaching with my hands and all that." Besides, Grace's prayer life was already jammed full: "I was praying every day three rosaries. Three o'clock I get up and by six o'clock I am on my knees saying the three rosaries and some novenas and all that. So, I didn't want the lifting of hands and all that."

Once her illness reached a critical point, Grace relented. Showing up at one of Jose's healing services, she described her shock at seeing her little brother, a shy stutterer as a child, standing up onstage holding a microphone. While she was still wondering what he could be doing up there, she heard him boom, "There is a man in the back. He has not been able to walk in fifteen years. In Jesus's name I command you, get up and walk!'" Grace lowered her voice, "I saw him walking. And I thought, 'This is my brother?' Can he talk like this with such authority?" Bowled over, Grace jumped from her seat, "shouting and screaming, praising God." Up to this point, she explained, her illness had depleted her energy and appetite. But now she rushed to the church canteen where, as she put it, "I had a *good meal*. A full stomach I had. And then I ran around and I said, 'Thank you Jesus, thank you Jesus.' Then I heard Jose shouting, 'Jesus loves Grace!'" Stopping to collect herself, Grace whispered. "And I thought 'Ah! Jesus loves Grace.' I was so happy."

After this, Grace started studying the Bible. Finding no support for devotion to Mary and the saints, she dismissed them along with her Catholicism and was baptized in the Pentecostal Church. Since then, the Holy Spirit has enabled her to do many things. In response to an inner voice, a book came through her in a day. "I just started writing. From ten o'clock in the morning to eleven o'clock at night, I only got up to go to the toilet or to have some food." Songs of praise also flowed through her, from which she's produced four albums.

In Iceland, the "gift" of openness to spirits, or *skyggnigáfa*, enables abilities such as healing, prophecy, automatic writing, and other gifts similar to

FIGURE 9.2 Grace signing her book. Photo by Haley Saba.

those attributed to the Holy Spirit.[2] Spirit practices in northern Iceland, known locally as *andleg mál*, include prayer circles, hands-on healing, and weekly trance sessions that, like Pentecostal Spirit dancing, involve the hosting of spirits bodily. In Iceland, inhabiting spirits use the medium's body to converse with still-conscious circle members, instructing or receiving

FIGURE 9.3 Olla and Auður with snacks. Photo by author.

emotional support.[3] Over half of the older women I met with in Akureyri mentioned friends or relatives born with this gift. Four out of the nineteen were formally involved in andleg mál activities themselves.

Auður at first resisted involvement. She told us how she'd grown up with two sisters and a father who were regular members of a trance circle. She, on the other hand, was more inclined to "math and sciences and things you could prove." Circling the side of her head with her index finger, she recalled how, as a teenager, she "wasn't quite sure about them." While comfortable praying to God, "I was not quite sure about this . . . that you could talk to dead people." In her twenties, Auður's sister talked her into joining a session with a well-known medium, Guðrún, where she had "a strange experience." She told us how, when all was quiet and circle members waited for Guðrún to go into trance, Auður "heard people coming." Making quick knocking noises on the table with her knuckles, she said, "It sounded like kids were running around. I was thinking about the people in this house, how they weren't being considerate of Guðrún while she's working." Auður laughed. "I was kind of annoyed with this noise. But eventually it stopped when she began to talk.

So, after the meeting I mentioned this and how I thought it was so strange. They laughed and said that this was the sound of the spirits who were coming to the meeting." Looking up at Olla and me, Auður said, "So, I was thinking: now I'm crazy too.'"

Decades later, soon after Auður had retired from nursing, one of her sisters died of cancer. Six months later, her other sister died, also of cancer. Not long after her second sister's passing, someone told Auður that she was showing up in trance meetings hosted by a medium named Bjössi. Since her sister participated in these circles while on earth, it seemed she now wanted to work from the other side. Invited to attend one of their meetings, Auður experienced what she felt to be undeniable communication, through Bjössi, with her sister. With her doubts put to rest, she became a regular at his weekly sessions. For this, Auður had no regrets. Describing for us how the work often focuses on easing spirit angst, she reflected, "It's beautiful. It's something that fills me up. There are so many people who come through who need help. There are people who have committed suicide or who have gone too fast and they are lost in the dark for a long time. And we are helping them." With a chuckle, she added, "There's just a lot of life there."

During our first meeting with Jenný, Olla and I heard how, although she wasn't active in andleg mál, her parents regularly hosted trance sessions. Jenný wasn't allowed to join these sessions until she turned fourteen when, later that same year, her mother died. She recalled how her mother's spirit came through at a session soon after she died, but only for a "quick hello." Her mother explained to those sitting in the circle that three sisters had just been killed in a house fire and needed her care on the other side. At the time, Jenný told us, this felt unfair, "that she had left me to take care of those three young girls." Olla and I assumed that her current noninvolvement in andleg mál stemmed from this hurtful experience.

Returning to Jenný's home eight months later, we were surprised to learn that she had become a member of Bjössi's trance circle, along with Auður. It turned out that Auður's sister who worked in Bjössi's circle from the other side was Jenný's best friend and a vital support when her father died soon after her mother had passed. Jenný had decided to visit a few of Bjössi's sessions and now was a regular. This news prompted Olla to tell Jenný how we had assumed she'd kept her distance from andleg mál after her mother had shown up at a home session and quickly left to care for other children. Jenný took this in stride. "My mom was a really advanced soul, so she moved on really quickly. So, she only came through that once, which was really nice. But my dad was a more down-to-earth kind of guy. He was more bound to the earth, so I feel his presence more." Just as Jený finished saying this, an enormous slab of snow slid off her slanted roof, shaking the ground as it landed. We all jumped.

"Boom!" I said.

"Exactly!" said Olla. The three of us burst out laughing.

Sonja, an andleg mál healer, discovered her abilities when she was twelve. It was on a dark winter afternoon when, arriving home from school, she found her house lit up inside and a priest performing a *skemmri skírn*, an emergency baptism, for her little brother who was dying. In a panic, Sonja recalled how she "hid in the closet, sat down, connected to God and prayed." To everyone's astonishment, including Sonja's, her brother revived.

Like other andleg mál healers, Sonja credited her ability to diagnose and treat ailments to her spirit partners, whose names and specialties she learned through her skyggnigáfa abilities. Three of her spirit-doctor partners are Icelandic, she told us, and one is British. Also typical of andleg mál healers, their arrival at healing sessions depended on what her clients needed. Sonja also told us of her struggles to feel worthy of this work, helped to remember that she was not the source but merely a conduit for the healing. "I know I am just an extension cord," she said. "Because when I'm healing it feels like I just plug into the wall. And that helps me a lot." As is the case for many Akureyri healers, Sonja doesn't take money for her work. "It's just something I have to do. All kinds of people have come to me or have written to tell me how they have benefited from my healing, how they have become whole. This, to me, is religion. This, to me, is something I can believe in."

As andleg mál practitioners describe it, relations with spirit partners, like Sonja's doctors, are reciprocal. Most recall spirit sensations and sightings in early childhood that, fading during adolescence, return with a vengeance in their late teens or early twenties. Initially terrifying, these sensations are eventually understood as prompted by spirits who prod for a purpose. From the spirits' perspective, aware that the earthly "gifted" can sense them, they target those they hope can join them in a healing practice. Once the earthly human relents, the spirits agree to hold up their end of the deal. Limiting their contact to working hours, life becomes more bearable for earthly participants and more productive for all involved.[4]

Although perceived and received differently, spirit encounters for Dalit women and andleg mál practitioners include similar practices of embodiment along with abilities with family resemblances. Bestowing "gifts" as such, the Spirit/spirits in both settings affirm the spiritual authority of the women themselves.

Real Presence: Christian Saints and Hindu Deities

"Real presence," a term coined by Robert Orsi, brings us to sacred entities in the form of saints and deities whose powers, typically mediated by material objects and sacred sites, are palpably present to devotees.[5] Just as angels are a decidedly Protestant genre, real presence is decidedly not. Accounts of real presence that I gathered were almost exclusively from Kerala. A few SSJs and California Catholics had some to share, yet these were mostly drawn from earlier generations. This fading of real presence within Euro-American Catholicism is telling, something I'll pursue below.

Lolly in California shared a story from her Italian Catholic childhood in Utica. It featured her younger brother who, stricken with polio when he was barely a year old, was sent to a Philadelphia children's hospital to quarantine for thirteen months. She recalled how the family would travel every Sunday to deliver food and to visit with him under his second-story window. At home, Lolly's mother had made her brother's bedroom into a shrine. When she wasn't cooking or cleaning, she would spend all her time there, lighting candles and praying to a host of saint images, especially focused on two small statues of St. Cosmas and St. Damian, doctor twins who were patrons of their Utica Catholic Church. Choked up by the memory, Lolly said, "That whole year, I lost my mother."

Returning home after spending the year in a crib, Lolly's brother's hips and knees were stabilized but he hadn't yet learned to walk. A few days after his arrival was the annual feast day of St. Cosmas and St. Damian. Living on the main street near the church, Lolly's family watched the festival procession from their front porch. Bringing up the rear behind the marching band, Lolly recalled, were two large statues of Cosmas and Damian. "My brother, who was in bed napping, could hear the band playing. And he walked from the back bedroom, through our flat, and came out to the front porch where we all were—just as the saints arrived." Her voice cracked. "And my mother was *crazed* by the fact that this was the miracle she had been praying for. I see this as if it happened yesterday." With a sigh, Lolly said, "But my mother was totally unavailable. And I understood it. She was in his bedroom every day, praying. She had such faith. Oh! Her Catholic faith was *daunting*."

Sr. Julie also shared memories of despairing parents who appealed to saintly powers, but stealthily so. Every summer they would go on long road trips to St. Anne's Church in Quebec and St. Anne de Beaupré and St. Joseph's Churches in Montreal. Her parents presented these trips as a lark, something fun for the family to enjoy. Yet in hindsight Julie understood their purpose, which was to appeal to the saints to heal her sister from a life-threatening case of diabetes. "I remember how there were crutches and canes all over the place. And as I look back now, I realize that we were making pilgrimages to pray for my sister's healing. *That's* what my parents were doing."

In Kerala, nearly every non-Protestant woman I met had at least one real presence anecdote to share. Ammini, who had married into the Protestantized Mar Thoma tradition and no longer prayed to saints, recalled childhood scenes from her Syrian Orthodox upbringing that, again, involved parental appeals to heal a sibling. In her case, her family made no secret of visiting churches reputed for their saintly powers, sometimes staying for up to two weeks at a time, praying to cure her brother who suffered from epileptic fits. Ammini recalled how, at the Parumala Syrian Orthodox Church, seat of a famous miracle-working bishop-saint, the saint sent her father a vision, assuring him that his son would be okay. From that point on, his fits stopped completely. Their family's story, she told us, is written in a book about the saint's miracles.

Teresa described her life as a series of big and small miracles, most of which she attributed to the Virgin Mary. She told us how, when she was a young mother, Mary would help her with her daily routine. After washing her babies in the nearby river, she would bring them home to sleep while she continued her work. Worried about leaving them, she draped rosary beads over their cradles, asking Mary to protect them. "Every morning, I would go back to the river to take a bath and wash the clothes. When I returned, the children would still be asleep. So, I knew that Mary and God were looking after them. Otherwise, I don't know how I would have been able to manage these things."

During our return visit to Teresa's house, when we asked if she had a song, poem, or object to share, she told us that any song about Mary made her happy. I mentioned how this reminded me of the stories she'd told during our last visit, about how Mary had kept her babies safe, rosary beads draped over their cribs. This prompted Teresa's grandson to mention his grandmother's new technique. To help his sister's second baby fall asleep, she was now putting a small Mother Mary booklet on his chest. Teresa nodded, "Whenever I feel any pain, any stomach pain or anything, I put the book on the area and it goes away." Getting up to fetch her books, she returned with Marian retreat center newsletters in one hand and a pilgrimage pamphlet in the other. "These are the ones I keep under my pillow," she said, holding up the newsletters. Holding out the pamphlet, she said, "This I put on the area with pain."

The powers of Hindu deities were similarly mediated by statues, sacred objects, holy sites, and an occasional vision. Ananda Lakshmi described how her family's special bond with the goddess Mukhambika began with her husband's dream vision. Receiving it as a sign that she was blessing their family, they stationed the goddess's image in their puja room and began making regular visits to her temple in Karnataka. The goddess had since blessed their family in many ways. One miracle that came to mind was when Ananda Lakshmi's sister was scheduled for a major operation. Just before the allotted time, Ananda Lakshmi went into their puja room and prayed before Mukhambika's image. At that moment, before her sister was to be wheeled into the operation theater, a specialist checking on her decided she didn't need the surgery after all. In thanksgiving, her sister's daughter made a special pilgrimage to the goddess's temple in Karnataka to give thanks.

As described in chapter 3, Jaya grew up honoring the Hindu goddess Durga yet switched allegiances to Mary when, at long last, her prayers to conceive were answered. From then on, the family would make annual pilgrimages to Mary's Velankanni shrine in Tamil Nadu. Bringing Jaya to new, Catholic terrain, her earlier system of reciprocity and material mediation remained.

To illustrate Mary's ongoing blessings, Jaya shared an incident that took place back when their home still had a palm leaf roof that needed replacing every year, ideally just before the monsoons hit. Yet this one year an early storm took them off guard. "It takes twenty-four hours to put on the roof and it was about to rain. I was worried about the children, so I prayed to Mary by offering *alrupam*—a house-shaped *rupam*." Alrupam, small metal objects traditionally shaped as body parts, are offered at both Hindu and Christian shrines, churches, and temples in Kerala. Delivering prayer-filled appeals or gratitude for miracles received, they are shared religious terrain.[6] After offering her prayer-infused rupam to Mary with pleas that their house be protected, rain poured all around them, Jaya told us. Yet their house stayed dry. "I have many examples, and this is just one," she said. "So, my faith is unwavering."

Reciprocity, Agency, and Religious "Progress"

In Selva Raj and William Harman's *Dealing with Deities: The Ritual Vow in South Asia*, contributors describe sacred dealmaking, the hallmark of real presence, as alive and well across South Asian religions, with Protestant Christianity the only outlier.[7] Yet in mainstream North America, Catholicism has long stepped away from the once-important place it gave to saintly exchange. It's no surprise therefore that Lolly and Julie's stories not only were from an earlier generation but were set in Catholic enclaves—Italian American and French Canadian, respectively. Meanwhile, the ethereal entity that has since made itself at home in the United States is the anonymous swooping angel who, as we've seen, is exceedingly self-sufficient.[8]

In her essay "Spirits and the Spirit of Capitalism," anthropologist Jane Schneider reflects on the impetus behind this shift, tracing it to the Protestant Reformation. She notes how reformers promoted sacred entities inclined to "selflessly promote the prosperity and morality of the people they protect to the neglect of their own well-being." Relieving the believer "of the obligation of a continuous give and take," this transition is often portrayed as a move away from superstition and toward reason and modernity. Yet Schneider argues that this might more accurately be understood as ethically driven, as a departure from an "ethic of reciprocity" expected of saint devotion and toward an "ethic of brotherly love" that, in turn, corresponds with an economic shift from reciprocally based systems to capitalism. She argues that "the peasants' worldview made them cautious about the exploitation of natural and human resources, whereas the Christian reformers, committed to an ethic of brotherly love and a belief in providence, de-emphasized personal accountability in this way. To the extent that lay populations internalized the reformers' outlook, the moral climate for the expansion of capitalism improved."[9] Just as an all-beneficent, self-sufficient divinity makes more sense in this modern context, so, it seems, do similarly inclined angels.

Schneider's reframing also calls into question colonizing assumptions that reciprocally based religious systems are necessarily less sophisticated than those promoted by the dominant Christian mainstream. Or, as Orsi puts it, that such systems are frozen "at an earlier stage on the timeline of human development and social and cultural evolution."[10] When we trace the demotion of real presence to particular political and economic forces rather than the natural advancement of Western rationality, the picture clarifies. More to the point of this chapter, we might ask whether angels who appear in the nick of time are necessarily a more valid, respectable specie of unearthly entity than transactionally geared saints and deities.

In addition to succumbing to economic and political pressures over time, real presence also takes a hit when it challenges institutional authority. While Mary and the saints are recognized as "effective emissaries of Roman authority," as Orsi puts it, these same entities can stir up mistrust among religious authorities when in the hands of ordinary people, especially when these people claim to have direct access to their powers. The ongoing conundrum for the

Vatican is that while it offers access to supernatural presence, it must find ways to control who gets this access and when.[11]

The Icelandic State Church faced a similar quandary. In the early 1900s, Church authorities welcomed Spiritualism as offering scientific proof of life beyond death. Taking place during a time when Icelanders were vying for independence from Denmark, Spiritualism helped boost Iceland's status as a scientifically inclined modern society contrasted with the "backwards" ultraorthodox Danish Church. Yet half a century later, decades after independence had been won, the Icelandic Church took its own turn toward neo-orthodoxy and set out to squash the same spirit work it earlier supported. Ostensibly aimed at banishing superstition, the switch also reflected a need to contain people's access to supernatural power.[12]

The flip side to the real threat that real presence poses to institutional authority is the access to sacred power it affords those outside the realm of officialdom. Although an obligation to "a continuous give and take" is not without its pitfalls, it is a price that, fueled by devotion, people are more than willing to pay. By contrast, spontaneous angelic rescues that expect nothing in return, although wondrously suggestive of divine favor, leave little room for sacred agency or authority.

A common sticking point for women who claimed access to supernatural powers, whether attributed to divinities, saints, or spirits, is its presumptuousness. Sr. Mechtilde, who boldly and accurately predicted that a kindly priest would someday be pope, maintained a delicate balance. Confident in the efficacy of her prayers yet mindful of her place, she wanted to ensure we understood that she always asked permission from her convent superior before responding to prayer requests. While Thankachikkuttan openly asserted the power of her prayers, she was careful to note how her imperfections made her pipeline to God all the more astounding. Sonja in Iceland, who struggled with the idea that she could heal people, was helped to remember that she was not the source but a conduit for this work.[13]

Amid the checks and balances, gains and losses, women's claims to sacred authority and intimacy resounded in Kerala like nowhere else. Along with plentiful accounts of brokered blessings, the plainest expression of this authority was the half dozen times that, after our interview was over, women offered us their parting blessings. With hands placed over our bowed heads or clasped each of us to our hearts, we were sent back into the world fortified and protected. The quiet gravity of these moments, something I cannot imagine happening elsewhere, was always moving for my students and me. Performed by elite women and Dalits, by Hindus and Christians of different

FIGURE 9.4 Annamma blesses Corinne. Photo by Paige Serpe-Miller.

stripes, and fueled by a confidence in their sacred connections, these gestures were a grand leveler on multiple fronts. Conveying longtime heavenly collaborations, they were also, I suspect, something to which women felt increasingly entitled as they aged. Over the many years I've spent learning about practices and beliefs in Kerala, with and without students in tow, it was only during this round of encounters with older women that such audaciously generous blessings have come my way.

10

Frameless Presence

• • • • • • • • • • • • • •

Encounters with the
Unshakable Unknown

The first woman I interviewed for this project was Helen. To prepare for our meeting, I'd read her published memoir featuring her father, David Park, a painter and founding member of the Bay Area Figurative Movement.[1] I learned that Helen had grown up in Berkeley surrounded by artists and intellectuals, so I wasn't surprised when she began our conversation by telling me that she had no religious exposure as a child and had little inclination since then. Once that was settled, she added, "But I did have experiences."

Helen had two to share. The first, as she put it, "always stayed very, very strongly in my mind. I can't even call it spiritual. But it was a... What do we call these things? It was a life lesson, a life gift. It was something that happened to me that helped form me." The event took place in the Colorado Rockies when Helen was around fourteen or fifteen. She had agreed to spend a summer with her father's distant cousin to help care for her nine-year-old daughter. From the moment their time together began, however, Helen realized she was out of her element, with endless mother-daughter yelling bouts, their rage regularly spilling out onto her.

One day, "in complete despair," Helen decided to walk to her great aunt's cabin about a quarter mile down a mountain path from where she was staying. "I was *so* over my head," she said. "And I was walking—and I was crying—along this mountain path. And you know what that means: it's this narrow little footpath and there's roots and there's rocks and there are pinecones and evergreens and a patch of grass because the sun shines right there so there's some yarrow blooming or yellow something or other. And I'm looking at the ground and all around." Slowing the pace, Helen continued, "And I realized while I was walking that I was as terrified and miserable and unhappy as I have ever been in my life. And at the same time, I was *melting* from the beauty. I had both experiences. Now, I was very young. That was just my experience. I didn't put words on it. I didn't say, 'Oh wow,' to myself or anything. I just . . . That was what that walk was." Looking back, Helen described the moment as instilling in her the conviction that "natural beauty *is*. It is. It's something that exists. And within it is an enormous resource, at any moment."

Moved by the intensity of her recollection, I asked, "Resource for what?"

"Resource for comfort, reassurance, reassessment. I learned that. I didn't know those words then. I don't mean to indicate that I was this brilliant child who had figured all this out. Not at all." Helen paused. "I doubt I've had a week in my life without my thinking about it."

Captivated by Helen's inexplicable jolt and its lasting impact, I assumed it was unique. Yet over the years I've heard similar accounts of what I now refer to as frameless presence events, delivered by just over a quarter of the women I met in California, in Iceland, and among the SSJs. In Kerala, only Grace had such a story to share. The reason for this dearth, I suspect, is that when traditionally framed presence abounds, as in Kerala, the frameless sort gets edged out. Yet the impact of these untethered events, typically lasting a matter of seconds, seems to be no less intense or meaningful for the women who experienced them. Leaving indelible impressions, they were invoked not simply as portals into "the more," but as full-on encounters.

A remarkable feature of frameless presence is the potency of memory. In the telling, women were swept back, recalling their encounters in vivid detail. The strong emotions that surfaced often took them off guard. Adding to their force was how the events felt unprovoked, as something that happened *to* them, unsolicited. Experienced as unanticipated and beyond comprehension, many women confided, through tears, that they rarely, if ever, spoke of such things.

These accounts bear the classic markings of mystical experiences as defined by William James: as fleeting, unanticipated, and undeniable encounters with a deeper, more profound reality for which language cannot do justice.[2] Noting their occurrence among the general populace, Dorothee Soelle describes such episodes "in which we are grasped by a remarkable, seemingly unshakable certainty" as everyday mysticism. Often buried over time, "the feeling of oneness and of being overcome arises anew" when they are recalled. "Memory clings to little, insignificant details, 'As if it were yesterday.'"[3] Skirting "the mediation of doctrine, sacred text, or sacrament," such events are powerfully felt to be moments when "time stands still in the presence of the mystical now."[4]

Everyday mystical encounters are not so rare according to Soelle, and I would agree. Yet we rarely hear about them. Lacking frameworks to give them shape, to give us a grip, they slip out of sight and, for some, out of mind. Because they are inexplicable, we keep them under wraps. Perhaps the reason these experiences surfaced so often during my conversations with older women relates to how life reprioritizes near its edge, where what really matters clarifies and overrides societal expectation. People admit to things they wouldn't otherwise. The edge is also where, as we've seen, programmed certainties can give way to the enticements of wonder. When all frames are off, space opens for recalling and reconsidering events as undeniable as they are inconceivable. It also makes sense that, as resources for "comfort, reassurance, reassessment," such experiences are especially welcomed in later life. When conditions are right, unforgotten moments can work their way into the light.

Although frameless presence events are by nature nearly impossible to rein in, I forge ahead by organizing them into three not-so-watertight categories: as beheld, revelatory, and embodied. Across these differences, the women who recalled them described coming into contact with an unshakable unknown that laid bare for them, as Helen intimated, what *is*.

Beholding

In *Effing the Ineffable*, Wesley Wildman describes the struggles of language to capture life's deepest experiences. The process of beholding, he writes, involves giving in to "the pressure to silence." While words fail us, we also fail at words "in the name of making us small so that the universe can expand in our imaginations, consuming us."[5] While a few women tried to explain their frameless presence encounters, most found it best to stop short.

Incapable of capturing their enormity, words seemed only to constrain. Beholding the event within the powerful outlines of memory, mystery was given the space it deserved. Prodding for more, I learned, was useless.

A few days after hearing Helen's account, Nora surprised me with another. In response to my question about how her view of God had shifted over the years, she related a "major experience" that happened when she was around ten or eleven. Growing up in China in an "American bubble," she told me how her family would spend summers at an oceanside spot far from the bustle of city life. She then recalled walking along the beach. "I was by myself, and it was quiet and beautiful. Suddenly, everything... It was as if the world clicked. Everything was absolutely..." Choking back her tears, she whispered, "*perfect*. Perfect. For about six seconds. Just perfect. And then it went back to the way it had been." With a sigh, she said, "Looking back, it had to be... there was something very holy about those few, that very, very, *very* short period of time."

"At such a young age, yet you'll never forget it."

Nora shook her head slowly, "Never forgot it. All these years." Wanting to be clear about what the event wasn't for her, she returned to my question, "But it doesn't define God for me."

Wanting to hear what it *was* for her, I asked. "So, what have you thought about this? As a kid what did you think it was and then later?" Met by silence, I added, hopefully, "Any thoughts?"

"You can't define it and I can't define what I think it was. Except that it had to do with the other side. And since then, I've heard people who've talked about the very thin veil between us and the other side." Pausing, Nora added, "I can't think of anything else to say about it, but I have to believe that that absolute, extraordinary, overwhelming beauty and perfection was a sudden pssssst," Nora slid her hand left to right, as though opening a curtain, "of the other side. And I don't know how to define it."

When I asked Sr. Joan Margaret what she considered to be sacred outside formal religion, she shared several frameless presence moments triggered by beauty. The first happened in the Grand Canyon where, as she described it, she was "drinking in the awesomeness of this..." Stopping short, she said, "You cannot contain it, it's so big. But these are only momentary experiences." This triggered another memory of a classroom moment at Nazareth. "It was the end of the period, and I looked out at the forty or fifty students." Joan Margaret paused. "They had such *beautiful* faces. Beautiful. And all of a sudden, I just felt, for that moment, just swept away with the beauty of those beautiful, young faces. All vibrant and alive. And then I said, 'You might think I'm off the wall as I say this. But,' I said, 'I just have to tell you what beautiful faces you have, what expression.'" John Margaret chuckled, "And some of them were probably thinking," she rolled her eyes, "Oh boy!"

"But how good you were able to tell them that."

Joan Margaret nodded. "And I said, 'I've never said that to another group.' But in that moment, there was something in that sea of young, beautiful, vibrant, interested faces. So, I had to tell them. I had to tell them. So that was another occasion." When I asked what she thought was behind these events, Joan Margaret said, "I don't know. It's something that takes hold of you. I don't think you can create it or make it. I think it's something that happens." With a shrug, she added, "How do you explain it? You don't."

A few women described isolated appearances of deceased loved ones that also lacked explanation. After recalling her seaside childhood encounter, Nora related another inexplicable event, this time involving her recently deceased husband. It happened while she was driving down the road in her new Volkswagen that she had just traded for his Cadillac. "Suddenly," she said, "Norm was sitting in the seat beside me. And I said, 'What?'" Nora and I laughed. "And then I said, 'I miss you! I don't miss your car, but I miss you.'"

Thinking I would probably have driven off the road, I asked, "You said that?"

Nora nodded. "And then he was gone."

My mother, who had joined us for the interview, prodded, "And what about your sister?" Nora turned to me, "And then on Good Friday, when I was with your mother at the Priory, suddenly Franny was there. We were standing during the Gospel reading and suddenly she was there, sort of in front of us." Thinking it through, Nora said, "I don't think it was because it was Good Friday. And I don't think it was because of that spot in the service. I think it was because Franny decided to say hello." When I asked whether she thought these experiences were in any way related, Nora shrugged. Both seemed to her to be a breaking through the veil in some way, as if to say, "I'm not that far away."

After Helen finished telling me about her experience in the Colorado Rockies, she tacked on a story featuring her mother-in-law, "a marvelous human being" who died from breast cancer at age fifty-nine. She later arrived unannounced in the kitchen as Helen was making peanut butter and jelly sandwiches for her daughters. Slowing down to recall, she said, "I don't remember how I was feeling right then, as I stood at the counter. I don't remember if I was feeling ordinary and fine or if I was in a moment of grief. What I know is that I was, and am, incapable of denying or forgetting or understanding it. I just simply knew. I knew the presence of my mother-in-law. I knew her outreach to me, which was, 'You're going to be fine.' And I didn't do anything. I went on making the peanut butter and jelly sandwiches. And the moment faded." Although Helen had lost many other loved ones before and since, this was a singular event for her. "Go figure," she said. "But what it gave me—and again it's something I've not been able to deny—is how very, very, very deeply much I do not know."

By the time I met with Sr. Barbara G., I had heard unsolicited frameless presence accounts from five other SSJ sisters. At this point, for the first time, I decided to start asking about them. After explaining to Barbara the kinds of stories I'd been hearing, I wondered if anything like this had happened to her. She had nothing to recall, so we moved on. Later, when I asked what had led her to join the convent, Barbara considered her response. Laughing lightly, she said, "Well then. I'm going to share something that probably fits into your other question."

Barbara told me that by the end of her senior year in high school, she had fully intended to start nursing school in the fall. "I had my roommate, everything was set, and it was May." She described how, on the first Friday of each month, her high school held the Exposition of the Blessed Sacrament in the chapel, where girls would filter in to pray during the day. On the first Friday in May, Barbara was up in the choir loft, alone. "I was praying and I started to cry. And I was crying and crying and crying. I thought, 'What's the matter with me?' And then I had all these thoughts that maybe God was calling me." Barbara teared up. "I'm going to start crying. I haven't told this story in a long time." Taking a breath, she continued, "So I thought maybe God was calling me to follow him in another way. Maybe that's what was happening. So, I finally got some control of myself and I walked out. And across the hall I could see my homeroom teacher. She was in the classroom and she was by herself. So, I . . ." Barbara stopped, tearing up again at the memory. "I'm sorry."

Touched by her emotion, I said, "Oh. Don't be sorry!"

"So, I walked in and I told her what happened. So, she said, 'Well, God must want you to enter!'" Barbara laughed. "And it was that fast."

"Wow. So, you did have one of those experiences."

"I guess so. I guess so."

I told Barbara how, when others shared these long-ago events with me, they were often taken right back, just like her. Their resurfaced emotions often brought them to tears, which seemed to surprise them almost as much as the experiences themselves. Shaking her head over this last point, Barbara said,

"No. No. No way. I couldn't even tell anybody about it back then either. They'd think I was crazy. Because it doesn't make any sense."

Sr. Marie Michael's frameless experience was one of two factors that led her to the convent. When I asked, as I did all the sisters, what prompted her to commit her life to God, she told me, with a laugh, that her siblings would say that she had always been a pious child. She then moved on to specifics. "And so, when I was in the fourth grade, and I was riding my bicycle in Carter Park, I had the knowledge that, when I grew up, I would be a sister. Now, how I got it . . . It was not a voice, but that stayed with me through all of the years." Marie Michael then went on to tell me about her priest friend, Fr. Carron, who inspired her, meeting with her regularly and writing letters of encouragement. When she'd finished telling me about Fr. Carron, I asked if we could go back to the fourth grade girl on the bike. I wondered if she had more to say about her.

Marie Michael looked at me in silence. As the seconds ticked by, hoping to diffuse the awkwardness, I suggested, "Maybe not. I'm not sure there are words for these experiences."

Eyes welling up, Marie Michael said, "There aren't."

Realizing we had arrived, once again, at this profound place, I also got choked up. I managed to say, "That's beautiful." For what seemed like forever, maybe fifteen seconds, Marie Michael and I simply sat, blinking away our tears. Finally, she said, with a sigh, "Anyhow, it's a gift from God. That's all I can say!"

"And I think there are often tears because, although you don't know what it is, it's so big." This choked me up again. "And I've been doing this now for years, talking to women who have these experiences, and I feel affected too. Obviously. So, thanks."

Laughing, Marie Michael said, "It did the trick!"

"And it's not something you can repeat or make happen," I said. "You can't make it happen." Marie Michael shook her head vigorously. "You can't, like, go to church extra or pray extra, or have a deeper faith."

"No, no," she said. "It's pure gift. *Pure* gift."

Presence as Revelation

No one who shared frameless events with me seemed interested in fully understanding them, likely because incomprehensibility was part of the impact.

Yet, for some, meaning was revealed in the moment itself and in ways that forever shifted a woman's sense of large things, such as the nature of reality, of divinity, or of her own life's purpose.

When Pat in California told me that she had a hard time applying "the sacred" to her life, an incident from decades ago came to her mind. It happened on a resort island while she was watching, from a distance, a stream of people walking toward a chapel up on a hill. Night was falling and they were holding lanterns, the dim light of the sky behind them. "And just suddenly I felt . . ." Pat paused. "I can't remember now exactly, except that it was very powerful emotionally. I just felt like I was one with the whole universe. And all these people walking up the path with their lanterns were part of me. It's just a moment. And I'm sure there have been others, but I can't remember them."

"So, is that sacred? Or is it an experience of reality?"

"That's a good word that you use. Because I used to think about whether this was *really* reality. Was this what reality *really* is? And now I've lost it. Because I couldn't stay there."

Pat's mention of staying "there" reminded her that this island experience was part of a monthlong period that began with a dream about her Great Aunt Cora. The dream let Pat know that Cora, a devout Christian Scientist who was bedridden and unable to read, needed her help. From that point forward, as Pat put it, "everything that I ever tried to do or wanted, everything opened up for me. Everything *opened*." Responding to her dream, she discovered the existence of portable tape recorders at Radio Shack. A Christian Science Reading Room librarian allowed her, against the rules, to take a book home so she could recite passages into the tape recorder for her aunt. Throughout this period, Pat felt "connected somehow to the world in a different way. It seemed like nothing I touched could go wrong. It wasn't any kind of power thing. I don't mean that. It's like I'm in a different world within this world. But it's not different. It's the same. And just *absolutely* comfortable."

"There's an ease."

"Yeah, just everything easy. And right. And I don't want to—I hate to use the word 'loving' because people use that too much and it sounds sappy. It also doesn't feel 'holy' to me because 'holy' is different from the everyday. And this felt like the everyday." Pat smiled. "This is the everyday that I wish it always were."

Edda shared her story after she explained that her Akureyri upbringing wasn't particularly religious. Sounding like Helen, she then said, "But when I was about six years old, something very strange happened to me." She set the scene by describing how her neighborhood had too many boys and not enough girls her age to play with. One day, while she was sulking around the house, her mother suggested she visit a cousin who lived about a ten-minute walk away. "So, I went there, and she wasn't at home. So, I started to walk home, feeling very sorry for myself." With a soft laugh, she added, "I think I was even crying. Then something very strange happened to me, in the middle of the street. It was like being in a shower of light . . . I heard a voice speaking to me. It said, 'You are not just a little girl who is sad because there is nobody to play with. You are a very, very old soul who has always existed and will always exist.'" Looking at me intently, Edda said, "This happened in the middle of the street."

Trying to imagine how this would feel to a six-year-old, I asked, "So, what did you *do*?"

Edda smiled, "I kept walking home. And when I talk about it now, it feels like it happened just today. When I tell you about it, it's as strong as when it happened." I asked if she told her mother, which she eventually did. "But the strange thing was that, from that time on, I felt older than my mom." Edda stopped to think. "I haven't told this story very often. Maybe once or twice." Shaking her head, she concluded, "Sometimes strange things happen to us."

Anna in Iceland related two formative frameless events. Intending to share them with me during our interview, she had prepared notes ahead of time. Responding to a question about how she perceived God, Anna explained how she had once envisioned God as an old man with golden shoes, but now God was an energy of love. When asked if she'd ever experienced this energy, Anna unfolded her notes. The first event took place in 1986, the night after she had undergone emergency surgery. Lying awake in her hospital bed, she had asked the nurse to give her something to help her sleep. "What happened next was so vivid," she recalled. "I could see a clock against the wall and I could hear out in the hallway the walkie-talkies that they used in those days, where the nurse was asking the doctor for permission to give me something to help me sleep. The doctor had left, so she couldn't ask and I couldn't get anything. I was just lying there, looking at the clock. I remember that it was midnight, then it was one, two, and then three." Departing from her notes, Anna related her experience that began at three o'clock:

> I was like a fetus. I was in the fetal position, but I was also like a drop of water. Everything around me was shaped like a drop of water. I was also looking at myself and saw this lady who was getting old. Her hair was starting to turn gray and she was wearing this striped hospital gown. I remember seeing that

the gown wasn't buttoned up right, it was slightly off. This really bugged me. I was thinking, "Oh, she looks really tired, and she has these strands of gray hair."

Then, suddenly, I was swept away. I went up, up in the air and I felt like I was part of everything. I was flying over this beautiful country. I saw fields and fields of dirt, ready for planting, and then I saw in a field that I was passing that there was a furrow made by a plow. I went into the furrow and felt like part of the earth. I felt like the dirt was a part of me and I was part of the dirt. And I remember how everything was so vivid and vibrant. There was also this sense of harmony, like a sound of harmony, that came with the dirt.

The next thing I saw was this man walking by. He was huge, and wearing old-fashioned riding breeches. He was good-looking and clean. I felt him pick me up. I was part of the dirt that he picked up, like I was an earthworm. And I could feel the heat coming from the palm of his hand. So, I crawled to the edge of his palm. Then he put me back down again.

At this point, Anna awoke. Soon after, a doctor arrived to ask how she was feeling. Thrown off by her experience, she told him, "I don't know. So many things happened to me last night, I don't know." Seeing his surprise, Anna realized how crazy she would have sounded if she continued. So, she told him she didn't want to talk about it. Yet ever since this event, Anna told us, "I've had this sense of harmony with everything that is. I was never the same after that. There was a new Anna after this experience."

Anna's second experience happened about a decade later, during harvest time. She had spent the day on her tractor, clearing plastic coverings off of the round bales of hay that dotted her fields. Deciding to check on a forest she had planted on a hill, she got off her tractor at one point and climbed up into the trees. Here, she was drawn to a small tree standing by itself in a clearing. Against her otherwise no-nonsense way, she felt compelled to give the tree a hug. When she did, she told us, "I felt this current coming from the earth. It went through me and there I felt I was one with the tree. And one with everything that is. I was part of the ground, the gravel." Anna's friend Sirra, who had hosted our meeting, asked whether she heard any sounds, like with her other experience. Shaking her head, she said, "But you know how it feels, it slides through you, this great energy. I felt this moment to be a holy moment for me. As I walked back to the tractor, I felt this merging... I knew that it was the soil and that I was part of the soil. I was the protector of the soil. You have to protect the soil. This, to me, was a holy moment."

Finished with her two accounts, Anna told us that she usually kept them to herself, not always sure how people will take them. Shen then asked that I use a pseudonym for her, which I have. Wrapping up our interview, her eyes settled on me. "You have heard everything that is known to me, the biggest moments for me in my beliefs. I hope you can use them for a good cause."

Grace was the only woman in Kerala to share a frameless presence story. She didn't think to tell us about the event until our second meeting, which shocked her given its weight. She was in her early sixties at the time, during a period when she regularly spent three hours every night in prayer, saying the rosary and reading from the Bible. On this night, she had been crying "about something that had happened sometime back," Grace recalled. "I was sobbing. I couldn't stop." She told us how, through her tears, she was saying to God, "There's nobody to help me. Father, you've also left me. Suddenly, in my mind came: 'Open your Bible.' So, I opened the Bible. I think it was from Isaiah. The verse was this: 'Do not look to the past. See what I am going to do to you now.' The moment I read that, I started crying. More crying."[6]

Grace paused to collect herself. Thinking she had finished, I said, "Beautiful."

She continued, "But at that moment, I felt as if someone was holding me *tight* like that." Grace wrapped her arms around her chest in a hug. "And I knew it was my Father. I *knew* it was my Father. I knew that it was not human. I knew it was God the Father. I couldn't touch him, but I knew he was touching me. He was holding me. *That* was an experience." Looking to the side, Grace softly said, "I'm still praying to get it back.

After a short silence, Haley, Paige, and I thanked Grace for her story. Aware of her God-filled life, I said, "So, if I were to ask about your most powerful experience of God, would that be it?" Grace nodded. But she still hadn't finished her story. After the embrace, a voice told her to write in her journal. She began writing furiously in Malayalam, although, since she had been living in Delhi and Bangalore, it had been twenty years since she'd read or written in her mother tongue. When she'd finished, she broke down into fits of laughter. "I was still laughing when I fell asleep."

Grace went on to explain how the event shifted her earlier sense of a stern God, who sounded more like the God of pre–Vatican II U.S. Catholicism than anything I'd heard in Kerala. "Before that day, I thought my Father was a father sitting there with a stick. The moment I sin, he will beat me up. That's how I thought about it. But from that day I knew he is such a *loving* father." Doing the math for a moment, Grace was startled to realize that this event happened while she was still a practicing Catholic, before converting to Pentecostalism where such experiences are more the norm. With her timeline corrected, the encounter seemed all the more extraordinary, a completely out of the blue gift.

Some of the SSJ sisters described frameless events as cracking open similar epiphanies. Sr. Julie's took place during a retreat in the early 1970s, when many of the sisters were adopting "the healthy God image," as she put it, in place of the severe pre–Vatican II God. Julie's experience cemented the transition. She described the physical setting in vivid detail, motioning around the convent parlor as she spoke. "I was in a room, just about this size. And it had cedar paneling all around and cushions to sit on. And there were a couple icons—one of the Blessed Mother and one of Jesus, with vigil lights hanging next to them. And then . . . well, it's very difficult to describe."

Surprised by the turn in her story, I said, "Oh!"

"And um . . . I just knew I was in the presence . . ." Julie hesitated. "It's very difficult . . . I just knew. I knew I was in the presence of God." Becoming self-conscious, she laughed lightly, "It wasn't shee-shee-foo-foo crazy . . . or nutty, or anything like that. I didn't levitate."

"But you'll never forget it."

"I'll never forget it. I always go back there. When you asked me that question about how my ideas of God have changed, I knew right away. I remember, I had a Jesuit director on the retreat. One of the things he suggested I pray was Psalm 139: 'I see you when you sit, I see you when you stand. I see you when you walk.' That's the sense of that psalm. I used to read it and think, 'Ohh, God is watching me and making sure I don't misstep.' But after that, it totally became, 'God is watching me with love. God never stops watching me with love.' It was a whole shift in my concept of God: I'm with you always."

Sr. Loretta's experience of God's loving magnificence happened before Vatican II gave her a framework for doing so. She told me how, despite the stern view of God promoted by the school nuns, one that was still thriving at the convent when she joined, she always knew for certain that God was loving. Her frameless presence event happened in her early twenties, before entering the convent. She was staying at Lake Placid with some friends and one morning decided to get up for seven o'clock mass while the others slept in. Arriving at the church to find she was half an hour early, she decided to hike out to nearby Mirror Lake instead. Standing on the lakeshore surrounded by high peaks, she was swept up by "the most sacred, most sacred, *cherished* moment" of her life. Tearing up then collecting herself, Loretta explained, "Because that was, you know, *majesty*. That's a word I would put on it. The majesty of those mountains. The beauty. And the sacred. Everything in one."

When I told Loretta that she wasn't alone in having such a moment, she said, "Good. I'm glad people can have that. And that certainly led me forth into wanting to spend my life with that God." Recalling how she had earlier mentioned that she'd always known that God was loving despite the prevailing Catholic culture, I suggested that this mountain event must have sealed her conviction. Loretta's eyes lit up. "Oh, true! Oh true!" Laughing, we agreed that she'd been ahead of the curve all along.

Wrapping up our interview, the intensity of Loretta's frameless account still reverberating, I told her how I relished hearing stories like hers. When I mentioned how the others who shared them were also moved in the telling, she said, "Well, they're precious. And I thank you for bringing them back. Bringing them out." With a sigh, she added, "That's a biggy."

Embodied Encounters

For some women, frameless presence made itself known through bodily sensations. Different from the others' experiences, they tended to happen intermittently and with recognizable triggers such as nature, art, music, prayer, or a sacred site. Yet they also served as profound resources, a connection to what *is* that happened *to* them, and in ways they couldn't fully anticipate or explain.

Margrét's experiences came to her mind when she told us how her goal in life wasn't happiness, which she felt was superficial and fleeting, but contentment. "It's amazing when it comes," she said. Moving her hands from her stomach up to her head, blowing air from her mouth, she said, "It's like you are in flames."

Surprised, I asked. "You can feel it in your body?"

Margrét nodded. "This inner contentment. You feel you are bursting with something." She went on to explain how this feeling was triggered by chaotic nature, by chaotic art, and while listening to Bach. At this point, our conversation flowed in other directions. The topic returned after we'd finished our formal interview and were sitting before the lavish spread Margrét had set out on her dining table. Margrét was looking through a half dozen rocks I'd painted for one to keep and, admiring their unruly designs, explained, "This is what makes chaotic art so great—anyone can splash paint across a canvas. Good artists contain their splashes in ways that are brilliant, so it works." This brought Margrét to the topic of Iceland's stunning landscapes created by volcanic activity. A sign of the earth's inner strength, they brought her to a deep sense of contentment in the face of uncontainable power. Hearing the intensity in her voice, I asked if this feeling ever made her cry. "Yes. I'm big crybaby." Margrét smiled. With her hands showing how the feeling moved through her body, rising from her gut upward, she added, "Whoosh."[7]

Auður described something similar, complete with hand motions. The subject came up when she reflected on how she experienced the sacred. "Maybe when I'm walking outside in nature, I feel this . . ." Auður closed her eyes and moved her hands from her torso up to her head. When I asked if she could say more, she said, "Sometimes I feel this feeling, like *upphafin*." Struggling to translate, Olla explained that the word typically means "resurrection." Auður elaborated, "It's where you are here but you are not here. I feel like I have risen." Sounding like Margrét, Auður added, "And there's a feeling of deep peace that comes over me." This same feeling, she explained, sometimes came over her in the evenings when she prayed, "But only sometimes. It's not every day. Sometimes not at all. Sometimes it comes and it's great."

When Olla and I returned to Auður's home the following spring, we heard how her Monday prayer circle meetings had recently become very important to her. When we asked why, she laughed at her loss for words and moved her hands down the sides of her body. I reminded Auður of how she had described something similar the last time we met, which she remembered. Wanting to understand how this worked, I asked, "And when you feel this in your body, is it coming from the ground, up your legs? How are you feeling this?"

"I think it's coming over." Auður made a motion from over her head and down her sides. "It's like a huge sense of peace. It's like I am very relaxed all over. And I'm so very comfortable. It's deep. But it doesn't happen every time. Not at all." When asked if she could compare the feelings from her prayer circle with what she felt in nature, Auður had to think. "They're kind of the same. But different. I can't tell you how they are different." Chuckling, she continued, "It's best to work in the forest, around the trees, because there's so much energy around you from the trees. I can feel that. I am kind of upphafin. I am raised up. It's something that . . ." Auður moved her hands upward alongside her body. With a sigh, she said, "I can't really explain it." Like for Margrét, certain classical music pieces also triggered these sensations for Auður. Still trying to compare, she said, "In nature, you get the energy from all the way around you. Not with music. Music is from above. Like in a prayer circle." Leaving technicalities behind, she shook her head and said, "It just *is*."

For Sr. Jackie, bodily sensations confirmed God's presence. Yet over the past few years, her frustration with the institutional Church had made it hard, as she put it, "to clue into that quiet time and that feeling of the presence of God." Yet this sense of "deep connection," to her relief, was starting to return. Listening to Jackie describe God's presence, using the word "feeling," I at first assumed she was referring to an emotion. So, I didn't pursue the topic. Later, when I asked what she considered to be sacred in her life, Jackie returned to this feeling that came over her, typically occurring in sacred places, out in nature, or while reading good theology. Catching on, I asked whether these feelings were emotional or physical. Placing her hand on the middle of her chest, she said, "I'm talking about a warmth right here. In my chest."

"Okay. That's awesome."

"Yes. And that is something I can identify from back in my early days, when I was in nursing school, when I was first becoming aware of God and all this. I can tell you exactly where I was in that chapel and what that feeling was. And I can still feel it today. And it's the same thread. And that's not me. That's God."

"Right. You can't make that happen."

Jackie shook her head. "And you don't know when it's going to happen. So, it's totally God's gift." When I told Jackie that I imagined she must have missed these feelings during her dry spell, she nodded. "Yes. Because that's the thing that reassured me and grounded me . . . I feel extremely blessed. I really do. And it's not that I'm any more spiritual or holy or blessed than any other person. But I have that connection. And it's extremely important to me."

Jackie was the first of the SSJs to share such an experience with me. So, I told her how she had "joined the ranks" of women in Iceland and California for whom similar physical phenomena were also points of contact and reassurance. Happy to hear this, Jackie admitted that this wasn't something she usually talked about. We laughed about how, even when it's okay to talk about such things, it's hard to find words. Reflecting on how the feeling had returned since her dry spell lifted, Jackie said, "I have to say, I feel it now, talking about it. With you."

Bringing home the unspeakability of these events was my mother. She and I were always close and openly talked about pretty much anything—or so I thought. It was during our second formal interview that she brought up her experiences in response to my question about what she found to be sacred her life. "Well, you see," she said, "it's not something you could put a word to."

Not sure where this was going, I said, "Right."

"That's the problem. You want a word?"

"No, a thing, a moment, a habit, a place that's sacred to you."

Mom tried again. "Well, for me, it seems when I'm particularly grateful, or particularly sad, like missing Tom [my father who had passed two years earlier], at particular times it can go through you, like a wave, in any of those situations. It's an indescribable feeling that sort of comes inside and sort of moves." Mom moved her hands from her torso upward. "And there's no object. It's a feeling. And I can *feeeel* it. And it is just at certain times. And it's so nice."

Rather blown away, I said, "Wow."

"And it's like two seconds."

Confessing my amazement, I told Mom that she sounded like some of the Icelandic women I'd met earlier that summer. Digging for more, I said, "So I want you to think about this some. You say it can be during a time of gratitude or it could be a time of missing someone. So, it's not necessarily connected to joy. It's about . . . What is it, then?"

"Well, I think it's a connection. To what *is*. It's that connection that we have to apply the word 'faith' to, because it's nothing that you can say, 'There it is.' It's nothing that you can put words to . . . and it's very, very quick."

"And you don't see it coming."

Mom shook her head. Thinking some more, she said, "I am in a place. And it's usually when I'm still. And it's probably when I'm prone. I'm lying down. And the feelings that come up are around me—of whatever. And then that nice . . ." Mom laughed, "*thing*. And I think, 'That's good!'"

"So, it's recognizable. It's like, 'Oh, there it is!'"

"Oh, I can feel it."

Taking advantage of the fact that this was my mother, I kept digging. When I asked about frequency, she said there was no pattern. She could go years between experiences and then have another three days later. When I asked if the feeling differed when triggered by joy or sorrow, she couldn't commit. "It's so short. It's just a lovely, short little moment." Feeling at a loss, Mom said, "I don't think I'm doing it justice."

I reassured her that no one seemed to find words adequate for the experience. Yet I persisted (I now admit begrudgingly). I explained how Auður and Margrét described a deep sense of peace or contentment when the feeling moved through them and wondered if this sounded right. Mom said, "Well, yes. Peace would work. There is peace. This is certainly peace, very definitely. Yeah." I nodded encouragingly. "It's just . . . I feel silly talking about it. Because it's so quick when it happens. And it's calm. But if anything, it's just so quick.

It's sort of like . . ." Mom laughed. "I'd better not go any further. Because it's too hard and it doesn't sound right in our words."

Finally letting Mom off the hook, we moved on to other topics. After we'd finished our interview and I'd switched off the recorder, she remembered two instances that were particularly strong. The first was in Delphi, where my parents visited temple ruins with a tour group. When they had reached the place where the female oracles had once held court, Mom told the group to go on without her. "I didn't want to leave it. Inside, I didn't *want to* leave it. So, they all went trudging up the hill and I stayed there. And that's where I felt it again. It was just *wow*. Just for a bit." The second was in Machu Picchu. Again, when their tour group reached a certain spot, Mom felt compelled to stay behind so she could, as she put it, "Just be. And be. And then I had that feeling of . . ." she whispered, "'*Wow*.' And then, '*Good*.'" She shook her head. "Oh boy. That was—your word—sacred."

What *Is*

In an essay from her collection *Long Life*, Mary Oliver includes what sounds like a frameless presence event. Recalled from decades earlier, she writes of a "sudden awareness" that came over her when she stepped out from the shade of a tree and into the sunlight.

> Time seemed to vanish. Urgency vanished. Any important difference between myself and all other things vanished. I knew that I belonged to the world and felt comfortably my own containment in the totality. I did not feel that I understood any mystery, not at all; rather that I could be happy and feel blessed within the perplexity—the summer morning, its gentleness, the sense of the great work being done through the grass where I stood scarcely trembled. As I say, it was the most casual of moments, not mystical as the word is usually meant, for there was no vision, or anything extraordinary at all, but only a sudden awareness of the citizenry of all things within one world: leaves, dust, thrushes and finches, men and women. And yet it was a moment I have never forgotten, and upon which I have based many decisions in the years since.[8]

A common foundation to women's frameless events, including Mary Oliver's, is that no one doubted their significance. While some needed nudging for the moment and its weight to return, many held their experiences close, touchstones upon which they based decisions, filters through which the profundity of ordinary existence shown through.

Janet, an avid gardener and civil rights activist most of her life, suffered a debilitating stroke in the fall of 2016. This landed her in the community's skilled nursing facility for several months during the time my father was finishing his life in the same building. One evening on my way out from visiting my dad, I met up with Janet sitting in a wheelchair in the entryway lounge. I squatted beside her so we could talk. Leaning in to catch her words, holding her right hand with my left, I heard of her difficulties, her work to regain mobility on her left side, and her determination to return to her campus apartment. She also spoke of her gratitude for her children's loving attention throughout the ordeal.

Janet also wanted to share with me a passage by the Buddhist monk-poet Thich Nhat Hanh that she had been repeating lately, like a mantra: "I have arrived. I am home in the here and the now. I am solid. I am free. In the ultimate I dwell." Staying next to her chair, holding her hand in the silence that followed, my eyes welled up and spilled over. I thanked her, kissed her cheek, and headed out into the night.

Six months later, Janet and I met at her apartment where she had returned to live. I reminded her of our exchange in the lounge and asked what it was about Thich Nhat Hanh's passage that drew her in. After some thought, she said, "Well, I guess one of the ideas is that we are on a level of experience in our lives with the day-to-day things—things that we keep busy with and things that we become involved in. But that's not what's real. Well, I mean, that's part of what's real. But there's another level of existence that's more . . ." Janet paused, "I don't want to use the word 'spiritual.' So, what is that?"

"Yeah. Please find a word for me."

Janet recited the passage again from memory: "I have arrived. I am home in the here and the now. I am solid. I am free. In the ultimate I dwell." She reflected, "So, 'in the ultimate I dwell.' There's another level of existence and the things that are going on in the world are part of that but they're not the things that have meaning."

"Which means that the everyday can't really break you? Because there's something deeper?"

"Yeah. So that's, I guess, what impressed me. Because it's pretty easy to get disillusioned and depressed, looking at what's happening in the world. So, this is inviting us to think of some other level of existence." Janet backed up. "But nobody really *knows* or has all the answers. And if you think you do, then you're just thinking that you're God and you're making the decisions." Watching me smile at her last point, Janet smiled back.

This promise of a more meaningful level of existence parallels what some Buddhists might refer to as *bodhichitta*, our true nature that abides despite appearances. It is also captured by the phrase "what *is*" to which women sometimes defaulted, with a shrug, when trying to describe what their frameless encounters touched into, when definitions felt not only impossible but, as Janet asserted, presumptuous. Like noetic certainties that William James describes as taking hold in the wake of mystical experiences, they are "states of insight into depths of truth unplumbed by the discursive intellect," they are "illuminations, revelations, full of significance and importance, all inarticulate though they remain."[9] As Helen put it, they become resources "for comfort, reassurance, reassessment" within our otherwise distracting and discouraging lives. Feeling "as if the world clicked," as Nora put it, we arrive home in the here and now.[10] Inciting "a sudden awareness of the citizenry of all things within one world," frameless encounters are ultimately capable, as Soelle puts it, of "breaking open the self's seclusion."[11]

While impossible to pin down, reassurances found at the heart of frameless presence are not, I'm convinced, the same as wishful thinking. Freed from everyday categories and logics, "the more" in this context echoes features of "The Real" as fleshed out in part II of this book. Just as the divinity that made sense to women was experienced as entrenched within earthly lives, frameless encounters were usually rooted in the ordinary. Similar to the poignancy that anchors meaning into women's life stories, where love is deepened by loss, frameless events often broke through during times of despair or disarray. Like the abiding goodness that women discovered when letting go of expectations, frameless presence revealed, in a flash, the "what is" that reassuringly streams beneath our control or conception.

Rather than leaving reality behind, the more threads itself throughout. We've seen how the humbling realities of later life clear the way for wonder. They prime us for counterintuitive, countercultural ways of being from which, this book repeatedly suggests, we could all benefit. How then, we might ask, can those not yet arrived claim its view as their own? How might we shift the view from life's edge closer to the center?

Conclusion

• • • • • • • • • • • • • •

Finding Our Place
at the Edge

> Who is heard and who is not defines
> the status quo.
>
> **REBECCA SOLNIT,** *The Mother of All
> Questions*

We finish by considering why what matters at life's edge matters. Helping to make the case are kindred perspectives from critical gerontology, disability studies, and mystical theologies that, each in their own way, defy societal norms that diminish, distract, and separate us. Offering a more expansive view of what it means to be human, they help us to consider what it might mean to move life's edge to the center, a place to call our own.

Ageism, Ableism, and the Mythical Norm

At its core, ageism stems from a fear of growing old and dying. According to terror management theory, one of the ways we try to keep this inevitability at bay is by creating symbolic identities. We elevate ourselves above our animal existence by identifying as intellectuals, artists, good parents, and so on, feeling indestructible as long as we can keep up with these identities. Pulling us off course is not just advancing age but the diminishments that often come with the aging process. Losing control over mental and bodily functions, we eventually have to face the fragility of our constructions, of who we think ourselves to be.[1]

Ageism and its fears thus tangle up with ableism, twin bigotries that flourish in the United States like nowhere else.[2] We equate normality with youthful, able bodies—a "normal" that is highly unstable—and we create labels to uphold this natural ordering of things through nonidentity. As such, "disability" serves as "a narrative prothesis," as dis/ability scholar Dan Goodley puts it, "a prop on which to lean in which to emphasize a preference for ability." "Old age," also an artificially fixed category, gathers ageist associations by a culture that clings to youth.[3]

In mainstream North America, we tend to address the "problem" of old age by reifying the category in one of two opposing ways. Standard gerontology, which often focuses on disease and dependency, tends to equate older age with diminishment. Successful aging campaigns on the other hand insist that our later years be filled with activity and enjoyment. Stepping outside this binary, critical gerontology questions the usefulness of "old age" as a category to begin with.[4] Rather than focusing on individual ailments, the field strives to uncover the social and cultural structures that uphold ideologies of age, those that feed into scientific discourses and create ageist policies. Emphasizing diversity among older adult populations, critical gerontologists also look to the social, economic, and biological factors that impact the aging process.[5]

Alongside critical gerontology, disability studies calls to task mainstream biomedical approaches that identify individuals as "disabled."[6] Shifting away from a microfocus on medical diagnoses and solutions, disability studies concerns itself with how ableist society isolates and excludes people with physical or psychological challenges. Rejecting the perception that disabled people are abnormal, deviant, or deficient, disability studies, like critical gerontology, questions assumptions about who does and doesn't count as a productive member of society.[7]

As critical gerontologists and disability scholars see it, ageism and ableism owe much of their enduring strength to consumer capitalism that calculates human worth according to people's ability to contribute to the labor market. Those who don't measure up, marked as expendable within this framework, are often diminished and dehumanized.[8] Racialized others, those outside the structures of power, are furthermore commodified and exploited. Some historians argue that the capitalist turn in Europe, which coincides with a devaluation of older adults, marks ageism's beginnings. The industrial revolution that favored younger workers, relocating them for new jobs, undermined the extended family system at around the same time that medical advances increased life expectancy, creating a growing aging population for which society was ill-prepared.[9] The resulting view of older adults as nonproductive burdens on society continues to make its way across the globe in sync with similar patterns of industrialization and population growth among this demographic.[10] Intensifying the challenges that older adults and other marginalized groups face is neoliberalism's emphasis on individual responsibility that, in turn, diminishes social supports.

Late-stage consumer capitalism also fuels successful aging campaigns that thrive in our culture of "compulsory youthfulness." In this case, rather than demeaning older people as nonproducers, they become consummate consumers. Especially compelling to women for whom the "normal" female body is young, able-bodied, slim, and attractive, the multibillion-dollar antiaging industry encourages futile efforts to uphold normative status. Depicting older-age infirmities as preventable, the industry leads us to believe that the way we age is up to individual effort, ignoring the actual variables of class, gender, race, education, and luck. Placing the onus on the individual, the state is further absolved of its responsibilities to provide support for older adults with disabilities.[11]

The work of both critical gerontology and disability studies is thus to chip away at what Audre Lorde refers to as a "mythical norm" that lies "somewhere, on the edge of consciousness . . . which each one of us within our hearts knows 'that is not me.'"[12] Questioning the artificial divide that structures this myth, one that cleanly separates the able from the disabled, disability scholars emphasize fluidity, given that "one is always dis/abled in relation to the context in which one is put."[13] The commonly inserted slash in dis/ability reminds us of how disability and ability cocreate one another.[14] Critical gerontologists likewise promote age as nonbinary. Rejecting fixed meanings to a number, Ashton Applewhite suggests we might together become "age queer."[15]

Also propping up both ageism and ableism is the mythical norm of independence for which dependence becomes a problem to be solved. Sunaura Taylor counters that "we are all vulnerable beings, who during our lives go in and out of dependency, who will be giving and receiving care." Rather than casting certain populations as caricatures of dependence while the able-bodied live "in a delusion of independence," she proposes a spectrum in which dependency is seen not "as negative and certainly not unnatural, but rather as an integral part of being alive."[16]

Widening the scope, critical gerontologist Jan Baars suggests that rather than attempting to banish finitude from life, we look to how it extends throughout. The American tendency to measure our lives according to "success, perfection, infinite youth, and innovation" misleadingly implies that "failing, decay, and vulnerability" are not critical to reality. A more expansive sense of finitude and limitation, Baars insists, can be "intensely life affirming."[17]

Dorothee Soelle and the Mythical Norm of Nonsuffering

Dorothee Soelle's critical theology parallels critical gerontology and dis/ability studies in its departure from traditional theology's microfocus on individual sin, concerned instead with societal sin and the suffering it causes. The mythical norm that Soelle takes to task is that of nonsuffering, fueled by Euro-American Christianity and consumer capitalism.

Soelle's classic 1975 work *Suffering* was born of her astonishment at our nonresponse to the horrors of Vietnamese suffering during the Vietnam War. The book explores the religious roots of what Soelle considers to be our modern-day norm of a suffering-free life that, in turn, obscures the sufferings of others. She begins by acknowledging how suffering was once deemed virtuous by mainstream Christianity, a means to break our pride and a test sent from God. Today's nonsuffering ethos, captured by the Greek term *apatheia*, connotes both a freedom from suffering as well as an inability to suffer. Our current "gratuitous avoidance of suffering," Soelle writes, "leaves us with no language or gesture with which to make sense of or to learn from suffering." Although apathetic people still feel pain, their suffering is stripped of significance. Lacking an awareness of our own suffering, we become insensitive to the suffering of others.[18]

For Soelle, Euro-American Christianity is emblematic of this nonsuffering approach, as "shrunken down into a purely personal affair without general interest." Its God, "a mild and apathetic being," is disengaged from the humanity of a suffering Christ, aligned instead with a perfectionism that "builds on a wish to be in God's image." The domain of rich, white, industrialized nations, this apathetic Christianity enables capitalist exploitation to flourish, ensuring that the suffering of others, required for our prosperity, goes unseen. Or, if it is seen, it has "nothing to do with us, too high a birth rate and inadequate industrialization, for example." Neither does this world of the rich, "sealed air-tight against hunger and disease," feel a need to address suffering even in its own midst. "Exploitation needs a certain amount of apathy in order to run its course smoothly."[19]

In *The Silent Cry*, written more than two decades after *Suffering*, Soelle portrays late-stage capitalism as superseding Christianity in bolstering expectations for nonsuffering perfection. The individual is now envisioned as having "unlimited capacity for utilization and consumption," in which "choice, purchase, presentation, and enjoyment" are promoted by "their own forms of religious staging and production." Adopting a "religion of consumerism," mainstream affluent society is cut loose from "the old and milder forms of the opiate of the people."[20] Echoing critical gerontologists and disability studies scholars who insist that aging, disability, and dependence are not only intrinsic to reality but essential to lives fully lived, Soelle submits that, in our determination to avoid suffering, we've created "a corresponding disappearance of passion for life and of the strength and intensity of its joys."[21] Blind to terror and despair in order to muffle our fears, "we have succeeded in banishing the demons together with all the angels."[22]

Medical anthropologist Arthur Kleinman likewise describes affluent societies today as portraying suffering as something "that one can and should avoid, that is without any redeeming virtue." Enticed by "the gratuitous optimism of Hollywood," we hastily resort to high-technology solutions, bypassing what really matters in life that can be found in suffering itself. For Kleinman this avoidance, part of "the disordering effects of advanced capitalism," ultimately leads to the erasure of the human.[23] Oncologist Rachel Remen maintains that our cultural addiction to perfection keeps us from recognizing how serious diseases can be a "foundation from which to live a good life." People living with terminal illnesses, forced to give up the struggle to be something they're not, discover a view of life that is "so much clearer than the view that most of us have—that what seems to be important is much more simple and accessible for everybody." This, she surmises, "is one of the best kept secrets in America."[24]

Yet the propensity for humans to avoid pain to their own detriment is nothing new. We learn this from Prince Siddhartha. It was only after fleeing the luxuries of the palace, unfettered from the illusions of nonsuffering created by his father, that he could find enlightenment. Awakened to the inevitable passing of all things—youth, health, and his own finite being—his Buddhahood emerges.

Unsurprisingly, as Buddhism adapts to the American mainstream, most notably within the Buddhist-inspired mindfulness industry, it bends to the same forces that have shaped apathetic Christianity. Heralded for relieving stress, its practices have been critiqued for bolstering rather than decentering the self-cherishing ego, thus directly departing from Buddhist principles. Critics see these adaptations as promoting a superficial form of happiness that keeps practitioners from questioning the conditions that trouble them to begin with. Although not enmeshed in global systems of neoliberal capitalism to the same degree as Christianity, popularized Buddhism is seen to be yet another opiating force working on its behalf.[25]

For a society gone awry, Soelle prescribes a three-step program: to be amazed, to let go, and to resist. Amazement arises when we genuinely engage the "bleak, terrifying side [of life] that our society attempts to expunge," freeing ourselves "from customs, viewpoints, and convictions, which, like layers of fat that make us untouchable and insensitive, accumulate around us." By letting go, Soelle refers to our dependence on consumerism that feeds our false desires and needs. The more we can let go, "the more we make room for amazement in day-to-day life." Soelle calls us to resist the strict divisions that we create "between day and night, summer and winter, seedtime and harvest, desert and fertile regions, youth and old age, living and dying." Otherwise, detached from life's full range of experience as well as from one another, the autonomous self vainly pursues "springtime forever available for sale." The remedy Soelle proposes is a *via unitiva* approach to life, a being-at-one with and through God.[26]

Soelle's three-step prescription closely follows the themes that structure this book. Clear-eyed amazement at the bleak side of life is one way of describing the realistic view at life's edge itself, where endings and losses are no longer so easily ignored. We also see this in the ways women consistently embedded their treasured memories in contexts of sorrow, deepening their worth. While older women rarely spoke of letting go of consumerism per se, their accounts consistently reflected a letting go of socially mandated certitudes similarly designed to rein in life's unwieldiness, stoking similarly futile desires. Resistance to dualisms forms the backbone of this book, where late-life precarity sharpens our sense of what matters and life's freefalls give way to solidity and joy. A nondualistic via unitiva approach emerges in how women discovered divinity, sanctity, and goodness as abiding in the middle of messy, flawed existence.

While philosophical and theological frameworks can encourage us against the flow of convention to embrace life's harsh fullness, there's no substitute for the realities that life forces upon us. In an interview with Ram Dass after the release of his final book, *Polishing the Mirror*, he admits to how, when writing *Still Here* two decades earlier, he thought his spiritual practices had granted him wisdom to impart on the subject of aging and dying. "But I was in my 60s," Dass said. "Now, I'm in my 80s and this new book talks about what it's really like. Now, I am aging. I am approaching death. I'm getting closer to the end. I was so naive when I wrote that earlier book."[27] In *Polishing the Mirror*, Dass reflects on how "facing death can help us open up to deeper parts of ourselves." Before reaching a certain age, however, "death scares the hell out of who you think you are."[28]

The Perks and Problems of Irrelevance

Another perk of older age is marginalization. By this I refer to how people, concepts, or objects demeaned and dismissed by normative society find space to thrive on their own terms. This is like the giant, oddly shaped redwoods that my mother taught me to look for when hiking along the California coastal range. Passed over by loggers, they now tower over the second-growth redwoods. There are benefits to being misshapen.[29]

Applied to older women, the perks of illegibility can include a freedom from the demands of sexist society. Feminist gerontologist Martha Holstein notes that, over time, women become "free in ways we haven't been free in decades," making it all the more important that we reject the successful aging movement and its mandates.[30] Anthropologist Barbara Myerhoff discovers that, amid diminishing status and lowered expectations, older people across cultures find they have little to lose. Becoming "liminal figures that buck societal rules," they display an "often-noted but little studied toughness, fearlessness, idiosyncrasy, and creativity."[31] With the wearing of the years, it becomes easier to come clean from society's opiates.

Yet despite an ever-circulating stream of courageous, nonconforming people arriving at life's edge, their illegibility—thanks to ageism—makes this hard to recognize. While we typically regard the innate creativity of unsocialized children "with affection and nostalgia," Myerhoff writes, we are often "blind to the creativity of de-socialized elders at the other end of the life cycle." Our "intolerance for 'bad behavior' among the elderly is part of our blindness to their gifts," resources that "have yet to be mined and appreciated."[32]

As Audre Lorde frames it, our incapacity to recognize older-age offerings feeds a generation gap that keeps younger people from learning. "Stuck in a historical amnesia that keeps us working to invent the wheel every time we have to go to the store for bread, we find ourselves having to repeat and relearn the same old lessons over and over that our mothers did because we do not pass on what we have learned, or because we are unable to listen." Lorde asks, "Who would have believed that once again our daughters are allowing their bodies to be hampered and purgatoried by girdles and high heels and hobble skirts?"[33]

Finding Our Place at the Edge

One way to respond to this segregation and silencing is to join forces. Intersectional analysis does so by revealing how social bigotries work as a team, as must their antidotes. A common shortcoming to this approach, however, is that ageism and ableism are often left out of the picture.[34] If we hope to strengthen nonnormative solidarity, the inclusion of older age and disability is critical not only because they reflect populations worthy of representation but because older age and disability are nearly universal conditions.

A real-time widened view into how intersectional realities work has been the COVID-19 debacle that, as Fayola Jacobs puts it, was caused not by a glitch in the system but by the system itself. While mainstream North American coverage about those hit hardest by the pandemic tended to focus on the vulnerabilities of particular groups, it largely ignored the structural causes that repeatedly force communities of color along with poor, disabled, elderly, and health-compromised people to bear the brunt of such disasters. Recognizing that structural inequities in the United States stem from histories of slavery and settler colonialism, the pandemic revealed how our gendered, ableist, and ageist impulses similarly devalue and render these populations disposable.[35]

Writing from the perspective of dis/ability studies, Goodley recommends that we build solidarity by recognizing that the "deeply insidious nature of normality" belongs to no one.[36] Letting go of the "entanglements of racism, heteronormativity, and compulsory able-bodiedness" that divide us (to which we could add ageism and others), we might realize how we are all, in fact, "mutually dependent and desiring interconnections."[37] Claiming our place beyond the bounds of an impossible normal, "celebrating our potential for abnormality," we gain strength not only in numbers but in the critical humility needed to widen understandings of and compassion for nonnormative realities we don't share. Dismantling socially mandated apatheia, it gets harder to turn a blind eye to the suffering of others.

Also in line to join forces are mystical perspectives that embed social justice concerns into a vision of human-divine interdependence. Soelle's via unitiva, made possible by letting go of our reliance on consumerism, helps us to realize that the other is "not of our making, not our product and that we, rather, are a dependent part of the whole."[38] As heard during the "Roots Alive!" Zoom program, the founding Sisters of St. Joseph experienced via unitiva during an era of social upheaval and in a region "awash in mysticism" through their work among society's forgotten, bound and fortified by a divinity they envisioned as "a dimensionless love," as Sr. Marcia put it. "We're in [divinity] and it's in us and all of us are in it together, as one."

In his final chapter of *Memories, Dreams, Reflections*, Carl Jung, well into his eighties, describes a newly emergent sense of boundless interconnectedness. Amid the limitations of older age, he writes, "there is so much that fills me: plants, animals, clouds, day and night, and the eternal in man. The more uncertain I have felt about myself, the more there has grown in me a feeling of kinship with all things."[39] Sr. Joan Chittister notes a similar expansiveness: "A blessing of these years is coming to see that behind everything so solid, so firm, so familiar in front of us runs a descant of a mystery and meaning to be experienced in ways we never thought of before. To become free of the prosaic and the scheduled and the pragmatic is to break the world open in ways we never dreamed of. In this new world, a mountain, a bench, a grassy path is far more than simply itself. It is a symbol of unprecedented possibilities, of the holiness of time."[40]

The accounts that fill this book show us how, as the prosaic fades and disarray closes in, a sense of what really matters can clarify and strengthen. Becoming more at home with uncertainty, possessed of a "higher incomprehension," older women deflect society's impossible norms. Their stories and reflections confirm that, in reality, nothing in life is under our control. Those who so generously shared with me are thus beacons, among the ranks of the socially illegible that must include older adults with little choice but to think differently. I lean on this point one last time because advancing age so often means getting left behind, even by social critics whose intersectional work is admirably broad. I also do so in recognition that older age with its attendant sorrows and joys is where we're all headed. Old age, sickness, and death, Buddha's trifecta of inevitability, become levelers for a larger cause. By acknowledging vulnerability and dependence as central to our existence, by centering life's edge itself, we can better understand what it means to be more fully alive—together.

Acknowledgments

It's taken many villages and villagers to raise this work to a full-fledged book. I gratefully acknowledge many of them here by name, mindful that many unnamed have been pivotal to the process, as well.

Residents of the San Francisco Bay Area retirement community where my mom lived for sixteen years are largely responsible for the conception and shaping of this book. While I limited our formal interviews to twenty women, countless others have also made their mark. I am grateful for their insights, recorded and unrecorded, yet more important to me have been the friendships we've forged along the way.

During my stays in Akureyri, I was graciously hosted, as always, by my friends Sólveig Hrafnsdóttir and Kiddi Kristjánssón. Akureyri friends who helped me locate women who were willing and able to meet with me include Anna Guðný Egilsdóttir, Ármann Hinriksson, Bobba Ásgeirsdóttir, Hlynur Hallson, Hólmkell Hreinsson, Jói Sigurðsson, Kristín Kristjánsdóttir, Sigrún Magnusdóttir, Sigrún Lilja Sigurðardóttir, Stebbi Jóhannsson, and Svavar Jónsson. Jón Haukur Ingimundarson smartly suggested his graduate student, Olla Brynjarsdóttir, to help arrange and accompany me to my interviews. Olla's reassuring presence and nuanced observations at our meetings as well as her insights into Icelandic culture and generational differences were indispensable to the process.

In Kerala, longtime friends Jyothi Mathew, Sujatha Menon, and Shobha Menon identified women interested in taking part and, in some cases, joined us at our meetings. Reeta Benoy in Rochester led me to her sister, Chachimma

Christy in Ernakulam, who opened up networks of older women, as did Sosa Varghese, Annah Chackola, Denny Jose, and Janena Oliver. Sanal Mohan recommended Jestin Varghese, his PhD student, to help arrange interviews and to accompany us to women's homes in Dalit colonies near Kottayam. Easing us into these conversations with grace, Jestin's expertise in Dalit Christian history was also critical to this project. Nazareth University students Haley Saba and Paige Serpe-Miller traveled with me twice to Kerala, bringing light and insight to our meetings and beyond and, back in Rochester, helped with interview transcriptions. Our shared experiences have been and will continue to be a tie that binds us.

The vital role that the Rochester Sisters of St. Joseph played in creating this book was their own excellent idea. The day after I gave a presentation on this project at their Motherhouse, I received a strong suggestion, spearheaded by Sr. Kay Heverin, that I interview them, as well. Director of resident services, Martha Mortensen, and my Nazareth colleague, Sr. Susan Nowak, helped break the ice by identifying sisters willing and able to meet with me.

I thank Nazareth University's Rose Marie Beston Chair for International Studies and the Kilian J. and Caroline F. Schmitt Chair for making this book possible. Between the two, I was afforded multiple trips to Iceland and India as well as a lightened teaching load that freed up the time I needed to organize my findings and to write.

I thank my Nazareth colleagues Christine Bochen, Thom Donlin-Smith, Bishal Karna, Susan Nowak, Rochelle Ruffer, and David Steitz for reading and helping me think through the book's framework. Beyond Nazareth, I am grateful to Ann Gold, Amanda Greenbaum, Ruben Habito, Patty Ingham, Alice Keefe, Sarah Lamb, Robert Orsi, Brian Pennington, Angela Rudert, and Luke Whitmore for supporting this project in various ways. Friends and family members Kathy Bannon, Jane Bleeg, Marsha Boelio, Kip Hargrave, Julie Hladky, Alyson Wood Illich, Sue Kochan, Ellen Nakhnikian, Stephen Remington, and Amy Rosa also thoughtfully read and responded to chapter drafts. My thanks also to anonymous readers at Rutgers University Press for their suggestions and to those at RUP who have ushered this book into existence: Emma-Li Downer, Elizabeth Graber, Kimberly Guinta, Benjamin Horner Karah Naseem, Vincent Nordhaus, Kiely Schuck, and Nicole Solano. Thanks also to Brian Ostrander from Westchester Publishing Services and copyeditor Joseph Dahm.

My sons, Jack and Sam Dempsey Garigliano, and their partners, Lilly Campbell and Libby Rosa, have regularly joined my ponderings over women's stories, thematic patterns, and book titles over the years. During a family trip to Kerala, Lilly and Libby came along for an interview. My husband, Nick Garigliano, who read and commented on drafts of every chapter, astounded me as he always does with his untiring support of my ethnographical work and writing.

One of the hardest parts of writing this book has been facing the fact that the gems I've collected across the globe over the years are enough to fill three books. My hope is that, for all who honored me with their stories, the process of reflection had value in itself, that our conversations gave them as much joy as they gave me, that they felt heard. Whether or not their accounts appear here, in ink, all have been instrumental to the shaping of this book.

This book's greatest champion from the start—also my greatest champion from the start—was my mother, Frances Dempsey. Although she never got to hold the finished product in her hands, she was thrilled to learn, during the final week of her life, that it was underway, under contract with Rutgers. If she were alive today, I would still have dedicated the book to her. Now I dedicate the book to her memory, to her indomitable spirit that I miss deeply and that lives on in countless ways.

Notes

Introduction

1. For other ethnographers with similar observations, see Lamb, *White Saris and Sweet Mangoes*, 23, and Kavedžija, "Attitude of Gratitude," 68.
2. Baars, *Aging and the Art of Living*, 237.
3. For a review of studies that support the idea that people become more spiritual as they age, see Moberg, *Aging and Spirituality*. For other work linking older age with spirituality, see Harris, "Growing while Going"; Ramsey and Bliezner, *Spiritual Resiliency and Aging*; David, "Aging, Religion, and Spirituality"; Cruikshank, *Learning to Be Old*; and Atchley, "Spirituality, Meaning, and the Experience of Aging."
4. Jackson, *Palm at the End of the Mind*, 233.
5. In his cross-cultural study of college students, Bodner concludes that "ageism has become a universal reality." "On the Origins of Ageism," 1004.
6. Baars, *Aging and the Art of Living*, 5.
7. Le Guin, *No Time to Spare*.
8. Lamb, *Successful Aging as a Contemporary Obsession*, n.p. See also Kavedžija and Lamb, "'Ends of Life,'" 111.
9. Cole and Winkler, *Oxford Book of Aging*, 7.
10. Morganroth Gullette, *Ending Ageism*, xvii, 1.
11. Nelson, "Ageism." See also Applewhite, *This Chair Rocks*, 17–18.
12. Lamb, "Introduction," in *Successful Aging as a Contemporary Obsession*, n.p.
13. Leavy, "Last of Life," 708, quoted in Kavedžija, "Introduction," 6.
14. Kavedžija and Lamb, "'Ends of Life,'" 112.
15. Thank you to Sue Kochan for alerting me to how the Four Thoughts fits this context.
16. In a presidential address at an American Academy of Religion Conference, Anne Taves argued that the study of religion, at its heart, deals in what matters most to people. See Taves, "2010 Presidential Address," 289–290.

17 A term often cited in the literature is "gerotranscendence," coined by Lars Tornstam, which equates older age with spiritual prowess. See *Gerotranscendence*, 40–41, 46–47. Critics of gerotranscendence worry that by posing "enlightened maturity" as a developmental goal, older people who still grieve losses deeply or don't feel a cosmic connection with the universe might feel they are not aging well. See McFadden and Ramsey, "Encountering the Numinous," 175.
18 Ortegren, *Middle Class Dharma*, 2–3.
19 Orsi, *History and Presence*, 3. See also Orsi, *Between Heaven and Earth*, 175–176, 187–188. As phrased by Fessenden, sanitized spirituality has become good religion's "most recent installment, the evanescence of Protestantism beyond Protestantism, the disappearance of religion into everyday life." "Problem of the Postsecular," 154–155, 165.
20 Braidotti, "In Spite of the Times," 6, 11–12.
21 Cruikshank, *Learning to Be Old*, 36.
22 From Le Guin's 1986 Bryn Mawr commencement speech, first published in Le Guin, *Dancing at the Edge of the World*, 147–160.

Chapter 1 Crossing Frontiers in the San Francisco Bay Area

1 Applewhite describes a preference for "olders" rather than elderly because it reflects a continuum, not simply an old/young divide. *This Chair Rocks*, 11, 49–51. Moon suggests "old at heart" rather than "young at heart." She reasons, "Wouldn't you like to be loved by people whose hearts have been practicing loving for a long time?" *This Is Getting Old*, xi.
2 For a discussion of ageism's impact in the United States compared with other countries and based on our naturalized idea of an "ageless self," see Lamb, "Debate," 107–110.

Chapter 2 The Forces of Nature in Northern Iceland

1 The Law of Jante was first identified by Aksel Sandemose in his 1933 satirical novel *A Fugitive Crosses His Tracks*.
2 Despite Icelanders' disinterest in organized religion, spirit practices have flourished. Yet true to form, spirit traditions never institutionalized in Iceland as they have elsewhere. See Dempsey, *Bridges between Worlds*, 30–41.

Chapter 3 Sacred Relations in South India

1 For discussions of how Hindu women serve as brokers of culture and religion in India and in the diaspora, see Kurien, *Place at the Multicultural Table*, 138; Prashad, *Karma of Brown Folk*, 130.
2 For an overview of how these theories evolved and have been fine-tuned over time, see Karl Smith, "From Dividual and Individual Selves to Porous Subjects," 50–64.
3 Kerala's Syrian Christians are currently split into a variety of denominations that include Catholic, Orthodox, and Protestant branches. See Stephen Neill's *History of Christianity in India* for an extensive overview.
4 See Thomas, *Privileged Minorities*, for a discussion of the interplay between religion and caste privilege as it pertains to women in Kerala. See especially pages 43–46 for a discussion of how domestic confinement for Syrian Christian and upper-caste Hindu women was a sign of social status.

5 For a description of how religious affiliation has little bearing on those who visit healing shrines in Kerala, see Dempsey, "Lessons in Miracles from Kerala."
6 Sectarian delineations in other parts of India are typically aligned with Shaiva, Vaishnava, and Shakta traditions, related to the deities Shiva, Vishnu, and the Great Goddess, respectively.
7 Traditional dress for Nair Hindu and Syrian Christian women was virtually identical except for the skirt in which the Nair *mundu* lacked the fan tail of the Syrian Christian *thuni*. For a discussion of how women's clothing in Kerala marked religious and communal belonging and privilege, see Thomas, *Privileged Minorities*, 35–66.
8 In Kerala, the abolition of slavery happened in stages: 1843 in British Malabar and 1855 in Travancore. As Mohan describes it, slaves in Kerala, property of upper-caste Hindus, Syrian Christians, and European planters and merchants, "endured the most oppressive conditions of existence, possibly unparalleled in any other part of India." "Caste Slavery and Structural Violence in Kerala," 31.
9 The song is from a 1972 Malayalam film, *Achanum Bappayum*. Jesudas, the vocalist, won a national film award for the best male playback singer.

Chapter 4 On Their Own Terms

1 By contrast, Corwin, who spent time with elderly Franciscan sisters at a Midwestern convent, describes these women as following aunts and uncles, older cousins and siblings, into the religious life. "Growing Old with God," 100.

Chapter 5 Where Does It Hurt?

1 Chittister, "Word from Joan," n.p.
2 Orsi, *Between Heaven and Earth*, 21, 33–35.
3 For a discussion of Dalit Christians in Tamil Nadu who, by contrast, cast their suffering as redemptive, see Roberts, *To Be Cared For*.
4 Soelle, *Suffering*, 93.
5 Boff, *Von der Würde der Erde*, 141, translated and quoted in Soelle, *Silent Cry*, 294.
6 Mayawati is also president of the Bahujan Samaj Party, which works for the rights of Dalits and other marginalized classes in India. Ayyankali, from the late nineteenth and early twentieth century, lives on through Cheramar Sangam, an organization that promotes Dalit rights in Kerala.
7 For a study of how Church Missionary Society (CMS) and London Missionary Society (LMS) members transformed the self-perceptions and material realities of Dalits in Kerala, see Mohan, *Modernity of Slavery*.
8 Thomas, *Privileged Minorities*, 37–46. See also Mohan, "Women and Religiosity."
9 Prejean, *River of Fire*, 47, 42. See also Corwin, *Embracing Age*, 148–152.
10 During the first half of the twentieth century, women entered convents in droves in order to run Catholic schools, hospitals, and orphanages that served the needs of Catholic immigrants at the time. Within Catholicism's self-contained sphere, the sisterhood also gave women status. When Vatican II opened the world to Catholics and did away with teachings of eternal damnation, many who had entered the convent felt free to leave. See Prejean, *River of Fire*, 123–124.
11 Médaille's theology draws from Ignatian spirituality, from scripture, and from his own mystical experiences.
12 Safi, *Radical Love*, 63.

Chapter 6 Critical Junctures

1. Kleinman, *What Really Matters*, 13–14.
2. Jackson, *Palm at the End of the Mind*, 37, 62, 102.
3. Soelle, *Suffering*, 124.
4. Solnit, "Foreword to Third Edition," in *Hope in the Dark*, xxiv–xxv.
5. Sneed and Whitbourne, "Models of the Aging Self," 375, 386. Kavedžija refers to this propensity as an "attitude of gratitude" based on her interactions with older adults in Japan. This reframing of hardship is also related to Erik Erikson's proposed eighth and final psychosocial life stage that helps promote late-life flourishing. "Attitude of Gratitude," 59, 67–68.
6. See Ersner-Hershfield et al., "Poignancy"; Reed and Carstensen, "Theory behind the Age-Related Positivity Effect"; and Cain, *Bittersweet*, 186–199.
7. According to Carstensen's socioemotional selectivity theory, people who perceive their time on earth to be limited tend to approach life more positively. Sneed and Whitbourne, "Models of the Aging Self," 379–380. Freya Dittmann-Kohli notes that "in the face of finitude and death, most elderly persons can maintain a positive attitude toward self and life" due to a "freedom from social norms and from constant striving to be more and more successful." "Temporal References," 115.
8. See Chopik, Weidman, and Purol, "Grateful Expectations." For more general studies of happiness in later life, see Blanchflower and Oswald, "Is Well-Being U-Shaped over the Life Cycle?," 1733–1749, and Yang, "Social Inequalities in Happiness."
9. The most commonly expressed reason for gratitude was for life's goodness. A close second was for family members, followed by positive mindsets, divine blessings, the beauty of nature, community, and health. While these were fairly equally represented across contexts, the SSJs were disproportionately thankful for life opportunities and women in Kerala for supportive husbands.
10. Gay, *Book of Delights*, 44.
11. Smith, "Joy."
12. See Lawrence, *Simply Imperfect*, 7–9.
13. Haidt argues that people need setbacks to reach the highest levels of personal development. He also notes how adversity makes for a good story that, in turn, helps to build coherence and makes sense of troubles in retrospect. *Happiness Hypothesis*, 144, 147–148.

Chapter 7 Lost and Found

1. Translator Brunnhölzl describes *The Heart Sutra* as teaching "emptiness through the epitome of compassion." *Heart Attack Sutra*, 8.
2. Chödrön, *When Things Fall Apart*, 87.
3. See Atchley, "Spirituality, Meaning, and the Experience of Aging"; Cruikshank. *Learning to Be Old*; David, "Aging, Religion, and Spirituality"; Harris, "Growing while Going"; Moberg, *Aging and Spirituality*; and Ramsey and Bliezner, *Spiritual Resiliency and Aging*.
4. Chödrön, *When Things Fall Apart*, 41–42.
5. Shannon, *Cloud of Witnesses*, 18; de Chardin, *Divine Milieu*, 89–90.
6. Chödrön, *When Things Fall Apart*, 8–9.
7. Kleinman, *What Really Matters*, 9.

8   Roberts, *To Be Cared For*, 227.
9   Stark argues against Marx's stance that religion is the opiate of the masses by noting how, across cultures and religions, asceticism is typically an upper-class pursuit. "Upper Class Asceticism."
10 Weinstein and Bell, *Saints and Society*, 229. For more on how silent suffering, categorized as "fortitude in illness," is the most common path to sainthood for women to date, see Dempsey, *Kerala Christian Sainthood*, 123–137.
11 Chacko, *Sister Alphonsa*, 62.
12 Teresa, *Come Be My Light*, 450–451.
13 See Corwin for an overview of how the Catholic Church has viewed pain as a path to holiness. *Embracing Age*, 118–122, 124–130.
14 See Dempsey, "Religioning of Anthropology," 198–199, for a discussion of this dynamic.
15 Bregman, *Humankind*, 17–20.
16 Chödrön, *When Things Fall Apart*, 87, 91.
17 Solnit, *Hope in the Dark*, 4. See also 22–23, 138.
18 Rohr, *Falling Upward*, 115–116.
19 Kavedžija refers to gratitude in later life as a "temporal reorientation of hope." While normally future-oriented, this "quiet hope" engages the past such that the present, amid its challenges, is inhabited "in a resolutely hopeful way. "Attitude of Gratitude," 66, 68.
20 Chittister, *Gift of Years*, 43.
21 Jung, *Memories, Dreams, Reflections*, 326.

Chapter 8   Death and Nature

1   I borrow from William James, who defines "the more" as encompassing a range of features, from religiously sanctioned unearthly beings to "stream[s] of ideal tendency embedded in the eternal structure of the world." *Varieties of Religious Experience*, 500.
2   See Rohr, *Falling Upward*, xxiii, xxix, 138–139, 146. See also Cole's commentary on Erikson's *Insight and Responsibility*, where he refers to late life as a "return to wonder." Cole and Winkler, *Oxford Book of Aging*, 43–44.
3   Jackson describes the basic function of religion as creating well-being through relationships with the dead, the natural environment, and divine presence—realms that exist "at the limits of what can be thought or said." The role of formal religion, he submits, is often to reduce, contain, and tame these unfathomable realms. *Palm at the End of the Mind*, 70, 5–8.
4   My experience differs from that of Sarah Lamb, who found that older women in India would bring up, unsolicited, their readiness to die, whereas her U.S. interlocutors tended not to raise the subject on their own. When Lamb did raise the subject, it was often dismissed rather than pursued. Kavedžija and Lamb, "'Ends of Life,'" 113–114.
5   This was corroborated by all but one of the ninety-one women I interviewed. See also Bodner, "On the Origins of Ageism," 1008–1009, for how fear of death diminishes with advancing age.
6   In interviews with self-identified atheists, Baggett notes their comfort with not knowing, a phenomenon he contends to be on the rise. His interlocutors often

218 • Notes to Pages 141–176

derided New Atheists such as Sam Harris, Richard Dawkins, and Christopher Hutchings as being "too all-knowing." *Varieties of Non-Religious Experience*, 173.
7   The title of *Gullnahliðið* translates to "the golden gates of heaven."
8   For studies that show how nonreligious Icelanders are more likely to believe in the afterlife when compared to their Nordic neighbors, see Haraldsson, "Psychic Experiences," 76–90.
9   Remen, *Kitchen Table Wisdom*, 293.
10 Wonder, though closely related to awe, more fully encompasses women's reflections on death and nature in that wonder lends itself to joy while awe is more closely connected to fear. See Burton, *Heaven and Hell*, 200, and Fuller, "Wonder and the Religious Sensibility," 380.
11 Fuentes likewise considers today's scientism as a form of fundamentalism. *Why We Believe*, 198–199.
12 Sideris, *Consecrating Science*, 172. Nussbaum similarly posits that wonder "redraws our world of concern, establishing true mutuality with a wider sphere of life." *Upheavals of Thought*, 55, quoted in Fuller, "Wonder and the Religious Sensibility," 384.
13 Rohr, "Utterly Humbled by Mystery," emphasis original. See also Baggett, *Varieties of Non-Religious Experience*, 169–170.
14 Heschel, *God in Search of Man*, 46–47.

Chapter 9   Unearthly Entities

1   Women's leadership in these contexts also departs from the ideal of female domesticity that British CSI missionaries tried to promote. Mohan, "Women and Religiosity."
2   As mentioned in chapter 1, Jan in California described experiences that, like those of Grace, included automatic writing along with other uncanny abilities.
3   These carry resemblances to the gifts of the Holy Spirit described in Corinthians as well as abilities known as *siddhis* built through yogic practices. See Dempsey, *Bringing the Sacred Down to Earth*, 109–142.
4   See Dempsey, *Bridges between Worlds*, 96–98.
5   See Orsi, *History and Presence*.
6   Dempsey, *Kerala Christian Sainthood*, 102–103.
7   Chapters on sacred dealmaking in Raj and Harman's *Dealing with Deities* cover a variety of Hindu traditions as well as Catholic Christianity, Islam, Sikhism, Buddhism, and Jainism.
8   For a fuller discussion of how U.S. angels are temperamentally different from South Asian saints, see Dempsey, *Kerala Christian Sainthood*, 158–159.
9   Schneider, "Spirits and the Spirit of Capitalism," 24–25, 32.
10 Orsi, *History and Presence*, 3.
11 Orsi, *History and Presence*, 29.
12 The Icelandic Church's efforts to squash spirit work have lightened up since the 1990s. Somewhat ironically, the only denomination still resolutely opposed to *andleg mál* today is Iceland's small Pentecostal community. Dempsey, *Bridges between Worlds*, 58–65.
13 This is a common refrain among healers as well as trance practitioners in Akureyri who insist that key to their success is getting out of the way. Dempsey, *Bridges between Worlds*, 144–148.

Chapter 10 Frameless Presence

1. Bigelow, *David Park*.
2. This is my rewording of William James's oft-cited mystical components that he lists as transient, passive, noetic, and ineffable. *Varieties of Religious Experience*, 371–372.
3. Regarding the vivid recall of these long-ago experience, Boyer argues that while life episodes are not necessarily recalled accurately, recollections of emotions are often "remarkably accurate" and can be relived. "What Are Memories For?," 20.
4. Soelle, *Silent Cry*, 11, 12, 15. Teresa of Ávila similarly contends that a sign of a genuine mystical experience is that it holds tight in one's memory. *Life of Teresa of Ávila*, 176.
5. Wildman, *Effing the Ineffable*, 176.
6. Isaiah 43:18–19.
7. See Elkins, *Pictures and Tears*, for discussions of weeping in front of art and on vulnerability and art.
8. Oliver, *Long Life*, 33–34.
9. James, *Varieties of Religious Experience*, 371.
10. Burton describes a sense of homecoming as essential to wonder, "returning us to the world that we came from and were in danger of losing." *Heaven and Hell*, 202. See also Rohr's description of a universal longing for home that he frames as a desire for "(re)union with God/Holy Spirit or with our True Self." *Falling Upward*, 91–95.
11. Soelle, *Silent Cry*, 21, 293.

Conclusion

1. Martens, Goldenberg, and Greenberg, "Terror Management Perspective on Ageism," 224, 226–228.
2. See Lamb's argument regarding "how deeply stigmatizing and terrifying it is to be 'old' in U.S. society and culture" when compared with other locations. "Debate," 108.
3. Goodley, *Dis/Ability Studies*, 115; Reynolds and Landre, "Ableism and Ageism," 118, 128.
4. In some contexts, such critical responses are referred to as countercultural gerontology, an umbrella term for humanistic gerontology, critical gerontology, and feminist gerontology. Cruikshank, *Learning to Be Old*, 161–184.
5. Baars et al., "Introduction," 3–4. See also Cruikshank, *Learning to Be Old*, 2–3, 60.
6. While critical gerontologists often cite ableism and disability studies to help build their case, the reverse seems less common.
7. Goodley, *Disability and Other Human Questions*, 12–13; Taylor, "Interdependent Animals," 146.
8. Pimentel and Monteleone, "Privileged Bodymind," 69–70, 78; Goodley, *Dis/Ability Studies*, 26.
9. Nelson, "Ageism." Tornstam traces ageism further back, to a "hidden contempt for weakness" held by Western, middle-class, middle-life society since the Reformation, characterized "by an overwhelmingly strong performance orientation." Tornstam, *Gerotranscendence*, 12–13.
10. We see this especially in China and Korea, where Confucian values that assign respect to elders are being replaced by a view of older people as potential burdens. North, "Modern Attitudes toward Older Adults," 1016. See also Bodner, "Cross-Cultural Differences in Ageism."

11 Cruikshank, *Learning to Be Old*, 2–3; Gibbons, "Compulsory Youthfulness," 7–10, 12; King and Calasanti, "Empowering the Old," 139, 144–145.
12 As Lorde describes it, the norm is "white, thin, male, young, heterosexual, Christian, and financially secure." "Age, Race, Class and Sex."
13 Pimentel and Monteleone, "Privileged Bodymind," 69.
14 Goodley, *Dis/Ability Studies*, xiii.
15 Applewhite, "Possibilities Even Where Our Darkest Fears Reside." See also Applewhite, *This Chair Rocks*, 9, 51–52, 54–55.
16 Taylor, "Interdependent Animals," 145–146. As Goodley words it, dependency is a part of "humanity and not human aberration." *Disability and Other Human Questions*, 37, 66–69.
17 Baars goes on to note that when we exclude the aged, the ill, and the disabled from the dignity of "normal" life, we put undue pressure on the young and healthy who "must try to keep up with these idols." "Philosophy of Aging, Time, and Finitude," 115.
18 Soelle, *Suffering*, 19, 20, 36, 37. Cain traces an "enforced positivity" particular to American culture to the New Thought movement at the turn of the twentieth century, which mostly applied to the pursuit of wealth, separating winners from losers. This, Cain argues, has only picked up steam since then. *Bittersweet*, 126–128. See also Ehrenreich's *Bright-Sited*.
19 Soelle, *Suffering*, 128, 131.
20 Soelle, *Silent Cry*, 192.
21 Soelle, *Suffering*, 36.
22 Soelle, *Silent Cry*, 90.
23 Kleinman, "'Everything That Really Matters,'" 332, 335.
24 From a Krista Tippett *On Being* interview, "How We Live with Loss."
25 See, for example, Dawson, "Zen and the Mindfulness Industry"; Huntington, "Triumph of Narcissism"; Nisbett, "Sciences, Publics, Politics"; and Purser, *McMindfulness*. In her overview of these perspectives, Wylie reminds us that Buddhism, like any religion, has long been used for less-than-spiritual ends such as worldly gain. "Mindfulness Explosion."
26 Soelle, *Silent Cry*, 90–92, 108, 110, 192.
27 Crum, "Ram Dass Interview."
28 Dass, *Polishing the Mirror*, 79.
29 Robert Orsi describes something similar in reference to the "real presence" of the gods who fly under the radar of modern religious sensibilities. Whereas real presence is left in the hands of the beholder, legitimate, legible practices remain "vulnerable to the schemes and demands of various officialdoms." *History and Presence*, 250.
30 Holstein, *Women in Late Life*, 61.
31 Myerhoff, "Experience at the Threshold," 223–224. Dittmann-Kohli also notes that the satisfaction one often finds in older age is likely a result of "freedom from social norms and from constant striving to be more and more successful." "Temporal References," 115.
32 Myerhoff, "Experience at the Threshold," 223–224.
33 Lorde, "Age, Race, Class and Sex."
34 Gibbons, "Compulsory Youthfulness," 5.
35 Jacobs, "Beyond Social Vulnerability," 57–59.

36 Goodley refers to "disability culture" as one to which we all belong in different ways and at different times, "a sense of shared and open-ended identity rooted in disability experience." *Dis/Ability Studies*, 134–135.
37 Goodley, *Dis/Ability Studies*, 49. Written from the perspective of racialization, Carter's *Anarchy of Black Religion* also reflects on the importance of recognizing the invariabilities of human entanglement.
38 Soelle, *Silent Cry*, 29, 92, 108.
39 Jung, "Retrospect," from *Memories, Dreams, Reflections*, quoted in Cole and Winkler, *Oxford Book of Aging*, 327–328.
40 Chittister, *Gift of Years*, 77.

Bibliography

Applewhite, Ashton. "The Possibilities Even Where Our Darkest Fears Reside." Silver Century Foundation, March 2021. https://www.silvercentury.org/2021/03/the-possibilities-even-where-our-darkest-fears-reside/.
———. *This Chair Rocks: A Manifesto against Ageism*. New York: Celedon Books, 2019.
Atchley, Robert. "Spirituality, Meaning, and the Experience of Aging." *Generations* 32, no. 2 (2001): 12–16.
Baars, Jan. *Aging and the Art of Living*. Baltimore: Johns Hopkins University Press, 2012.
———. "Aging: Learning to Live a Finite Life." *Gerontologist* 57, no. 5 (2017): 969–976.
———. "Philosophy of Aging, Time, and Finitude." In *A Guide to Humanistic Studies in Aging*, edited by Thomas Cole, Ruth Ray, and Robert Kastenbaum, 105–120. Baltimore: Johns Hopkins University Press, 2010.
Baars, Jan, Dale Dannefer, Chris Phillipson, and Alan Walker. "Introduction: Critical Perspectives in Social Gerontology." In *Aging, Globalization, and Inequality: The New Critical Gerontology*, edited by Jan Baars, Dale Dannefer, Chris Phillipson, and Alan Walker, 1–14. Amityville, NY: Baywood, 2006.
Baggett, Jerome. *Varieties of Non-Religious Experience: Atheism in American Culture*. New York: New York University Press, 2019.
Bakhtin, Mikhail. *Rabalais and His World*. Translated by Helen Iswolsky. Cambridge, MA: MIT Press, 1968.
Bigelow, Helen Park. *David Park, Painter: Nothing Held Back*. Berkeley, CA: Counterpoint, 2009.
Blanchflower, David, and Andrew Oswald. "Is Well-Being U-Shaped over the Life Cycle?" *Social Science & Medicine* 66, no. 8 (2008): 1733–1749.
Bodner, Ehud. "Cross-Cultural Differences in Ageism." In *Ageism: Stereotyping and Prejudice against Older Persons*, 2nd ed., edited by Todd Nelson, 291–318. Cambridge, MA: MIT Press, 2002.
———. "On the Origins of Ageism among Older and Younger Adults." *International Psychogeriatrics* 21, no. 6 (2009): 1003–1014.
Boff, Leonardo. *Von der Würde der Erde*. Düsseldorf: Patmos Verlag, 1994.

Boyer, Pascal. "What Are Memories For?" In *Memory in Mind and Culture*, edited by Pascal Boyer and James Wersch, 3–28. Cambridge: Cambridge University Press, 2009.

Braidotti, Rosi. "In Spite of the Times: The Postsecular Turn in Feminism." *Theory, Culture, and Society* 25, no. 6 (2008): 1–23.

Bregman, Rutger. *Humankind: A Hopeful History*. Boston: Little, Brown, 2021.

Brunnhölzl, Karl. *The Heart Attack Sutra: A New Commentary on the Heart Sutra*. Boulder, CO: Snow Lion, 2012.

Burton, Neel. *Heaven and Hell: The Psychology of Emotions*. Oxford: Acheron Press, 2015.

Cain, Susan. *Bittersweet: How Sorrow and Longing Make Us Whole*. New York: Crown, 2023.

Carter, J. Kameron. *The Anarchy of Black Religion: A Mystic Song*. Durham, NC: Duke University Press, 2023.

Chacko, Chevalier C. K. *Sister Alphonsa*. 1949. Ernakulam: Saint Francis De Sales Press, 1990.

Chittister, Joan. *The Gift of Years: Growing Older Gracefully*. Chanbersburg, PA: Blue Ridge Publishing, 2008.

———. "Word from Joan: Where Is God?" Benetvision. http://www.joanchittister.org/word-from-joan/where-god.

Chödrön, Pema. *When Things Fall Apart: Heart Advice for Difficult Times*. Boulder, CO: Shambhala, 2016.

Chopik, William, Rebekka Weidman, and Mariah Purol. "Grateful Expectations: Cultural Differences in the Curvilinear Association between Age and Gratitude." *Journal of Social and Personal Relationships* 39, no. 10 (2022): 3001–3014.

Cole, Thomas, and Mary Winkler, eds. *The Oxford Book of Aging*. New York: Oxford University Press, 1994.

Corwin, Anna. "Changing God, Changing Bodies: The Impact of New Prayer Practices on Elderly Catholic Nuns' Embodied Experiences." *Ethos* 40, no. 4 (2012): 390–410.

———. *Embracing Age: How Catholic Nuns Became Models of Aging Well*. New Brunswick, NJ: Rutgers University Press, 2021.

———. "Growing Old with God: An Alternative Vision of Successful Aging among Catholic Nuns." In *Successful Aging as a Contemporary Obsession: Global Perspectives*, edited by Sarah Lamb, 98–111. New Brunswick, NJ: Rutgers University Press, 2017.

Cruikshank, Margaret. *Learning to Be Old: Gender, Culture, and Aging*. Lanham, MD: Rowman & Littlefield, 2013.

Crum, David. "The Ram Dass Interview: Smiling as He Teaches about *Polishing the Mirror*." *Reading the Spirit*, July 14, 2013. https://readthespirit.com/explore/the-ram-dass-interview-on-polishing-the-mirror-you-cant-help-but-smile-hes-still-teaching-us/.

Dass, Ram. *Polishing the Mirror: How to Live from Your Spiritual Heart*. Boulder, CO: Sounds True, 2013.

David, Gerson. "Aging, Religion, and Spirituality: Advancing Meaning in Later Life." *Social Thought* 20, no. 3–4 (2001): 129–140.

Dawson, Geoff. "Zen and the Mindfulness Industry." *Humanist Psychologist* 49, no. 1 (2021): 133–146.

de Chardin, Teilhard. *The Divine Milieu*. London: William Collins and Sons, 1960.

Dempsey, Corinne. *Bridges between Worlds: Spirits and Spirit Work in Northern Iceland*. New York: Oxford University Press, 2018.

———. *Bringing the Sacred Down to Earth: Adventures in Comparative Religion*. New York: Oxford University Press, 2012.

———. *Kerala Christian Sainthood: Collisions of Cultures and Worldviews in South India.* New York: Oxford University Press, 2001.

———. "Lessons in Miracles from Kerala, South India: Stories of Three 'Christian' Saints." *History of Religions* 39, no. 2 (1999): 150–176.

———. "The Religioning of Anthropology: New Directions for the Ethnographer-Pilgrim." *Culture and Religion* 1, no. 2 (2000): 189–210.

Dittmann-Kohli, Freya. "Temporal References in the Construction of Self-Identity: A Life-Span Approach." In *Aging and Time: Multidisciplinary Perspectives*, edited by Jan Baars and Henk Visser, 83–119. Amityville, NY: Baywood, 2007.

Ehrenreich, Barbara. *Bright-Sited: How the Relentless Promotion of Positive Thinking Has Undermined America.* New York: Metropolitan Books, 2009.

Elkins, James. *Pictures and Tears: A History of People Who Have Cried in Front of Paintings.* New York: Routledge, 2004.

Erikson, Erik. *Insight and Responsibility: Lectures on the Ethical Implications of Psychoanalytic Insight.* New York: Norton, 1964.

Ersner-Hershfield, Hal, Joseph Mikels, Sarah Sullivan, and Laura Carstensen. "Poignancy: Mixed Emotional Experience in the Face of Meaningful Endings." *Journal of Personal Social Psychology* 94, no. 1 (2008): 158–167.

Fessenden, Tracy. "The Problem of the Postsecular." *American Literary History* 26, no. 1 (2014): 154–167.

Fuentes, Agustín. *Why We Believe: Evolution and the Human Way of Being.* New Haven, CT: Yale University Press, 2019.

Fuller, Robert. "Wonder and the Religious Sensibility: A Study in Religion and Emotion." *Journal of Religion* 86, no. 3 (2006): 364–384.

Gay, Ross. *Book of Delights: Essays.* Chapel Hill, NC: Algonquin Books, 2019.

———. *Inciting Joy: Essays.* Chapel Hill, NC: Algonquin Books, 2022.

Gibbons, Hailee. "Compulsory Youthfulness: Intersections of Ableism and Ageism in 'Successful Aging' Discourses." *Review of Disability Studies* 12, no. 2–3 (2016): 1–19.

Goodley, Dan. *Disability and Other Human Questions.* Bingley, UK: Emerald, 2021.

———. *Dis/Ability Studies: Theorizing Disablism and Ableism.* New York: Routledge, 2014.

Haidt, Jonathan. *The Happiness Hypothesis: Finding Modern Truth in Ancient Wisdom.* New York: Basic Books, 2006.

Haraldsson, Erlendur. "Psychic Experiences a Third of a Century Apart: Two Representative Surveys in Iceland with an International Comparison." *Journal of Society for Psychical Research* 75, no. 903 (2011): 76–90.

Harris, Helen. "Growing while Going: Spiritual Formation at the End of Life." In *Methods in Religion, Spirituality and Aging*, edited by James W. Ellor, 218–236. New York: Routledge, 2009.

Heschel, Abraham. *God in Search of Man: A Philosophy of Judaism.* New York: Farrar, Straus and Giroux, 1976.

Holstein, Martha. *Women in Late Life: Critical Perspectives on Gender and Age.* Lanham, MD: Rowman & Littlefield, 2015.

Huntington, C. W., Jr. "The Triumph of Narcissism: Theravada Buddhist Meditation in the Marketplace." *Journal of the American Academy of Religion* 83, no. 3 (2015): 624–648.

Jackson, Michael. *The Palm at the End of the Mind: Relatedness, Religiosity, and the Real.* Durham, NC: Duke University Press, 2009.

Jacobs, Fayola. "Beyond Social Vulnerability: COVID 19 as a Disaster of Racial Capitalism." *Sociologica* 15, no. 1 (2021): 55–65.

James, William. *Varieties of Religious Experience: A Study in Human Nature*. 1902. New York: Random House, 1929.

Jones, James. *Living Religion: Embodiment, Theology, and the Possibility of a Spiritual Sense*. New York: Oxford University Press, 2019.

Juergensmeyer, Mark, and Jack Hawley. *Songs of the Saints of India*. New York: Oxford University Press, 2004.

Jung, Carl. *Memories, Dreams, Reflections*. Translated by Clara Winston. New York: Vintage, 1989.

Kavedžija, Iza. "An Attitude of Gratitude: Older Japanese in the Hopeful Present." *Anthropology and Aging* 41, no. 2 (2020): 59–71.

———. "Introduction. The Ends of Life: Time and Meaning in Later Years." *Anthropology and Aging* 41, no. 2 (2020): 1–8.

Kavedžija, Iza, and Sarah Lamb. "'Ends of Life': An Interview with Sarah Lamb." *Anthropology and Aging* 41, no. 2 (2020): 110–125.

King, Neal, and Toni Calasanti. "Empowering the Old: Critical Gerontology and Anti-Aging in a Global Context." In *Aging, Globalization, and Inequality: The New Critical Gerontology*, edited by Jan Baars, Dale Dannefer, Chris Phillipson, and Alan Walker, 139–157. Amityville, NY: Baywood, 2006.

Kleinman, Arthur. "'Everything That Really Matters': Social Suffering, Subjectivity, and the Remaking of Human Experience in a Disordering World." *Harvard Theological Review* 90, no. 3 (1997): 315–335.

———. *What Really Matters: Living a Moral Life amidst Uncertainty and Danger*. New York: Oxford University Press, 2006.

Kreider, Tim. "You Are Going to Die." *Opinionator*, January 20, 2013. https://opinionator.blogs.nytimes.com/2013/01/20/you-are-going-to-die/.

Kurien, Prema. *A Place at the Multicultural Table: The Development of an American Hinduism*. New Brunswick, NJ: Rutgers University Press, 2007.

Lamb, Sarah. "Debate: Who Wants to Have an Aged Self if Aging Is so Bad? Ageless and Aged Selves as Cultural Constructs." *Anthropology and Aging* 44, no. 1 (2023): 107–110.

———, ed. *Successful Aging as a Contemporary Obsession: Global Perspectives*. New Brunswick, NJ: Rutgers University Press, 2017.

———. *White Saris and Sweet Mangoes: Aging, Gender, and Body in North India*. Oakland: University of California Press, 2000.

Lawrence, Robyn Griggs. *Simply Imperfect: Revisiting the Wabi Sabi House*. Gabriola, BC, Canada: New Society, 2011.

Leavy, Stanley. "The Last of Life: Psychological Reflections on Old age and Death." *Psychoanalytic Quarterly* 80, no. 3 (2011): 699–715.

Le Guin, Ursula. *Dancing at the Edge of the World: Thoughts on Words, Women, Places*. New York: Harper & Row, 1989.

———. *No Time to Spare: Thinking about What Matters*. Boston: Mariner Books, 2019.

Leibing, Annette. "Recognizing Older Individuals: An Essay on Critical Gerontology, Robin Hood, and the COVID-19 Crisis." *Anthropology and Aging* 41, no. 2 (2020): 221–229.

Lorde, Audre. "Age, Race, Class and Sex: Women Redefining Difference." Paper delivered at the Copeland Colloquium, Amherst College, April 1980. Reproduced in Sister Outsider Crossing Press, 1984.

Martens, Andy, Jamie Goldenberg, and Jeff Greenberg. "A Terror Management Perspective on Ageism." *Journal of Social Issues* 61, no. 2 (2005): 223–239.
Massumi, Brian. *Parables for the Virtual: Movement, Affect, Sensation*. Durham, NC: Duke University Press, 2002.
McFadden, Susan, and Janet Ramsey. "Encountering the Numinous: Relationality, the Arts, and Religion in Later Life." In *A Guide to Humanistic Studies in Aging: What Does It Mean to Grow Old?*, edited by Thomas Cole, Ruth Ray, and Robert Kastenbaum, 163–181. Baltimore: Johns Hopkins University Press, 2010.
Moberg, David, ed. *Aging and Spirituality: Spiritual Dimensions of Aging Theory, Research, Practice, and Policy*. New York: Routledge, 2009.
Mohan, Sanal. "Caste Slavery and Structural Violence in Kerala." *Marg: A Magazine of the Arts* 68, no. 2 (2016): 30–36.
———. *Modernity of Slavery: Struggles against Caste Inequality in Colonial Kerala*. Delhi: Oxford University Press, 2015.
———. "Women and Religiosity: Dalit Christianity in Kerala." *Economic & Political Weekly* 52, no. 42–43 (2017). https://www.epw.in/journal/2017/42-43/review-issues/women-and-religiosity.html.
Moon, Susan. *This Is Getting Old: Zen Thoughts on Aging with Humor and Dignity*. Boulder, CO: Shambhala, 2010.
Morganroth Gullette, Margaret. *Ending Ageism, or How Not to Shoot Old People*. New Brunswick, NJ: Rutgers University Press, 2017.
Myerhoff, Barbara. "Experience at the Threshold: The Interplay of Aging and Ritual." In *Remembered Lives: The Work of Ritual, Storytelling, and Growing Older*. Ann Arbor: University of Michigan Press, 1992.
Neill, Stephen. *A History of Christianity in India*. Vol. 1, *The Beginnings to AD 1707*. Cambridge: Cambridge University Press, 1984.
———. *A History of Christianity in India*. Vol. 2, *1707–1858*. Cambridge: Cambridge University Press, 1985.
Nelson, Todd D. "Ageism: Prejudice against Our Feared Future Self." *Journal of Social Issues* 61, no. 2 (2005): 207–221.
Nisbett, Mathew. "Sciences, Publics, Politics: Mindfulness Inc." *Issues in Science and Technology* 36, no. 1 (Fall 2019): 33–35.
North, Mike. "Modern Attitudes toward Older Adults in the Aging World: A Cross-Cultural Meta Analysis." *Psychological Bulletin* 141, no. 5 (2015): 993–1021.
Nussbaum, Martha. *Upheavals of Thought: The Intelligence of Emotions*. Cambridge: Cambridge University Press, 2001.
Oliver, Mary. *Long Life: Essays and Other Writings*. Cambridge, MA: Da Capo Press, 2004.
Orsi, Robert. *Between Heaven and Earth: The Religious Worlds People Make and the Scholars Who Study Them*. Princeton, NJ: Princeton University Press, 2006.
———. *History and Presence*. Cambridge, MA: Belknap, 2016.
Ortegren, Jennifer. *Middle Class Dharma: Women, Aspiration and the Making of Contemporary Hinduism*. New York: Oxford University Press, 2023.
Pimentel, Mateo, and Rebecca Monteleone. "A Privileged Bodymind: The Entanglement of Ableism and Capitalism." *International Journal of Economic Development* 12, no. 1 (2019): 63–81.
Prashad, Vijay. *The Karma of Brown Folk*. Minneapolis: University of Minnesota Press, 2000.
Prejean, Helen. *River of Fire: My Spiritual Journey*. New York: Random House, 2019.

Purser, Ronald. *McMindfulness: How Mindfulness Became the New Capitalist Spirituality*. London: Repeater Books, 2019.

Raj, Selva, and William Harman, eds. *Dealing with Deities: The Ritual Vow in South Asia*. Albany: State University of New York Press, 2006.

Ramsey, Janet, and Rosemary Bliezner. *Spiritual Resiliency and Aging: Hope, Relationality, and the Creative Self*. Amityville, NY: Baywood, 2012.

Reed, Andrew, and Laura Carstensen. "The Theory behind the Age-Related Positivity Effect." *Frontiers in Psychology* 3 (September 2012). https://www.frontiersin.org/articles/10.3389/fpsyg.2012.00339/full.

Remen, Rachel Naomi. "Being Old." Zoom lecture, New School at Commonweal, August 4, 2020. https://www.youtube.com/watch?v=2hfHcybsEiA&t=2s.

———. *Kitchen Table Wisdom: Stories That Heal*. New York: Riverhead Books, 1996.

Reynolds, Joel Michael, and Anna Landre. "Ableism and Ageism: Insights from Disability Studies for Aging Studies." In *Critical Humanities and Ageing: Forging Interdisciplinary Dialogues*, edited by Marlene Goldman, Thomas Cole, and Kate De Medeiros, 118–129. New York: Routledge, 2022.

Roberts, Nathaniel. *To Be Cared For: The Power of Conversion and Foreignness of Belonging in an Indian Slum*. Oakland: University of California Press, 2016.

Rohr, Richard. *Falling Upward: A Spirituality for the Two Halves of Life*. San Francisco: Jossey-Bass, 2011.

———. "Utterly Humbled by Mystery." *On Being*, November 6, 2017. https://onbeing.org/blog/richard-rohr-utterly-humbled-by-mystery/.

Safi, Omid. *Radical Love: Teachings from the Islamic Mystical Tradition*. New Haven, CT: Yale University Press, 2018.

Schneider, Jane. "Spirits and the Spirit of Capitalism." In *Religious Orthodoxy and Popular Faith in European Society*, edited by Ellen Badone, 24–54. Princeton, NJ: Princeton University Press, 1990.

Shannon, William. *Cloud of Witnesses: Sisters of St. Joseph of Rochester*. Rochester, NY: Shannon, 2006.

Sideris, Lisa. *Consecrating Science: Wonder, Knowledge, and the Natural World*. Oakland: University of California Press, 2017.

Smith, Karl. "From Dividual and Individual Selves to Porous Subjects." *Australian Journal of Anthropology* 23, no. 1 (2012): 50–64.

Smith, Zadie. "Joy." *New York Review of Books*, January 10, 2013. https://www.nybooks.com/articles/2013/01/10/joy/.

Sneed, Joel, and Susan Krauss Whitbourne. "Models of the Aging Self." *Journal of Social Issues* 61, no. 2 (2005): 375–388.

Soelle, Dorothee. *The Silent Cry: Mysticism and Resistance*. Translated by Barbara and Marin Rumscheidt. Minneapolis, MN: Fortress Press, 2001.

———. *Suffering*. 1975. Reprint, Minneapolis, MN: Fortress Press, 1984.

Solnit, Rebecca. *Hope in the Dark: Untold Histories, Wild Possibilities*. Chicago: Haymarket Books, 2016.

———. *The Mother of All Questions*. Chicago: Haymarket Books, 2017.

Stark, Rodney. "Upper Class Asceticism: Social Origins of Ascetic Movements and Medieval Saints." *Review of Religious Research* 45, no. 1 (September 2003): 5–19.

Taves, Anne. "2010 Presidential Address: 'Religion' in the Humanities and the Humanities in the University." *Journal of the American Academy of Religion* 79, no. 2 (2011): 287–314.

Taylor, Sunaura. "Interdependent Animals: A Feminist Disability Ethic-of-Care." In *Ecofeminism: Feminist Intersections with Other Animals and the Earth*, edited by Carol Adams and Lori Gruen, 141–158. New York: Bloomsbury, 2014.
Teresa, Mother. *Come Be My Light: The Private Writings of the Saint of Calcutta*. Edited by Brian Kolodiejchuk. New York: Doubleday Religion, 1994.
Teresa of Ávila. *The Life of Teresa of Ávila by Herself*. Translated by J. M. Cohen. London: Penguin, 1957.
Thomas, Sonja. *Privileged Minorities: Syrian Christianity, Gender, and Minority Rights in Postcolonial India*. Seattle: University of Washington Press, 2018.
Tippett, Krista, "How We Live with Loss." *On Being Project* interview with Rachel Naomi Remen, August 11, 2005.
Tornstam, Lars. *Gerotranscendence: A Developmental Theory of Positive Aging*. New York: Spring, 2005.
Upton, Charles. *Doorkeeper of the Heart: Versions of Rabi'a*. New York: Pir Press, 2004.
Verbruggen, Christine, Britteny Howell, and Kaylee Simmons. "How We Talk about Aging during a Global Pandemic Matters: On Ageist Othering and Aging 'Others' Talking Back." *Anthropology and Aging* 41, no. 2 (2020): 230–245.
Weinstein, Donald, and Rudolph Bell. *Saints and Society: The Two Worlds of Western Christendom 1000–1700*. Chicago: University of Chicago Press, 1982.
Whyte, David. *Consolations: The Solace, Nourishment, and Underlying Meaning of Everyday Words*. Langley, WA: Many Rivers Press, 2014.
Wildman, Wesley. *Effing the Ineffable: Existential Mumblings at the Limits of Language*. Albany: State University of New York Press, 2018.
Wylie, Mary Sykes. "The Mindfulness Explosion." *Psychotherapy Networker Magazine*, January–February 2015, 19–45.
Yang, Yang. "Social Inequalities in Happiness in the U.S. 1972–2004: An Age-Period-Cohort Analysis." *American Sociological Review* 73, no. 2 (2008): 204–226.

Index

ableism, 199–202, 206, 209n3, 209n6. *See also* disability studies
Abraham and Isaac, 103
adoption, child, 23, 24, 107–108, 132
afterlife: certainty about, 23, 141, 218n8 (chap. 8); rejection of, 77, 141; sense of humor about, 143; uncertainty about, 77, 141–145. *See also* heaven
ageism, 2, 5–6, 24–27, 46, 206, 213nn10–11; and capitalism, 200–201; global spread of, 213n5, 219n10 (concl.); mixed with ableism, 200–202; prevalence in U.S., 214n2 (chap. 1); root causes of, 199, 217n5, 219n1 (concl.), 219n9 (concl.); women as targets of, 9
agency, 5, 7, 111, 176
agricultural work: in Iceland, 33, 107, 149, 188; in Kerala, 108, 111; by prisoners of war, 128. *See also* farm life, Icelandic; rice paddy labor
Akureyri, descriptions of, 3, 29–30, 95
Alabama. *See* Selma, Alabama
Allen, Sr. Marcia, 92–94, 207
alrupam, 174
amazement as virtue, 156, 204
Ambedkar, B. R., 81
ancestral home, 45, 108–109
andleg mál, 35, 167–171; history of, 176, 218n12 (chap. 9); spirit-human relations in, 171. *See also skyggnigáfa*; spirits in ritual settings
angel accounts: from California, 158–159; from Iceland, 160–161; from Kerala, 159–160
angels, characteristic of, 157–158, 176, 218n8 (chap. 9)
anicca, 112–113, 116, 119. *See also* impermanence
animals, appreciation for, 47, 107, 146–147, 149, 150–151. *See also* farm life, Icelandic
anthropocentrism. *See* new cosmology
antiaging industry, 5, 6, 201. *See also* successful aging
apatheia, 202, 206. *See also* nonsuffering, culture of
Applewhite, Ashton, 201, 213n11, 214n1 (chap. 1), 220n15
atheism, 8, 21–24, 40, 217n6
Ayyankali, 81, 215n6 (chap. 5)

Baars, Jan, 1, 2, 5, 202, 219n5 (concl.), 220n17
Baggett, Jerome, 217n6, 218n3
baptism, 23, 171
Baptist Church, 65
Bay Area Figurative Movement, 179
beauty, overwhelmed by, 107, 131, 146, 150, 152, 180, 182, 191
Bible, 18, 19, 33, 34, 37, 38, 48, 167; quotes from, 52–53, 189

blessings: in life, 52, 54, 55, 87, 207, 216n9; from older women, 51, 163, 165, 176–177; from sacred sites and entities, 43, 56–58, 77, 90–91, 174
Bloody Sunday, 86–87
bodhichitta, 116, 119, 131, 133, 134, 197
Bodhisattva of Compassion, 116
bodily experience. *See* frameless presence, experiences of; spirits in ritual settings: as embodied
Bodner, Ehud, 213n5, 217n5, 219n10 (concl.)
Boff, Leonardo, 80–81, 215n5 (chap. 5)
Brahman. *See* caste in Kerala
Braidotti, Rosi, 9, 214n20
Brazil, 59–61, 71, 72, 80–81, 85–86
Bregman, Rutger, 130, 217n15
Buddha, 203
Buddhism, 204, 218n7 (chap. 9), 220n25; concepts applied, 6–7, 112–113, 116, 118, 133, 207; older women as inspired by, 2, 17, 121–122, 142, 196. See also *anicca*; *bodhichitta*; Mahayana Buddhism; Zen Buddhism
Byrne, Patricia, 92–93

Cain, Susan, 216n6 (chap. 6), 220n18
California, 4, 16; as frontier, 15–16, 27; as religiously fluid, 15–16
Canada, 18, 173–174
capitalism, 5, 174, 200–202, 204, 218n9 (chap. 9); and culture of nonsuffering, 202–203. *See also* ageism
Carstensen, Laura, 97, 216n6 (chap. 6)
caste in Kerala: Brahman, 56; Nair, 45, 82, 91, 215n7 (chap. 3); Thiyya, 48; within Christianity, 44–45, 82, 214n4, 215n8 (chap. 3), 215n7 (chap. 5). *See also* Dalits in Kerala; Syrian Christianity
catastrophe, lessons learned from, 96–102
Catholicism, Euro American, 172, 174–175; as immigrant community, 16, 66, 175, 179–180; popular devotion, 66–67, 70, 172–173; pre-Vatican II severity, 78–79, 85, 126–127, 179–180, 189, 191, 217n13. *See also* convent life; ethic of reciprocity; Sisters of St. Joseph
Catholicism in Kerala, 79, 126–127, 167, 189–190, 214n3, 218n7 (chap. 9);

devotional, 50–51, 56–57, 173–174. *See also* Mother Teresa; Saint Alphonsa
certitude, benefits of letting go of, 11, 116, 123, 134, 155–156, 204. *See also* letting go
childhood home, love for, 31–33, 106–109
childhood memories: of death of parent, 38, 45, 52, 54–56, 67, 80, 103, 105; of death of sibling, 55, 69, 98, 104; of love in family, 101–102, 103–106, 132; of neglect, 107–108; of poverty, 31, 34, 40, 51, 52–56, 80, 104, 121; of validation, 104–105, 107–111
childhood religion: practices in, 31, 35, 39, 40, 45–46, 47, 50–51, 56, 62, 65–67, 70; rejection of, 2–3, 15–20, 22–23, 51, 167
China, 182; changing views in, 219n10 (concl.)
Chittister, Joan, 79, 134, 207, 215n1 (chap. 5), 217n20, 221n40
Chödrön, Pema, 116, 121–123, 131, 133
Christianity, Protestant, 51, 173–175, 214n19; and angels, 158–160, 172; as parents of SSJ Sisters, 65–66, 68–69. *See also individual denominations*
Christianity in Kerala, overview of, 44–45, 51, 214n3. *See also* Catholicism in Kerala; Church of South India; Syrian Christianity
Christian Scientism, 186
Church of South India (CSI), 51, 52, 83, 166, 218n1
circle of life, 146, 152–153, 155. *See also* humus
Civil Rights Movement, 86–87. *See also* Lewis, John
colonialist assumptions, 9, 175, 206; inversions of, 83
compulsory ablebodiedness, 206. *See also* mythical norms
compulsory youthfulness, 201, 220n11, 220n34. *See also* antiaging industry; mythical norms
Congregationalist Church, 18, 19
consumerism, 5, 200–202, 204, 207; as opiate, 203, 204. *See also* capitalism
convent entry: and heartbroken parents, 4, 62, 63–67, 69, 103; new names given upon, 62, 68, 72; reasons for, 63, 65, 67, 69, 70, 71, 184–185
convent life: opportunities opened by, 81, 85–87, 89, 92–93, 215n10; strict rule

within, 4, 61–62, 78, 84–86. *See also* school nuns; Vatican II
conversion, religious, 45, 82–83, 96, 166, 167, 189–190
Corwin, Anna, 215n1 (chap. 4), 215n9 (chap. 5), 217n13
countercultural perspectives, 2, 6, 12, 116, 197, 219n4 (concl.). *See also* older age: as countercultural
counterintuitive, 12, 197
COVID-19, 130, 206
critical gerontology, 11, 199–202, 219n4 (concl.)
critical junctures, 96–97
critical theology, 202
Cruikshank, Margaret, 9, 213n3, 216n3 (chap. 7), 219nn4–5 (concl.)
CSI. *See* Church of South India

Dalits in Kerala, 45, 51, 52, 54, 162, 210; discrimination against, 81–84, 163, 251; and history of enslavement, 51, 81, 215n8 (chap. 3), 215n7 (chap. 5); and resistance against discrimination, 81–84, 215n6 (chap. 5). *See also* Church of South India; prayer meetings; rice paddy labor
Dalits in Tamil Nadu, 215n3
Dass, Ram, 205, 220nn27–28
Day of the Spirit, 8
death: comfort with in older age, 79, 138–140, 217n5; as intrinsic to nature, 11, 146, 151–153, 155–156; as normalized in Iceland, 138–139; fear of, 2, 6, 138, 199, 244; as sparking curiosity, 140–145; as taboo topic, 138, 139. *See also* childhood memories; dying process; Saint Joseph
death-denying culture, 5, 6
de Chardin, Teilhard, 123, 216n5 (chap. 7)
despair, 21, 203; as bringing God closer, 80–81, 122–123, 133; as opening new perspectives, 131, 134, 196–197; as triggering mystical experiences, 180, 186–187, 189–190. See also *bodhichitta*
dharma, 6, 7, 214n18. *See also* religion: definitions of
disability studies, 11–12, 199–203, 206. *See also* Goodley, Dan
Dittmann-Kohli, Freya, 216n7 (chap. 6), 220n31

divinity as problem: as judgmental, 76–78, 80, 92, 143, 189, 190; as remote, 18, 22–23, 76, 82, 89–90, 153–154; as source of betrayal, 76–77, 122; as rejected over time, 22–24, 76–77, 154; as transformed over time, 4, 77–78, 82, 189, 190
divinity as resource: as abiding in hardship, 56, 79–81, 97, 122; as enduring presence, 23, 47, 89, 93–94, 122, 160–161, 189–190, 193; experienced in nature, 146–148, 153, 154; as source of blessing, 52–53, 77, 79, 90–92, 173, 174; as source of miracles, 161–163. *See also* faith in divinity; nondualistic theologies
dying process, fear of, 141

earth energies, 99, 146, 153, 187–189, 192
elderly, rejection of term, 24–25
embodiment. *See* spirits in ritual settings: as embodied
enchanted worldviews, 44
enforced positivity, 220n18
epiphany, 23, 96, 97, 153, 190
Erikson, Erik, 216n5 (chap. 6), 217n2
ethic of reciprocity, 58, 175
ethnography. *See* interview process
Evangelical Christianity, 24
Eyjafjörður, 29, 35

faith in divinity: as kept under wraps, 31, 40–42; by letting go, 122–123; as unshakeable, 36–37, 54–55, 67–68, 80–81, 172, 174
faith in goodness. *See* goodness, belief in
farm life, Icelandic, 3, 31–35, 37, 38, 40, 107–108, 149; as demanding, 30, 32–35, 40, 107; *farskóli* (traveling school), 31–32, 34; fond memories of, 31, 34, 107–108, 149; *húslestur* (house service), 33, 34, 40
farskóli. *See* farm life, Icelandic
fathers, memories of: in California, 19, 21, 22, 179; in Iceland, 32, 34, 35, 37, 39, 40, 105, 169–171; in Kerala, 45, 50–53, 80, 100, 101, 103, 107–108, 173; among the SSJs, 62–70, 78, 104, 120
fear of aging, 2, 5–6, 200–201. *See also* ageism: root causes of

feminism, 205, 219n4 (concl.); Western feminist assumptions, 9, 214n20. *See also* colonialist assumptions
finitude, 2, 202, 216n7 (chap. 6)
fishing livelihood, 32, 37, 153. *See also* farm life, Icelandic
flowers, 65, 100, 132, 149, 150, 169; wondrous stories about, 151, 152
Four Thoughts That Turn the Mind to the Dharma, 6, 213n15
frameless presence, descriptions of: as an enduring resource, 180, 182, 188, 190–193, 195–197; as inexplicable, 181–185, 192, 194–195, 197; as kept to oneself, 180, 185, 187, 189, 193–194; as tearful, 182, 184, 185, 189, 190–192
frameless presence, experiences of: as bodily, 191–195; feeling at one with everything, 181, 186, 188, 195, 197; as tapping into *what is*, 180, 181, 186, 191, 192, 194, 195, 197; as transformative, 185–191. *See also* interconnection
frameless presence, qualities of, 11, 180–181
freedom. *See* older women: as free
funerals, 59–61, 70–72. *See also* vigil

Gay, Ross, 112
generational differences: in California, 15, 16, 25–26, 175; in Iceland, 31, 33, 34, 41–42, 139, 209; in Kerala, 45, 47, 51, 83–84, 108–109; among the SSJs, 61–62, 79–80, 84–85, 87, 172
generation gap, 205–206
gerotranscendence, 214n17, 219n9 (concl.)
God. *See* divinity
Goodley, Dan, 200, 206, 219n3 (concl.), 219n8 (concl.), 220n16, 221n36
goodness, belief in: as abiding, 11, 115–116, 127–132; as human essence, 127–130, 132–133; in nature, 130–133; as revealed in letting go, 115–116, 133; viewed differently in Kerala, 130. *See also bodhichitta*; hope; ripple effect
Good Samaritan Hospital, 86–87
gratitude, 37, 41, 100, 122, 124, 194, 196, 150; for blessings, 150, 174, 216n9; as context dependent, 102, 216n9; for life in general, 95, 99, 102, 216n9; and non-entitlement, 99; in older age, 102, 216n5 (chap. 6), 216n8, 217n19; as response to catastrophe, 96, 97, 102, 112
grief, 17, 144, 183
Guillain-Barré, 99
Gullette, Margaret Morganroth, 5, 213n10

happiness in later life, 216n8. *See also* poignancy near life's end
healing: through energy work, 99; Pentecostal, 51, 167–168; through prayer, 17, 90, 163; at sacred sites, 173, 215n5 (chap. 3); with spirits, 167–168, 171, 218n13 (chap. 9); as unsuccessful, 76, 77; through yoga, 17, 20. *See also andleg mál*
Heart Sutra, 116, 216n1 (chap. 7)
heaven, 76–79, 103, 140–144, 158. *See also* afterlife
heiligur (holy), 145, 148, 149
hell, 18, 75, 76, 143
Heschel, Abraham, 137, 156
higher incomprehension, 151, 207
Hindu deities: Great Goddess, 46, 48, 50, 56, 57, 90–91; Krishna, 46–47, 80; Mukhambika, 174; Rama, 46, 82; Shiva, 46, 56, 57, 58. *See also* Kerala: nonsectarian Hinduism in
Hindu nationalism, 58
Holstein, Martha, 205, 220n30
holy objects. *See* images, household; rosary
Holy Spirit, 93, 150, 166, 218n3, 219n10 (chap. 10); in Dalit Christianity, 51, 52, 55, 166–167; gifts of, 167–168
homecoming, 196–197; California frontier as, 20–21, 24; experienced in nature, 131; found in wonder, 219n10 (chap. 10); as universal longing, 219n10 (chap. 10)
hope: in hardship, 96, 145; in older age, 11, 133–134, 217n19; pitfalls of, 121–122, 133; as realistic, 96, 133–134; as sustaining, 122. *See also* goodness, belief in
humility: as aim of novitiate training, 84; forged by nature, 11, 42; as intrinsic to wonder, 155–156, 218n13 (chap. 8); as paradoxical, 92; as requisite for compassion, 206. *See also* humus
humor, 143, 152
humus, 155–156
húslestur. *See* farm life, Icelandic

Icelandic irreligiosity, 30–31, 38–41; as non-churchgoing, 33–35, 37, 41; as tied to landscape, 33, 34, 42
illegibility. *See* irrelevance, perks of
images, household: of family members, 29, 35, 43, 45, 47, 107; of deities, 43, 45–47, 58, 82, 101, 163; of saints, 43, 47, 50, 70, 82. *See also* statues, sacred
impermanence, 6–7, 116, 119. *See also* anicca
interconnection: through creation, 132, 146, 147, 149, 152–153; through divinity, 193; through goodness, 132–133. *See also* frameless presence, experiences of; interdependence; nondualistic theologies
interdependence: as human reality, 119–120, 206, 207, 219n7 (concl.), 220n16; and human-divine activity, 90–94, 207. *See also* nondualistic theologies
intersectional analysis, 206, 207
interview process: as emotional, 4, 62, 65, 98, 101, 103, 122, 126, 128, 131, 132, 145, 150, 172, 180, 182, 184, 185, 189–192, 196; and Icelandic women's reticence, 30–31, 40–42; laughter in, 4, 8, 21, 38, 50, 52, 60, 70, 91, 107, 118, 128, 141, 154, 158, 185, 187; and older-adult willingness, 2, 213n1; women as subjects, 9–10
irrelevance, perks of, 205–206
Islam, 3, 44, 57, 82, 218n7 (chap. 9)

Jackson, Jimmie Lee, 86
Jackson, Michael, 5, 96, 217n3
James, William, 181, 197, 217n1
Jesus: in California, 19–20, 23–24, 142; in Kerala, 50–51, 55, 57, 58, 82, 91, 126, 141, 144, 165, 167; for the SSJs, 89, 93, 143; images of, 47, 58, 82, 101, 163, 190
joy, grown up, 112
Judaism, 2, 5
Jung, Carl, 134, 207

Kavedžija, Iza, 213n1, 213n8, 216n5 (chap. 6), 217n19, 217n4
Kerala: missionary activity in, 45, 51, 82–83, 215n7 (chap. 5), 218n1; nonsectarian Hinduism in, 45, 215n6 (chap. 3); religious pluralism in, 57–58; tropical terrain in, 43, 44. *See also* Dalits in Kerala; Syrian Christianity

kintsugi repair, 112
Kleinman, Arthur, 96, 123, 203
Kothadu elder care center, 55–56, 80, 121, 124

Lamb, Sarah, 6, 213n1, 213n8, 213n12, 214n2 (chap. 1), 217n4, 219n2 (concl.)
landscapes, worldviews shaped by, 3, 11, 16, 42, 44–45
laughter. *See* interview process
Law of Jante, 42, 214n1 (chap. 2)
Leavy, Stanley, 6, 213n13
Le Guin, Ursula, 5, 10, 12, 214n22
LePuy, France, 85
letting go: of control, 117, 119, 121–123, 134, 204; eased by hope, 133–134; of expectation, 116, 120–122, 133, 197; of judgement, 127–130; of negative emotions, 120–124, 132; of reliance on consumerism, 204, 207; resistance to, 116–119, 123. *See also* certitude, benefits of letting go of
Lewis, John, 86–87
Liberation Theology, 80–81
life lessons, 11, 115–117, 134; in California, 20, 98–100, 120–124, 128, 179; in Iceland, 127, 132; in Kerala, 91, 121; among the SSJs, 120–121, 127–130
Lorde, Audre, 201, 205–206, 220n12
Lutheran Church, 3, 36, 144, 158, 176

Mahayana Buddhism, 116, 133
Malayalam (language spoken in Kerala), 8, 51, 52, 80, 189
manual labor. *See* occupations
Manushyan Mathangale, 57–58
Marx, Karl, 81, 217n9
Mary, Virgin, 50, 56–58, 69, 140, 167, 173–175; images of, 47, 82. *See also* Velankanni Mary
Mayawati, Kumari, 81, 215n6 (chap. 5)
Médaille, Jean Pierre, 92, 94, 215n11
Mendel, Menachem, 95
Methodist Church, 23
mindfulness industry, 204, 220n25
miracles, 91, 161, 162, 172–174. *See also* angel accounts; prayer: power of; saint stories
missionaries, 18–20, 37, 71, 72
Mohan, Sanal, 210, 215n8 (chap. 3), 215n7 (chap. 5), 218n1
Moral Re-armament (MRA), 21–23

more, the, 134, 157, 180; definition of, 137–138, 197, 217n1; as countercultural, 197
Morgunblaðið, 41
Motherhouse, SSJ, 29, 59, 67, 68, 99, 146, 210
mothers, memories of: in California, 17, 18, 19–20, 22, 23, 76, 104–105, 172; in Iceland, 33–35, 38, 77, 105, 107, 170, 187; in Kerala, 45, 50–52, 54, 55, 80, 83, 91, 101–102, 166; among the SSJs, 62, 64–72, 104
Mother Teresa, 124–125
music, 34, 55, 80, 111, 128; choir, 19, 34, 38–39; drumming, 166; Icelandic hymns, 33–35, 37, 40–41, 107; Malayalam devotional songs, 52, 57, 103, 166, 167, 173; Malayalam film songs, 57–58, 80, 215n9 (chap. 3); at Motherhouse, 61, 140; trigger for mystical experiences, 148, 191, 192
Myerhoff, Barbara, 205, 220n31
mystical experience. *See* frameless presence, experiences of
mythical norms: of able-bodied youth, 199–201; defiance of, 206–207; of independence, 201–202; of non-suffering, 202–203

Nair. *See* caste in Kerala
naivete, 127, 130, 133–134, 205; second naivete, 134
National Poetry Day (Iceland), 152–153
nature: as humbling, 11, 138, 147, 149, 154–156; as majestic, 147; as source of abiding goodness, 127, 130–132, 146, 148; as synonymous with divinity, 146–149, 153, 154; as unwieldy, 3, 30–35, 42, 148–151. *See also* landscapes
nature as sacred, 138; for Californians, 145, 149–151, 153; for Icelanders, 3, 42, 145–146, 148–149, 152, 153; among the SSJs, 146–148
Nazareth University (College), 59, 69, 85, 123, 182
neoliberalism, 201, 204
new cosmology, 155–156
noetic, 197, 219n2 (chap. 10)
nonbinary perspectives: related to ability, 201; related to age and aging, 6, 200, 201; related to life fully lived, 201–205. *See also* nondualistic theologies; paradox

nondualistic theologies, 76, 79–81, 89; and human-divine activity, 90–94, 133, 207; as locating God in nature, 131–132; for Soelle, 202–204, 207; for SSJs, 93–94, 133, 207. *See also* interconnection; nature: as synonymous with divinity; *via unitiva*
nonnormative solidarity, 206
nonsuffering, culture of, 202–204. *See also* mythical norms
nuns. *See* religious orders, women's; school nuns; Sisters of St. Joseph
nursing. *See* occupations

object, song, or poem of significance: in California, 130–131, 150; in Iceland, 105, 107; in Kerala, 57, 110, 173; among the SSJs, 148
occupations: author, 179; business owner, 50; farmer, 34, 188; head mistress, 40; journalist, 41, 95; lawyer, 89; nurse, 65, 89, 163, 170, 184, 193; manual laborer, 52, 80, 121, 166; physician's assistant, 59; prison chaplain, 88–89; professor, 69, 87, 123; school principal, 89; teacher, 40, 85, 89. *See also* rice paddy labor; school nuns
older age: clarity in, 2, 10, 41; as countercultural, 2, 6, 12, 116, 197, 204–205; drawn to mystery in, 137–138, 156, 181; as spiritual exercise (or not), 117, 119
older age diminishment, 123, 200, 205; as instructive, 6, 10, 134; as inviting wonder, 137–138, 155; as purported spiritual path, 116–120. *See also* poignancy near life's end; wonder: as older age specialty
older women: as self-confident, 2, 41, 44, 176–177; as expressive, 2, 9–10; as free, 205
Old Norse beliefs, 132
Oliver, Mary, 130–131, 195
opiate: consumer capitalism as, 203–204; religion as, 81, 202–204, 217n9
optimism, 16, 126, 130, 203. *See also* hope
Orsi, Robert, 9, 79, 172, 175–176, 220n29
out-of-body experience, 187–188
Oxford Group, 21

Panther, The. *See* Rilke, Rainer Maria
paradox, 92, 155; as central to religion, 96; as late-life theme, 6, 116, 134. *See also* critical junctures; older age diminishment; poignancy near life's end
parapsychology, 24
Park, David, 179
parochial school, 67, 77–78
patriarchy, 108–109
peace, sense of, 7, 56, 92; within frameless presence, 192, 194; in letting go, 121
Pentecostalism, 51, 190
perfection: experienced in nature, 182; as illusion, 7, 12, 76, 95–96, 113, 206, 207
perfectionism, 113; religious, 12, 97, 203; societal, 12, 76, 97, 202, 203, 206, 207
Peter, T. J., 83
pilgrimage, 57, 159, 173, 174
pluralism, religious. *See* Kerala
poetry: in California, 130–131, 150–151, 155–156; in Iceland, 152–153; among the SSJs, 63, 148, 153
poignancy near life's end, 11, 97, 113, 152, 197, 216n6 (chap. 6)
polio, 40, 172
Pope Francis, 163–164
pottery, 112–113
poverty: in Iceland, 30, 34, 35, 40; in Kerala, 51, 52, 80, 121; work among the poor, 9, 89–92, 124–125, 133, 206
prayer, 18, 24, 92, 123, 150; as daily routine, 47–50, 57, 126, 165, 189; learned in childhood, 31, 45, 47, 50–51, 62, 82; power of, 161–163, 174, 176. *See also* healing: through prayer; prayer meetings
prayer meetings: in Iceland, 37, 168, 192; in Kerala, 52, 55, 166–167, 171
precarity: lessons learned from, 5, 11, 12, 42, 204; as source of gratitude, 102. *See* critical junctures; poignancy near life's end
Prejean, Helen, 84, 215n10
Presbyterian Church, 19–21
prophesy, 167–168
Protestant Reformation, 175
puja room, 45, 46, 48–49, 50, 174

Rabi'a al 'Adawiyya, 75, 76, 94
racism, 5, 206

Raj, Selva, 174–175, 218n7 (chap. 9)
real, the: definitions of, 11, 76, 96–97, 116, 176, 197. *See also* critical junctures
real presence, 172–176, 220n29
reciprocity: as challenge to institutional authority, 176; systems of, 58, 157–158, 171, 174–176. *See also* ethic of reciprocity
religion: as both harmful and helpful, 81–90; definitions of, 6–7, 213n16, 214n18
religious orders, women's: Belgian, 100–101; Carmelite, 79, 103, 144, 164; Maryknoll, 71; Sisters of Mercy, 63, 68. *See also* Sisters of St. Joseph
religious uprooting, 2–3, 15–16
Remen, Rachel Naomi, 145, 203
retreat, religious, 52, 147, 166, 173, 190
rice paddy labor, 52, 55–56, 80, 162. *See also* occupations
Rilke, Rainer Maria, 150–151, 155
ripple effect, 132–133
rituals, domestic: at sunset, 33, 35–36, 46; in prayer and puja rooms, 46, 48–49, 50, 172
Rohr, Richard, 134, 156
"Roots Alive!," 92–94, 207
rosary: beads, 66, 72, 164–165, 176; prayers, 47–48, 50, 51, 70, 189

sacred sites. *See* healing: at sacred sites; pilgrimage
Saint Alphonsa, 124, 125, 127
Saint Anne de Beaupré, 172–173
Saint Cosmas and Saint Damian, 172
Saint George, 162
Saint Joseph, 50–51, 140. *See also* Sisters of St. Joseph
saint stories: from California, 172; from Kerala, 173–174; from SSJs, 172–173. *See also* Mary, Virgin; Velankanni Mary; *names of individual saints*
Saint Teresa of Ávila, 219n4 (chap. 10)
Saint Thomas (the apostle), 44
Saint Thomas Christianity. *See* Syrian Christianity
Schneider, Jane, 175
school nuns: as inspiring, 63, 68–70, 78, 100–101; as severe, 63, 67–68, 77–78, 85, 100–101, 190

scientific discovery: as magnifying or replacing divinity, 154–155; as squelching or triggering wonder, 155–156
scientism, 155, 156
Selma, Alabama, 86–88
September 11. *See* Twin Towers
sexism, 5, 9, 41. *See also* patriarchy
Shannon, William, 123
Sideris, Lisa, 155
Sidhartha Gautama, 203
sin, 16, 189, 202
sisters, religious. *See* religious orders, women's; school nuns; Sisters of St. Joseph
Sisters of St. Joseph (SSJs): charism, 85; French founders, 85, 92–93; in India, 93–94. *See also* convent life; LePuy, France; Médaille, Jean Pierre; Motherhouse
skyggnigáfa. See *andleg mál*
Smith, Zadie, 112
social justice, 207. *See also* Sisters of St. Joseph: charism
socially porous societies, 44
socioemotional selectivity theory, 216n7 (chap. 6). *See also* Carstensen, Laura
Soelle, Dorothee, 80, 96, 181, 197; and nonsuffering, 202–204, 207
Solnit, Rebecca, 96, 133–134, 199
songs. *See* music
soul, 126, 141–142, 170, 187
spirits, unanticipated, 183–184; as unwanted, 166–167
spirits in ritual settings: as embodied, 166–171; in Iceland, 167–171; in Kerala, 166–167. See also *andleg mál*; Holy Spirit
Spiritualism, 176
spirituality, use of term, 2, 7, 117, 156; as code for "safe" religion, 9, 214n19; by SSJs, 8; as unhelpful, 7–8
SSJs. *See* Sisters of St. Joseph
statues, sacred, 47, 67, 172, 174
storm stories, 161, 162, 174
structural inequities, 206
successful aging, 5, 200, 201, 205. *See also* antiaging industry
suffering: as Christ-like, 124–125; eased by letting go, 122–123; as intrinsic to life's fullness, 96–97, 123, 133; as virtuous, 79–80, 124, 126, 215n3. *See also* Mother Teresa; nonsuffering, culture of; Saint Alphonsa
suicide, 23, 170
superstition, 175, 176
Syrian Christianity, 44, 110, 214n3; and caste privilege, 45, 214n4, 215n8 (chap. 3); and women's attire, 47, 214n7

Taylor, Sunaura, 201–202
terminal illness, perspectives gained from, 4–5, 97
terror management theory, 199–200
Theosophical Society, 35
Thich Nhat Hanh, 196–197
Thiyya. *See* caste in Kerala
Tornstam, Lars, 214n17, 219n9 (concl.)
trance possession, 168–170, 218n13 (chap. 9). See *andleg mál*; spirits in ritual settings: as embodied
Trinity, 93
true nature. See *bodhichitta*
tuberculosis, 18, 76, 161
Twin Towers, 131

United States mainstream: as ageist, 5, 9, 200, 214n2 (chap. 1); belief in angels, 175; as death-denying, 5, 139; as perfectionistic, 202–203; as success-driven, 5, 220n18

Vatican City, 163–164
Vatican II reforms: and convent life, 4, 80, 84–85, 92, 215n10; theological, 4, 78, 79, 189, 190
Velankanni Mary, 57, 174
Venbanad Lake, 162
via unitiva, 204, 207
Vietnam War, 128, 202
vigil, 59–60, 70–72. *See also* funerals
Virgin Mary. *See* Mary, Virgin
vision, supernatural, 173, 174, 195
vowed offerings, 45, 57, 58, 82, 174–176. *See also* ethic of reciprocity; saint stories
vulnerability, fruits of, 115, 116, 155, 202, 207. *See also* suffering

wabi sabi, 112
what is, 181, 191, 194, 197
white clothing, ban on, 83

wisdom in older age, 1, 7, 25, 117, 205; rejected by older women, 25, 117
women as interviewees. *See* interview process
women's ordination, 90
wonder, 137, 218n10 (chap. 8); humility within, 155–156, 197; at nature's magnificence, 146, 153–155; as older age specialty, 2, 6, 11, 138, 156, 181, 197, 217n2; in praise of, 137, 151, 156, 218n12 (chap. 8), 219n10 (chap. 10); at scientific discovery, 155
World War II, 21, 104, 128; prisoners of war, 128

yoga, 16, 17, 20, 35, 49

Zen Buddhism, 112, 220n25

About the Author

CORINNE G. DEMPSEY is professor and chair at the religious studies department at Nazareth University in Rochester, New York. Her published research as an ethnographer of religion includes monographs on Indian Christianity (*Kerala Christian Sainthood: Collisions of Culture and Worldview in South India*), on Hinduism in the United States (*The Goddess Lives in Upstate New York: Breaking Convention and Making Home at a North American Hindu Temple*), and on spirit traditions in Iceland (*Bridges between Worlds: Spirits and Spirit Work in Northern Iceland*). A comparative study is published in *Bringing the Sacred down to Earth: Adventures in Comparative Religion*. If asked, she will tell you that some of her favorite fieldwork encounters yet have been with older women, upon which this book is based.